Bradford Washburn
A Life of Exploration

Bradford Washburn: A Life of Exploration is supported by the Denali Foundation. Since 1989 the Denali Foundation has earned a reputation for connecting people to Denali's subarctic ecosystem through education, research and communication. The Denali Foundation offers diverse, outdoor educational programs for youth and adults providing a forum for conversation about Denali and our natural world.
www.denali.org

Bradford Washburn
A Life of Exploration

Michael Sfraga

Oregon State University Press
Corvallis

The paper in this book meets the guidelines for permanence and durability of the Committee on Production Guidelines for Book Longevity of the Council on Library Resources and the minimum requirements of the American National Standard for Permanence of Paper for Printed Library Materials Z39.48-1984.

Library of Congress Cataloging-in-Publication Data
Sfraga, Michael.
  Bradford Washburn : a life of exploration / Michael Sfraga.
      p. cm.
  Includes bibliographical references and index.
  ISBN 0-87071-010-9 (alk. paper)
  1. Washburn, Bradford, 1910-   2. Mountaineers—United States—
Biography. 3. Photographers—United States—Biography. 4. Natural
history museum directors—Massachusetts—Boston—Biography.
I. Title.
  GV199.92.W35S47 2004
  796.52'2'092—dc22

                              2004001436

Oregon State University Press
101 Waldo Hall
Corvallis OR 97331-6407
541-737-3166 • fax 541-737-3170
www.oregonstate.edu/dept/press

OREGON STATE
UNIVERSITY

To my wife Evelyn,
and daughters Megan Denali and Hanna Rose Marie

*Allow me to introduce myself – I'm your husband and father,
you might have seen photos of me around the house!*

Contents

Preface

Along Boston's Charles River stands a monument to the tireless efforts of countless volunteers and donors who shared in one man's vision—a vision to create a science museum where children and adults could explore, experience, and appreciate the natural world. Bradford Washburn's vision for Boston's Museum of Science began on December 29, 1939, when at the age of twenty-nine he assumed the directorship of what was then known as the New England Museum of Natural History. Through the next forty-one years he purposefully transformed a quaint natural history museum into a thriving international institution of interactive displays that demystify the world of science for hundreds of thousands of visitors each year.

I first met Bradford Washburn, a boyhood hero, more than a decade ago on a cold, damp February New England evening. Washburn was the first person to scale Mount McKinley three times, complete the first aerial photographic survey of the mountain, and produce the authoritative map of the peak. In addition, Washburn made first ascents throughout Southeast Alaska and Western Canada. Washburn's life of dramatic exploration into uncharted lands came alive to me in the books and articles that I read in my family's tiny Brooklyn apartment. To a kid from the inner city, Washburn's life was as exciting as it was mysterious. When we finally met, I thought of my childhood in Brooklyn, New York, and the countless hours spent on my front stoop immersed in the pages of Terris Moore's now classic volume *Mount McKinley, The Pioneer Climbs*.[1] The book introduced me to the world of mountaineering and eventually lured me north to live in Alaska. At that time I had no idea that years later I would become close friends with both men. Nor did I think I would have the opportunity to share the speaker's podium with Washburn at such venues as the Explorers Club in New York City, or jointly develop programs and research opportunities as we did in the early 1990s on Dr. Cook and Mount McKinley.[2] I have had the opportunity to work with Washburn on many issues related to the history of exploration, and such opportunities have been enjoyable, never dull, and wonderful learning experiences.

As a result of this relationship, Washburn gave me, as early as 1989, unrestricted access to his private diaries, photographs, letters, and papers. On behalf of the University of Alaska Fairbanks, I was able to work with Washburn and secure these documents (which also include over nine thousand photographs, pictures, equipment, clothing, cameras, diaries, notes, and expedition logbooks) for the University's Alaska and Polar Regions Archives. Through his generosity, these materials now constitute the core of the Bradford Washburn Collection. In many instances, he has allowed me access to these materials prior to their inclusion in his collection. I am forever grateful to Brad and his wife Barbara, for their friendship, trust, and commitment to me and to the University of Alaska Fairbanks.

From 1949 through 1953 Dr. Terris Moore served as president of the University of Alaska, but the mountaineering community knew him best as one of this nation's leading climbers throughout the 1930s and 1940s. Before his death in 1993, I had the pleasure and honor of spending many memorable days in his home, sharing and recording his recollections of climbs and expeditions throughout the world. I will be forever grateful for his kindness, as well as that of his lovely wife Katrina, and for the opportunity to share with him the positive impact his book had on my life.[3] This, of course, is not the subject of this work, but it should be noted that it was Moore who convinced a hurried Bradford Washburn to meet with me so many years ago.[4]

On that wet New England evening I negotiated hordes of school children and frantic teachers amassed in the Museum of Science's lobby, eventually making my way below a walkway that spans the breadth of this large open area. A bold engraving in the walkway's front piece grabbed my attention despite the hectic activity. Etched in the marble span is a dedication to the tireless efforts and bold vision of Bradford Washburn and his wife Barbara. Here, prominently displayed, the museum's trustees chose to recognize the couple for their innovative work in the creation of this now-vibrant institution. Dedicated to the Washburns in 1974, the honor reads: "This Hall Is Given In Honor Of Bradford and Barbara Washburn, Our Museum Epitomizes Their Love of Youth and Discovery."

Staring at the span above me I soon realized that Mount McKinley was not Washburn's only passion. He had, in ways I had yet to discover, fashioned multiple career paths. The singularly focused mountaineer that I envisioned did not exist. My perception, born from the pages of books and journals, was far too narrow and restrictive. In the years that followed, I discovered the many sides and talents of Bradford Washburn–the explorer, administrator, visionary, entrepreneur, scientist, politician, geographer, cartographer, photographer, and educator. Almost as striking as his list of talents and accomplishments is the ease with which he embodies each role.

At the time of our first meeting, as Director Emeritus of the Museum of Science Washburn worked in an office that overlooked the peaceful Charles River. With thinning gray hair and a slight build, he was not a physically daunting individual, but he was every bit as intense as I had imagined. The long room was filled with maps and models of McKinley and Mount Everest, as well as scores of photographs of the Alps, the

Himalayas, Mount McKinley, and Mount Washington. We was surrounded by evidence of his life-long pursuits of exploring, documenting, and describing the unexplored. Seconds after I introduced myself to him, he yanked at my sleeve, pulled me to the back of the room, and declared, "I bet you've never seen one of these before!" The grand old man of the mountains laid before me the most beautiful large-format photograph of Mount Everest I had ever seen. With the pride of a father showing off his child to a friend, Washburn explained that the picture was just one of many he had taken on his recently completed mapping project of Mount Everest. The National Geographic Society published Washburn's Everest map in the fall of 1988.[5]

He and I (accompanied by Alaskan videographer Tom Wolf) chatted late into the evening and closed the Museum that memorable night. We then went to his home to meet his wife Barbara and talk about exploration over a wonderful dinner of Ritz Crackers, grape jelly, and a splash of 7UP. Washburn would accent a particular point in the conversation by either slapping the jelly down hard on the crackers or by sliding a fully prepared snack down the coffee table to me, where I was graded on how well I could catch the food before it hit the floor. From that day forward we have been friends and colleagues.[6]

Wherever possible, I have used original sources (including personal diaries, manuscripts, correspondence, and interviews) to frame and explore various themes regarding Washburn's participation in and impact on expeditionary science and geographic exploration. By focusing this work on the time period of 1910-1960, I have tried to capture the most dynamic and perhaps most important period of Washburn's work. However, it should be noted that the final chapter not only analyzes Washburn's career throughout those fifty years, but also discusses his work in later years, that includes path-breaking survey and mapping work of the Grand Canyon, and a re-survey and subsequent mapping of the Mount Everest massif. The timeframe I have established is significant not only for a review of Washburn's personal accomplishments, but because it also allows one to discuss geographic exploration, scientific trends, and associated funding opportunities in a period that experienced a global economic depression, a world war, the emergence of a political and military cold war, advances in technology, aviation, communications, and the emergence of Big Science.

Acknowledgements

This manuscript was originally written as a dissertation in partial fulfillment of the requirements for an interdisciplinary Ph.D. in Northern Studies and Geography. Many individuals influenced my work including Ad Carter, former editor of the American Alpine Journal who cautioned early that I not write "another one of those climbing stories about Brad." He challenged, "steer clear of a more popular piece; make sure there is a bigger context." I will always appreciate Ad's guiding words of advice.

I thank legendary mountaineer Bob Bates for his support of my work and (like Ad) for submitting himself to countless inquiries and interviews. Celebrated American mountaineer and former president of the University of Alaska, Dr. Terris Moore became a close friend and avid supporter in the early stages of research. I was very fortunate to have many pioneers and scientists take interest in my studies and a debt of gratitude is owed to Dr. William Field, Dr. Walter Wood, Dr. Troy Pewe', Dr. Carl Benson, Bill Hackett, and Galen Rowell. A special thank you is owed to mountaineer and author Jon Waterman, whose early encouragement has never been forgotten.

Many individuals helped to make this work possible. Dr. Judith Kleinfeld, Director, Northern Studies Program at the University of Alaska Fairbanks, was the chief architect of my doctoral program. Her enthusiastic and relentless advocacy can never be adequately stated and will forever be appreciated. Andrew Kleinfeld was equally supportive and enthusiastic. Dr. Roger Pearson, who chaired my doctoral committee, did so with immeasurable commitment and patience. I am indebted to him for guiding my work and seeing early on the value of such a study. Committee members included Dr. Ralph Gabrielli, whom I thank for his never-ending commitment and constructive criticisms. Dr. Ron Doel played a central role in developing the many themes found within this manuscript. Dr. Marvin Falk, early on a strong and enthusiastic partner, ably guided my studies in the history of science and Russian America. Dr. Jack Townshend provided careful analysis of early U.S. field science. I benefited from discussions with Dr. Carol Lewis regarding cosmic ray physics and geography. Dr. Bruce Molnia of the U.S.G.S. carefully reviewed sections of this manuscript and made it a more accurate study.

My formal doctoral work was informed and influenced by the insight and expertise Dr. Fae Korsmo, who also reviewed earlier versions of the dissertation. Dr. Carl Benson provided critical context for early glacial studies in Alaska and the Yukon. Advice and direction from Dr. William Hunt made initial research more focused and fruitful. Dr. Carol Gold and Dr. Art Buswell were both early and vocal supporters. Dr. Jonathan

Anderson and Dr. James Gladden offered helpful guidance in the closing days of my defense preparation.

Many archivists, librarians, and organizations helped beyond measure. The staff of the Elmer Rasmuson Library, University of Alaska Fairbanks, were of particular assistance, including Director Paul McCarthy, Dr. Susan Grigg, Gretchen Lake, and Richard Veazey. Members of the Research and Exploration Committee of the National Geographic Society granted permission to access the correspondence files of both Gilbert Grosvenor and Bradford Washburn. I thank the dedicated staff of the United States Library of Congress, the Denver Public Library, the Lyndon Baynes Johnson Library, and the Franklin Delano Roosevelt Library for their assistance over the years.

A very special thank you to Mary Braun, Acquisitions Editor at the Oregon State University Press, whose unwavering interest and enthusiasm for this work was the catalyst I needed to resurrect my dissertation and transform it into a viable manuscript. Dr. Paul Merchant's guiding hand and critical analysis helped shape the final text, yet I alone am accountable for any shortcomings the reader may identify. And a special thank you to OSU Managing Editor Jo Alexander, who carefully guided me and this manuscript through to publication. Greg Glade of Top of the World Books has been a long-time advocate and generously provided images found within the text. Gary Gavone was always available for consultation.

To mom, Sophia, who instilled in me a love of books, history, and exploration. She challenged a young boy from Brooklyn to see past buildings and train stations and search for distant horizons. To my father Tom, who provided a rare balance of humor, compassion, and support to go where the known gives way to the unknown. Paula Sfraga, T.J. Sfraga, Josephine Sfraga, and Christine Sfraga have always been there for me – and I thank them all. Ann Tremarello has been there from the beginning and provided tireless support and endless dedication. And finally, I am forever indebted to my wife and children for filling the void left by a nearly absentee father and husband while we all tried to balance work, family, and academic pursuits.

Introduction

Born on June 7, 1910, Bradford Washburn remains a dynamic and unique individual whose genius is easily identifiable. Mountaineering historian Audrey Saulkeld has called Washburn a Renaissance man.[1] Indeed, he is a complex mix of intellect, physical and mental fortitude, and perfectionism. Washburn is a cunning and critical thinker, a graceful and effective communicator, and an efficient and creative field scientist, educator, and visionary. "You recognize the explorer in Bradford Washburn at first sight," noted celebrated American photographer Ansel Adams. "There is something about his eyes, the set of the chin. . . the consistent energy of mind and spirit."[2] For nearly nine decades this energy has fueled an internal fire of desire for scientific exploration and geographic discovery.

Washburn's career has evolved from a lifetime of dedicated work, detailed preparation, and an encyclopedic, uncanny knowledge of his subjects. He has conducted mountaineers and scientists high atop the mountains of Alaska, Canada, Nepal, and the continental United States. His results include stunning photographs and maps as well as first ascents. At the very core of each of Washburn's expeditions can be found a few primary motifs: a fundamental love for high and distant places, a yearning to discover the unknown, and the desire to share with others the world's natural beauty and scientific wonders.[3]

Bradford Washburn's life can be viewed as an intersection between twentieth-century geographic exploration and field science. Washburn is an explorer who understands the scientific and aesthetic value of photographs, sharing this passion with such colleagues and friends as Ansel Adams. He is an entrepreneur who often brought together scientists from varied scientific disciplines; the most advanced technologies available, as well as patrons and powerful marketing plans to carry out a broad range of interdisciplinary fieldwork.

Through the second decade of the twentieth century, the most prized geographic trophies had been claimed by some of the most ingenious, stubborn, ardent, and persistent explorers of the time. For centuries, the conquest of both geographic poles and the Northwest Passage had captured the imagination of entire nations. To the victorious explorer lay the promise of fame and financial reward.[4] In 1907, just three years before Washburn's birth, Norwegian explorer Roald Amundsen made the first successful navigation of the Northwest Passage. In 1911 he was the expedition leader of a Norwegian team to be the first to reach the geographic South Pole.[5] In the span of just a few years, Amundsen had achieved two of the most renowned feats in exploration history. Yet these seemingly marvelous accomplishments did not fulfill Amundsen's true desires. The subsequent fame he enjoyed from the South Pole expedition did little to satisfy a long-desired goal to become the first person to set foot at the geographic North Pole. Nor did it help to overcome the subsequent controversy that clouded his achievement.[6] The "heroic" death of British explorer Robert Scott in his race with Amundsen to reach the South Pole first eclipsed and then tarnished the Norwegian's reputation and spoiled the victory.

Amundsen's dream of reaching the North Pole first was dashed in September of 1909 when news reached the outside world of New York physician Dr. Frederick A. Cook's claim to have discovered the geographic North Pole the previous year (1908). Just days after the world learned of Cook's discovery, fellow American Robert Peary dispatched word from Greenland that he, not Cook, had reached the Pole and claimed sole and rightful ownership of the honor. Peary declared Cook's expedition a fake and supported this with statements from Cook's Eskimo companions. This testimony, given to members of the Peary Arctic Club, supported Peary's claim that Cook had not journeyed far from sight of land.[7] Nevertheless, word of Cook's claim forced Amundsen to scrap his own planned North Pole expedition and secretly set sail to the Antarctic, thereby creating his race for the South Pole with Scott.[8]

In the spring of 1909, the two Americans, Cook and Peary, and their supporters, were engaged in the first of what would become a blizzard of claims and counter claims regarding the discovery of the Pole. The war of words escalated frequently, and the conflict was dramatically covered in the pages of the world's largest newspapers. As a result, the actual accomplishment of reaching the Pole often took second place to the ensuing firestorm of accusations and character assassination between the two men.[9] Because of disputes like this, polar exploration and geographic conquest during the first two decades of the twentieth century were followed with great interest by the American public who, as historian William Goetzmann points out, "wanted sensation and adventure."[10]

American fascination with unknown and distant lands reflected the nation's very character and was a palpable component of the society's framework and structure. As a matter of sheer geography, U.S. expansion was directed westward through the heart of the "frontier," supporting Goetzmann's assertion that "America has indeed been 'exploration's nation.'"[11] As Frederick Jackson Turner wrote in 1893, "Up to our own day American history has been in large degree the history of the colonization of the Great West." However, by the 1880s, Turner argues, the western United States was developed and populated to such a degree that the nation's frontier was no longer clearly discernible. For Turner, this marked the "closing of a great historic movement" which explained and indeed characterized the evolution and development of the nation.[12]

By the late nineteenth and early twentieth century, explorers had defined most of the large geographic regions within the United States. These explorations included, for example, the magnificent exploring and scientific expeditions of John Wesley Powell along the Colorado River and the scores of Federal geographic and geologic survey parties.[13] By the earliest part of the twentieth century the American public was well aware of the explorers and their discoveries and developed a taste for fantastic accounts of strange and distant lands within their diminishing frontier. Early western exploration, Goetzmann argues, had "set the values, tone and rhythm of American culture from the eighteenth century to the present."[14]

The degree to which geographic exploration captured the interests of the masses as well as the academic community can be easily demonstrated. Proliferation around the world of geographic societies, whose membership consisted of professional geographers and laymen alike, occurred at about the same time as the American frontier drew to a close. In 1866, for example, eighteen geographic societies were in existence. By the time Bradford Washburn embarked on his first expedition to Alaska in 1930, the number of geographic societies had reached 137. In the United States, the American Geographical Society was founded in 1852, the National Geographic Society was established in 1888, and the Association of American Geographers was founded in 1904. Each organization served to disseminate the ever-increasing geographic knowledge secured by continued exploration. Perhaps this is why the great polar expeditions at the turn of the twentieth century so captured public attention.[15]

Newspapers in the 1880s quickly discovered the art of selling copy by exploiting many of the period's more imaginative and controversial explorers. The promise of patronage carried with it specific expectations and demands. Moreover, the lure of such financial support and widespread publicity often overshadowed any moral reservations the explorer may have had in using the newspaper as both a public relations vehicle and expedition underwriter.[16] Explorers have long been viewed as heroes, and their published exploits served as a means through which common men experienced romantic portrayals of personal sacrifice and national pride. Late nineteenth and early twentieth century explorers reaffirmed America's intent to conquer the natural world and tame the frontier, from which a civilized framework would make possible future development. The explorer represented all that was daring and right in man's perpetual drive to discover, understand, and control the unknown.[17]

Historians such as Stephen Pyne and William Goetzmann have defined three separate and distinct phases of discovery and exploration. However, these delineations are made in broad terms and describe significant differences in the manner scientific and geographic exploration has been carried out. The First Great Age of Discovery occurred at about the time of the European Renaissance and, as Goetzmann points out, its focus "became that of mapping terrestrial space," in particular, the charting of the world's oceans. Moreover, great surveys were undertaken to identify and document the distribution and composition of the earth's minerals, fossils, flora and fauna.[18]

During the eighteenth and nineteenth centuries, the Second Great Age of Discovery emerged. This period is broadly defined by the geographic exploration of the continents and the formation of partnerships between explorers and academic institutions in field-based scientific investigations.[19] Large-scale expeditions traveled into the heart of the world's continents, first expanding outside of Europe to Siberia and then, as historian Stephen Pyne notes, across North America, "where one of the best known is the trek by Lewis and Clark."[20] Pyne argues that the current Third Great Age of Discovery emerged in the mid-twentieth century, underscored by the scientific undertakings of the International Geophysical Year (1957). He suggests that the geographic domain of exploration shifted to include the solar system, beginning with space-based exploration of earth.[21]

As the three "Great Ages" of discovery focused on varying geographies, they also employed different modes of exploration. The First Age was characterized by ship-borne exploration, while the Second Age utilized a wide array of transportation tools such as canoes, pack animals and spectacular overland treks.[22] In the present Third Age of Discovery, geographic exploration has relied, to a large degree, on remote sensing platforms and satellites, that have revealed in greater detail the geographic detail, inventory, and landscape of our planet.

The career of pioneer American explorer Bradford Washburn reflects the fundamental goals, structure, and framework of expeditionary science in both the Second and Third Ages of Discovery. Washburn's geographic "inventory" of the mountain landscape has been obtained through the use of similar modes of exploration found throughout the latter two periods. Indeed, Washburn's expeditions and associated use of emerging technologies may be viewed as a bridge from the Second era to the present. By investigating Washburn's work within this larger context, his career and the themes that emerge from its study will serve as a unique window into broader developments in American science, exploration, and culture in the twentieth century. Since windows provide two-way views, this will also create a context and forum for an analysis of Washburn's many contributions across and within numerous academic disciplines including geophysics, physics, glaciology, geography, cartography, and photography.

First, Washburn's role as an innovative expeditionary scientist will be examined by analyzing his interdisciplinary approach to field-based research and his commitment to the utilization of the most advanced technologies. By studying the ways in which field scientists conducted such expeditions, we can better understand broader issues such as social stratification, organizational skills and, as historians Kuklick and Kohler point out, the "heterogeneity of field science workers and tasks."[23] Through dramatic aerial photographs, Washburn's role as vivid "describer" will emerge, framing the geographic landscape in such a way as to capture the dynamic geologic processes at work within the alpine world.

Throughout the history of geographic exploration, explorers and scientists employed numerous mediums to describe the natural world. As

Goetzmann argues, expeditionary geographers provided a visual representation of their discoveries and travels, "mapping, describing, and characterizing the unexpected that they set out to find." Many explorers took along artists and illustrators whose visual representations were essential tools for scientific understanding and classification and who generated scientific thinking." Washburn's aerial photographs provided a "whole new way of looking at nature" and underscored his ability to capture and "describe" the landscape. [24] "Aerial photography," wrote Pyne in 1979, "has perhaps become the dominant form of geological illustration."[25]

The second theme is the study of geography as an integrating discipline. Through Washburn's work the field of geography emerges as a bridge for natural and social sciences, a conduit through which multidisciplinary field research, exploration, mountaineering, and photography is made possible.[26] Indeed, geography and geographic exploration are the primary catalysts, a framework for Washburn's expeditionary fieldwork.

The third and final theme is the role of the independent geographer and explorer in the pre and post World War II and Cold War eras. Although early on in his career, between 1937 and 1942, Washburn served as an instructor at Harvard's Institute for Geographic Exploration, he was, for the most part, an independent geographer and explorer. He relied almost exclusively on his ability to attract financial support through private patrons, and the sale of his many photographs as well as upon large corporate entities and organizations such as the National Geographic Society. When he assumed the position of director (from 1939 to 1981) of Boston's Museum of Science, he negotiated with the institution a contract that made possible frequent "paid" expeditionary sabbaticals to Alaska and the Yukon. Although the Museum covered his salary for such work, it provided minimal funding to support large-scale field research. Without the benefit of a permanent university affiliation from which to draw financial backing, he was continually forced to "sell" his ideas, stories, and photographs to numerous news and magazine organizations. However, Washburn, the independent geographer, field scientist and entrepreneur, returned enormous aesthetic and scientific dividends to his many investors and to those countless scientists who continue today to benefit from his scientific and photographic legacy.[27]

These three underlying themes will be amplified and analyzed by exploring Washburn's formative childhood years and the many factors that shaped his life and subsequent career. We will discover the critical role his parents and family played in providing the support and opportunity that would became the foundation for his lifelong interest in exploration. For instance, at the height of the Depression, he was afforded the benefit of private preparatory school and a Harvard education. Summer vacations through the 1920s to the White Mountains of New Hampshire and the European Alps shaped his interest in and passion for mountaineering, photography, geography, geology and cartography.[28]

Indeed, Washburn's Harvard education, social status, and his ability to integrate mountaineering and scientific investigations parallels "gentleman scientists" of the Victorian period, such as glaciologists James Forbes and John Tyndall. Historian Bruce Hevly notes that the Victorians, who often linked social status with scientific investigation, established a bridge between mountaineering and field science, and argues that "mountaineering should be wed to mountain science." Washburn's mountaineering accomplishments and geographic fieldwork in New Hampshire and the European Alps through the 1920s were nurtured and encouraged by family members and reflect a true Victorian style and character.

By 1930 Washburn was an accomplished and celebrated mountaineer, making first ascents in the Alps and publishing popular accounts and photographs of his adventures. He transferred these skills and experiences from the mountains of New Hampshire and Europe to the rugged peaks of Alaska and the Yukon in the 1930s. Here, in the glaciated peaks of the Wrangell-St. Elias Range, we can see the development of Washburn's mountaineering skills and strategies for large-scale interdisciplinary field science.[29] Adopting the airplane as a central means of exploration, Washburn utilized the plane for remote transportation, field supply, aerial photography, and reconnaissance.

By the mid 1930s, Washburn had joined a small brotherhood of pioneers using the airplane to carry out photographic and cartographic surveys throughout previously unexplored regions of Alaska and Canada. Thus the airplane became a critical tool in the development of our still-emerging understanding of the mountain landscape.[30] Private patronage as well as personal relationships made possible the majority of Washburn's North American expeditions. The most interesting and perhaps most significant has been his nearly eight decades of partnership with the National Geographic Society. In cooperation with the Society, Washburn executed numerous expeditions to Alaska and Canada throughout the 1930s on which he mapped and photographed previously unexplored mountain ranges and glaciers. His expeditions also incorporated the latest radio technology and communications, cutting edge geophysical techniques and monitoring strategies, and scaled remote and unclimbed peaks in North America including Mount Crillon (12,728 feet), Mount Sanford (16,200 feet), and Mount Lucania (17,150 feet). Washburn's scientific and mountaineering accomplishments in remote North America will be the focus of the second chapter.

During the Second World War Bradford Washburn played a critical role in the research and development of cold weather equipment and clothing for the United States Army Air Force. A discussion of his efforts during the war years is important in two ways. First, it provides further insight into Washburn's personality, underscoring his focused, determined drive and commitment to a single goal. For example, through personal connections, Washburn was able to suggest changes to President Franklin Roosevelt in the military's development of cold weather clothing and equipment. Washburn's military service is indicative of the style and ferocity he would later exhibit throughout the post-war years in his determination to carry out increasingly complex and comprehensive geographic and scientific investigations.

Second, field testing in Alaska of military equipment and clothing provided numerous opportunities for Washburn to explore, for the first time, the Mount McKinley region; the landscape he is most associated with today. In 1942 Washburn participated in one such field test along the slopes of the mountain, and eventually stood atop its summit, the first of three successful attempts over the course of his career. It was Washburn's subsequent familiarity with the McKinley region that qualified him to assume a critical role in a daring winter recovery effort of a downed U.S. military transport plane just below the summit of an adjacent unnamed peak.

In the waning months of the war, Washburn executed preliminary surveys of the McKinley region upon which he expanded after the war. The result of Washburn's survey work was the production of the authoritative map of the mountain, still used today by mountaineers eager to scale North America's tallest peak. Washburn's military service and personal associations, Alaskan fieldwork, and mountaineering accomplishments will be examined in the third chapter. Chapter Four examines and analyzes Washburn's unique relationship with Mount McKinley, beginning in 1936 when, at the age of twenty-six, he led an aerial photographic reconnaissance of the peak for the National Geographic Society.

In 1947 and 1951, with considerable assistance from the U.S. military, and the encouragement of several major figures in the American scientific community including Harvard astrophysicist Harlow Shapley, he returned to McKinley. On each occasion he incorporated an energetic research agenda that often included topographic surveys, geological identification and samplings, as well as high altitude geophysical investigation. With the emergence of the Cold War, Washburn capitalized on the military's interest in cosmic ray physics, photogrammetry, remote aerial resupply, and tactics in remote and inhospitable regions. Through the financial and logistical support of private institutions and federal agencies, including Harvard University and the Office of Naval Research, Washburn secured sufficient political and financial resources to undertake numerous large-scale mapping and mountaineering expeditions to the Mount McKinley region. It should be noted that Washburn secured such funding in the period historian Harvey Sapolsky called the "golden age of academic science" in which a steady flow of military funding was supplied to U.S. universities. [31]

It was through such support that Washburn, over the course of fifteen years, secured a complete survey and photographic record of the peak, and produced, in 1960, the authoritative map of Mount McKinley. Washburn's intimate knowledge of the peak makes him the unrivaled expert on the region's mountaineering history, geology, and topography. He has become McKinley's knowledge-keeper and "guide" to thousands of climbers who each year rely upon his map, photographs, and personal knowledge of the mountain to plan and execute increasingly difficult ascents.

In the final chapter, the numerous themes that emerge from a discussion of Washburn's career will be drawn together and analyzed. Washburn's continued use of evolving technologies in subsequent mapping projects such as an extensive survey throughout the 1970s of the Grand Canyon and of Mount Everest throughout the 1980s and 1990s will be examined. Still active today in his nineties, Washburn increasingly relies upon the world's brightest scientific minds and skilled mountaineers to assist him in a continuing whirlwind of research.

1

Tools of the Trade

"Every child in Miss Leatherbee's fifth grade geography class grew up with an intense interest in the world . . . and a keen desire to learn by seeing, touching, experiencing." Bradford Washburn

The Roots of Discovery

Henry Bradford Washburn Jr. was born on June 7, 1910. Although the American West was settled, dramatic tales of international exploration and discovery continually fed the public's desire for epic accounts of geographic conquest. The human drama in the ongoing debate about the rightful conqueror of the North Pole was played out in newspapers across the globe. Growing up in Cambridge, Massachusetts, young Washburn was surrounded by tales of exploration and the lure of distant adventure, an environment that would shape his subsequent interest in far and distant lands. Like many within Cambridge's social elite, the Washburn family followed the unceasing Polar debate between Cook and Peary with great interest. After all, Peary was the "establishment's man," an easterner and Naval officer funded and supported by the United States military as well as by the powerful and influential National Geographic Society.

When Washburn was five years old, his mother Edith gave to him a copy of *The Snow Baby*.[1] Written by Josephine Peary, wife of Admiral Robert Peary, the book recounts the birth and early life of their daughter Mary, the first documented white child born in the Arctic. Washburn and his mother spent hours with the small book, his introduction to distant and exotic lands. This modest book sparked a lifelong passion for the remote, mysterious, and uncharted landscapes of North America and beyond.

Heroes play a significant and influential role in many youngsters' development. Heroes are found in the pages of books, on movie screens, or in newspapers and magazines. Although such books and stories of

11

exploration had a great impact upon the young Bradford Washburn, his parents influenced him the most. "My father and mother were, in a way, my first heroes," Washburn would recall, nearly eighty years later, "they took me on my first airplane ride . . . . It was also, unquestionably my mother who opened my eyes to both the fun and importance of photography."[2]

Through his mother's encouragement, Washburn recognized early in life the power of combining his love for flying and photography, and that the two could make possible a fruitful career in geographic exploration and mountaineering. Washburn's parents also instilled in him values against which he measured each day's accomplishments. As he later recalled, "My parents used to say to me, sort of in unison, 'whatever you do, try to do it well,' and that rubbed off on me."[3] Henry and Edith Washburn gave to their son the most cherished gifts of all: opportunity, support and love.[4] Washburn's father Henry Bradford Sr., one of seven children, was born in Worcester, Massachusetts, on December 2, 1869 to Mary Elizabeth Whiton and Charles Francis Washburn. Charles was a direct descendent of William Brewster, a signatory of the Mayflower Compact and an original settler of the Plymouth Rock Bay colony in 1620. The Washburns were a relatively affluent family with a long-standing history in the Boston area where Charles served as President of the Washburn Wire Company. Henry Washburn graduated from Harvard in 1891, and later graduated from the Episcopal Theological School of Cambridge.[5] Henry followed in the footsteps of his older brother Philip, a Harvard graduate who pursued theological studies in Berlin. In 1893, Philip relocated to Colorado Springs where he led a growing congregation at St. Stephen's until his death in 1898 at age thirty-seven. In five short years Philip Washburn became an important community member and strong proponent for the fledgling Colorado College.[6]

With the encouragement of his parents, Henry pursued advanced theological studies in Oxford and Berlin. While attending the University of Berlin he met Samuel Colgate, a young American theological student, and his new bride Edith Hall Colgate. Both came from wealthy and influential families. Samuel's brother Gilbert was the president of the family's Colgate Soap Company. Edith's brother Edward J. Hall developed for AT&T the first long-distance phone service.[7] The three became close friends and spent a great deal of time together. However, this new friendship affected the lives of both Washburn and Edith Colgate to a far greater extent than the two realized at the time.

Completing his studies in 1896, Washburn returned to the United States, and in 1898 became rector of St. Mark's Church in his hometown of Worcester, Massachusetts. Henry also was appointed to the Episcopal Theological School as an instructor, the institution from which he had graduated just a few years earlier.[8]

By this time the Colgates and their newborn daughter Mabel had relocated to New York State, where Samuel served as rector of the First Presbyterian Church. However, tragedy soon stuck the Colgate family, when Samuel contracted typhoid fever. After a prolonged battle with the illness, he died in the summer of 1902. Through the next six years, Henry Washburn and Edith Colgate enjoyed an extended yet discreet courtship, built on their friendship from years earlier in Europe. The couple married in New York City on May 20, 1908.[9] Shortly after the wedding, Washburn became a professor of church history at the Episcopal Theological School, and moved his new family to Cambridge, Massachusetts. On June 7, 1910, Henry Bradford Washburn Jr. was born, and one year later the family expanded to include their second son Sherwood Larned Washburn.

The Washburns took great care to provide a home environment in which love, inquiry, and discovery were fostered. In one instance, the boys were introduced to the great mysteries and pyramids of Egypt, a subject that intrigued nine-year-old Bradford.[10] Washburn was so taken with the subject that he initiated correspondence with eminent archeologist and family friend Dr. G. A. Reisner at his field camp near Cairo. Reisner's correspondence to Washburn detailed camp life in the 1920 Egyptian desert, and further intrigued the would-be explorer.[11] Pursuing this interest with unbridled enthusiasm, the boys acquired a guinea pig from the Harvard Medical School and, after thorough research, mummified and buried the animal behind the Episcopal Theological School where their father was now Dean.[12] Before Washburn had reached the age of ten he was captivated by the intrigue of unknown regions and the explorers who traveled in these far-off lands.

With the outbreak of World War I Washburn Sr. moved his family to New York City, where he selected chaplains for war duty as part of the

Commission of Episcopal Churches.[13] Bradford spent a good deal of time fishing from inner city piers, and published his first article at the age of nine, entitled "Fishing: What a Boy Thinks." The story, published in 1919, demonstrated Washburn's early enthusiasm for the detailed explanation of processes, as it described the most effective means of inner-city fishing.

> Solder a bell onto the end of a strong piece of wire, on the other end a screw. Fasten this on the dock by means of the screw. Have about a hundred feet of line with about three hooks on the end of the line with a sinker. Tie the loose end of the line to the wire and throw the line into the water. When the fish bite the bell will ring.[14]

The young writer then instructs would-be fishermen to reel the creature in and remove the hook, noting, "they make a little groan and are off to the happy hunting grounds."[15]

Washburn's fascination with the natural world continued. After the war the family relocated to Cambridge, Massachusetts, where young Bradford's life would be forever changed by two powerful experiences that would impact the course of his adult life.

A Passion for Heights

Bradford Washburn's interest in geography and geographic exploration can be traced to two events that occurred relatively early in his life. The first was the experience of Miss Florence Leatherbee's fifth-grade geography lessons: "Every child in Miss Leatherbee's class grew up with an intense interest in the world," Washburn would later note, and "a keen desire to learn by seeing, touching, experiencing."

The second event occurred during the summer of 1921 while the family vacationed at Squam Lake, New Hampshire. That summer eleven-year-old Bradford hiked in the purified air of the surrounding hills, and discovered a "world where there was no hay fever."[16] And it was during this outing that he discovered the exhilaration and sense of accomplishment that come from climbing. On July 21, 1921, Bradford Washburn, accompanied by his cousin Sherman Hall, made his first of many ascents of Mount Washington. Washburn later recalled the joys of "hiking on mountain trails and sharing the thrills of discovery with close friends."[17]

"hiking on mountain trails and sharing the thrills of discovery with close friends"

Fifteen-year-old Bradford Washburn and friends climbing Mount Morgan in 1925. Washburn is second from right.

Courtesy of Bradford Washburn

In the years that followed, the Washburn's family frequented the lakes and mountains of New England. Washburn's wealthy Uncle Charles, a pioneer in the wire industry, took great interest in both Bradford and his younger brother, Sherry, and often joined the boys on their outings.[18] Long fishing excursions to Maine solidified the uncle's relationship with the boys, and when Bradford entered the prestigious all-boy private Massachusetts boarding institution of Groton School in the fall of 1923, Uncle Charles (a Groton School Trustee) paid the entire cost of six years' tuition – a gift of "discovery" for his nephew. [19]

Washburn's Groton years between the ages of thirteen and eighteen shaped his character, his interests in the outdoors, and his future career. In 1923 Washburn turned thirteen, and his parents scheduled his first plane flight as a birthday present. He experienced the joy of flying that would later evolve into a trademark of his professional career. As Washburn later recalled, his mother also encouraged him to purchase his first camera, a widely popular Kodak "Vest Pocket Autographic" to record the "details and the highlights of what we see and what we do."[20] Neither Washburn nor his parents could have realized the degree to which the young boy would some day merge his passion for flying and skills with a camera to explore, map, and photograph vast tracts of unknown mountains and glaciers in the far north.[21]

During his time at Groton, Washburn's passion for climbing intensified. Accompanied by his father and brother, the teenager made numerous summer ascents throughout the White Mountains, as well as several winter climbs of Mount Washington, known as one of the most challenging winter environments in the eastern United States. Washburn used these outings to sharpen his mountaineering skills, and began experimenting with winter photography.

One particular trip tested the teenager's skills in winter survival, navigation, and ability to remain levelheaded in adverse conditions, attributes he would later rely upon in the far-off reaches of Alaska and Canada. On one particularly eventful winter ascent of Mount Washington, a ferocious storm forced Washburn and classmate Tappy Turner to spend the night stranded in the "Halfway House" shelter on the mountain's upper slopes. With the temperature hovering in the teens and wind cutting through the walls of the cabin, the boys chopped wood and stoked the fire to stay warm throughout the night.[22]

The following morning found the boys fatigued from lack of food and sleep, yet confident of their skills. They even made light of the situation. As Turner noted in the cabin's log:

4:04 [A.M.] Have yelled no less than three times at an unresponsive Brad to get him to relieve me . . . . Maybe he has frozen to death—In this event I may have enough breakfast![23]

Washburn and Turner returned home safely the next day, and although the trip taxed the boys, Washburn immediately developed the photographs he had taken throughout the climb. Washburn was in need of facilities to develop his growing collection of negatives. So he had earlier built a makeshift darkroom in the school's basement.[24] With each experience and photograph taken, Washburn was slowly building the skills of mountain photography. He reveled in the quality of his pictures and budding knowledge of mountain terrain. Indeed, after one particular climb,

"Here is the view as you see it with Sandwich underlined"

Washburn often wrote to his stepsister Mabel while at Groton

Courtesy of Bradford Washburn

Washburn confessed in a letter to his stepsister Mabel that he knew "more about the trail than the guide did."[25]

Washburn's addiction to climbing, photography, and geography blossomed at Groton where such avocations occupied a significant part of his life. Correspondence between the teenager and Mabel reveals the degree to which the mountains of New England consumed his thoughts. His letters include numerous questions regarding the mountains, and often contain detailed hand-drawn "maps" of the terrain for reference in many his inquiries:

> How do the mountains look? Is there any snow on Chocorua . . . Sandwich Dome? (The mountain to the right behind the Squam Range with two poorly defined tops.) Here is the view as you see it with Sandwich underlined.[26]

Washburn worked diligently on his landscape drawings and emerging cartographic skills, and published in the Groton School newspaper his

"He found great satisfaction in producing such maps"

Washburn's Squam Lake map was published in the Groton School newspaper

Courtesy of Bradford Washburn

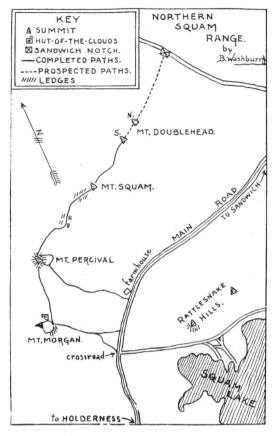

KEY
▲ SUMMIT
▥ HUT-OF-THE-CLOUDS
▧ SANDWICH NOTCH.
— COMPLETED PATHS.
---- PROSPECTED PATHS.
///// LEDGES

NORTHERN
SQUAM
RANGE.
by
B. Washburn

MT. DOUBLEHEAD.

MT. SQUAM.

MT. PERCIVAL

MT. MORGAN.

crossroad→

ROAD TO SANDWICH

MAIN

farmhouse

RATTLESNAKE HILLS.

SQUAM LAKE

to HOLDERNESS→

first map and guide, "Trails on The Squam Range." He found great satisfaction in producing such maps, and shared them enthusiastically with his friends and family.[27]

Mabel wrote faithfully to her brother throughout his Groton years, and Washburn kept her up to date on his studies, school activities, triumphs, and difficulties.[28] Many of his letters contain such information as the precise time at which the letter was written, temperature, precipitation, snow level, and weather forecasts. This compulsive attention to details of the natural world is reflected in every facet of Washburn's life and future career.[29]

Mabel became a confidante to the teenager, who relied on her for advice and news of home. Washburn even devised a plan to simplify and guarantee a constant flow of letters to and from his sister:

I have thought over the correspondence idea and have decided that as soon as either of us receives a letter from the other it is his (or her) duty to send one back.[30]

This strong commitment to family was no doubt fostered in all of the Washburn children. Mabel did not disappoint her brother, and their faithful correspondence and unique relationship continued throughout adulthood.[31]

Groton's curriculum and extracurricular activities challenged Washburn, and provided a showcase for his athletic and academic prowess. He played baseball, football, and hockey, was a member of the school's wall scaling team, and served as chairman of the Athletic Association, captain of the Debating Team, and managing editor of the school's *Third Form Weekly* newspaper.[32] Washburn's active and physical schedule is indicative, at an early age, of his utter dislike for idle time. His physical skills and talents were matched by his academic abilities. In addition to standard classes in history, mathematics, and English, each student at Groton was required to study Latin, a subject Washburn did not much enjoy.[33]

A Mr. Sturgis taught the dreaded Latin class in which Washburn studied. At the beginning of each school year Mr. Sturgis scrambled the boys' last names on the class roster from which the students would be called to recite. Washburn and classmate "Tappy" Turner soon figured out the instructor's method and prepared more diligently for the days when they might be called upon. Without the boys' knowledge, the teacher re-scrambled the list every six weeks. According to Washburn, having been called upon to recite the day before, neither he nor Turner came prepared to recite on one particular day. To his horror, Washburn was selected first to read and then translate several lines from Virgil's *Aeneid*. His ingenuity, creativity, and showmanship carried him through the crisis. Unable to translate any part of the text, he put heart and soul into the pronunciation and inflexion of each word.[34] As Washburn later recalled, the teacher interrupted him and announced to the entire class, "I have been teaching the *Aeneid* for many years, but I have never before heard a boy read those difficult passages so superbly." Stunned, Washburn stood in fear of the next exercise. "Washburn," the teacher continued, "you read so well that it is clear you understand every word of what you said. You may be seated." As a relieved Washburn returned to his seat, Sturgis turned his attention to Washburn's companion and ordered, "Turner you may rise and translate." Washburn received an "A" for his efforts; Tappy Turner received a "D."[35] Washburn's showmanship would serve him well in years to come; whether lecturing before larger audiences, speaking before Presidents and Kings, negotiating international agreements with foreign governments, crafting covert memorandum to President Franklin D. Roosevelt, or raising much-needed capital to support scores of future expeditions.

In 1926 Bradford Washburn was sixteen and had climbed every large peak in the Presidential Range of New Hampshire's White Mountains. Although large numbers of people frequently hiked through the area, Washburn was intent on playing a much larger role in the region. With his acquired knowledge of the area, and with no other comprehensive guide to the region available at that time, he published *The Trails and Peaks of the Presidential Range of the White Mountains*. This little vest-pocket guide, published with money given to him by a wealthy uncle, presented clear and concise trail descriptions, and contained his first widely published map, a meticulous hand-drawn work entitled "Trails of Mt. Washington and Near Vicinity."[36] The significance to Washburn of this relatively small map was far-reaching, as it signaled a clear and discernible moment when he wove together his love of the mountain landscape, joy of climbing, and passion for the outdoors. Decades later, Washburn would declare that the modest little book marked the "beginning of a lifelong career of sharing with others."[37]

The Mountains Take Hold

Family members continued to encourage Washburn's growing interest in the mountain world. In 1925, at the age of fifteen and still attending Groton School, Washburn received as a Christmas gift from his Uncle Charles a copy of Roger Tissot's classic alpine work, *Mont Blanc*. Tissot's book, vividly illustrated with striking photographs of alpine meadows and lofty glaciers, recounted the mountain's epic history, and ignited Washburn's interest in Europe's high glaciated peaks.[38] The fledgling explorer was drawn to the dramatic landscape of the Alps, and considered the region an ideal place to hone both his photographic and mountaineering skills.

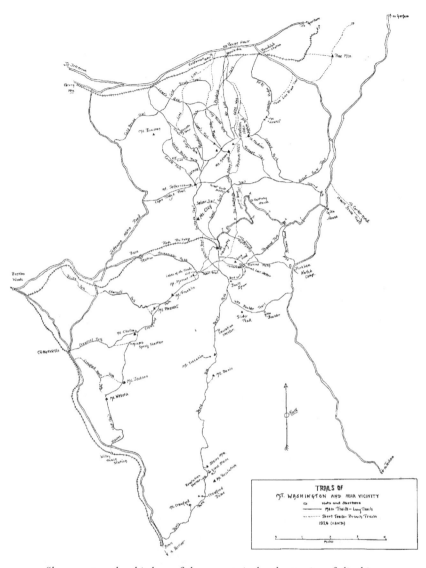

"he wove together his love of the mountain landscape, joy of climbing, and passion for the outdoors"

Washburn's first widely published map was included in his guide
The Trails and Peaks of the Presidential Range of the White Mountains
Courtesy of Bradford Washburn

Tissot's work exposed Washburn for the first time to the still fledgling scientific discipline of glacier studies and to the brilliant scientist and naturalist Horace Benedict de Saussure. Born in Geneva in 1740, de Saussure first saw the Mont Blanc massif during his travels to Chamonix before the Napoleonic Wars. The large and dynamic glaciers of the mountain fascinated de Saussure, who longed to study the composition of the ice as well as other facets of the peak. So enamored with the mountain was de Saussure that he offered a cash reward for the discovery of a practicable route to the mountain's summit.[39] In 1786 Michael Paccard, the local doctor, and crystal-hunter Jacques Balmat made the first ascent of the mountain. With a route now established, de Saussure returned to Chamonix the following year with ambitious plans to climb the peak and execute a number of research studies along the way.[40]

The 1788 expedition was unique in that upon reaching the summit, de Saussure erected a research tent and spent several hours recording temperature, mercurial barometric pressures, testing the boiling point of water at high altitude, and documenting physiological changes from the effect of altitude on the human body. He also "measured" the color of the sky from the summit, later comparing it with similar observations made in Chamonix. De Saussure continued his work on Mont Blanc the following year with a large contingent of guides and porters in support of an even more aggressive scientific expedition.[41]

Tissot's *Mont Blanc* had a profound impact on Washburn, who later described reading the little book as one of the most influential events in his life.[42] Indeed, it introduced Washburn to de Saussure's innovative combination of the sport of mountaineering, the art of large-scale expedition management, and interdisciplinary field science.[43]

A lecture presented on October 9, 1926, at Groton School by Captain John Noel, a member of the 1924 British Mount Everest expedition, also had a profound impact on young Washburn. Noel, the expedition's official photographer, presented the tragic story of the expedition on which George Mallory and Andrew Irvine perished just below Everest's summit.[44] As Managing Editor of Groton's *Third Form Weekly* newspaper, Washburn reported "a most enjoyable evening," with "vivid pictures of both the beauty and hardship."[45] Noel's presentation of daring mountaineering feats and glorious photographs of the Himalayas further intensified Washburn's interest in mountain photography. Sixty-two years later Washburn would lead the multi-national team of scientists and explorers that made the most detailed large-scale map of the world's highest mountain.[46]

By the age of sixteen, Washburn had further refined his keen skills through frequent climbs in both summer and winter months. So it was welcome news to the would-be explorer that the family would visit the mountains of France, in the summer of 1926. Bradford and his younger brother Sherwood (Sherry) accompanied their family to Europe where their father, now a professor of church history, was on a special sabbatical. The boys spent three glorious weeks in the heart of the French Alps surrounding Chamonix and Zermatt; then as now, a mecca for mountaineers. Under the tutelage of local mountain guides, the Washburn brothers refined the skills they had developed in the White Mountains on the ice-encrusted slopes of Europe's most challenging peaks.

It was a glorious summer. Bradford, sixteen years old, and Sherry, fifteen, achieved an impressive list of successful ascents including the Matterhorn (14,690 feet), Mont Rosa (15,217 feet) and Mont Blanc (15,780 feet).[47] Washburn also seized the opportunity to work on his photographic techniques. Despite the rather limited ability of his small Kodak pocket camera to capture the full grandeur of the region, a number of pictures were of fine enough quality to accompany two climbing articles Washburn authored for *The Youth's Companion*.[48]

Washburn's stories and photographs captured the attention of American publishing tycoon George Putnam, founder of G. P. Putnam and Sons, who considered such mountaineering stories a perfect fit for his newly created series *Boys' Books for Boys*.[49] Before his second visit to Europe in the summer of 1927, the seventeen-year-old met with Putnam in New York to solidify plans for a book chronicling his forthcoming mountaineering adventures. Putnam's order for two hundred thousand advertising sheets to support future book sales showed his confidence in Washburn's manuscript.[50]

Later that summer, the Washburn brothers spent another two months in Chamonix, completing a number of difficult climbs, including a traverse of the rather difficult Grand Charmoz and Grepon. With boundless energy drawn from the successful climbing season, Washburn completed his manuscript in less than two weeks. *Among the Alps with Bradford* was his

"the 'impossible' first ascent of the north face of the Aiguille Verte (13,520 feet)"
Washburn and guides on the summit of the Aiguille Verte.
Left to right: Nineteen-year-old Washburn with legendary alpine guides
Alfred Couttet and George Charlet

Negative 57-266, copyright Bradford Washburn, courtesy Panopticon Gallery, Waltham, MA

first of three books for Putnam's series.[51] In 1928 Putnam published Washburn's second book entitled *Bradford on Mt. Washington,* which recounted the young man's experiences climbing the peak that had opened to him the world of mountaineering.

The brothers returned to the Alps twice more in the coming years, where they continued their apprenticeship under the famous French alpine guides Alfred Couttet, Georges Charlet, and Antoine Ravanel. During this time Washburn made a number of impressive climbs, including the "course classic"–Charmoz-Grepon, the traverse of the Drus, the first traverse of the arête des Rochassiers, and the second ascent of the Col des

Deux Aigles.[52] Even by today's standards, these climbs were extremely difficult.

However, the Washburn climb most celebrated, and the one that caught the eye of most European mountaineers at the time, was the "impossible" first ascent of the north face of the Aiguille Verte (13,520 feet) in the summer of 1929. The soon-to-be Harvard freshmen accomplished that summer what is still considered by the mountaineering community an alpine classic. What makes this climb so impressive is that it traversed mixed rock and ice at a sustained angle of over sixty degrees, yet the endeavor took a mere four hours and twenty minutes to complete from base camp to summit.[53] Washburn's accomplishments were acknowledged that same summer by France's elite alpinists, who elected the young American to membership of the Groupe de Haute Montagne of the French Alpine Club.

Washburn continually improved his photographic skills by taking hundreds of pictures in various types of terrain and weather conditions. Once again, his mother played a central role in his development when she convinced her son that, although his pictures were of good quality, they were too small to capture the true aesthetic value of the region. Washburn soon retired his tiny "vest pocket Kodak" and applied the proceeds from his book and magazine sales to purchase a superior 4"X 6" "Ica Trix" camera. The camera enabled him to take large-format photographs of his climbs, and instantly enhanced the quality of his work.[54]

Washburn's photographic career advanced significantly when he came under the tutelage of famed Chamonix photographer and filmmaker Georges Tairraz. With Tairraz's assistance, Washburn filmed and directed his first 16mm movie during a traverse of the Grands Charmoz and Grepon in 1927.[55] Although pleased with the film's climbing content, Washburn believed a sequence of aerial photographs of the region "would help give scale and dimension" to the mountain terrain and more accurately capture and portray the region's topography "than ground photographs from any conceivable location."[56]

So Washburn hired renowned French pilot Thoret to fly him high above the surrounding peaks. The pair took off from nearby Le Fayet airport and circled the skies overlooking Chamonix. With the wind lashing his face, Washburn leaned out of the plane's open cockpit and snapped his first aerial photographs of Mont Blanc and the surrounding region, and in doing so, conducted one of the earliest aerial surveys made of the French Alps.[57] The power of aerial photography for the investigation of landscape and in the selection of potential climbing routes became clear to Washburn. He continued producing motion pictures, and joined George Tarraiz to make the first complete and commercially viable mountaineering motion picture of a traverse of the Grepon on 35mm film. Washburn would later use this film in public lectures at Harvard, to raise much needed income to support several expeditions throughout his undergraduate years.[58]

Washburn's photographic equipment as well as Thoret's tiny monoplane would be considered rather crude tools of the trade by modern standards. Nevertheless, their flight was among the few that ushered in a new and dynamic era of aerial photography and contributed to the practicability of the emerging field of photogrammetry.[59] As Washburn notes, the experience crystallized his passions and lured him closer to a career in the "study of mountains, glaciers, and geomorphology from the air."[60] He realized that aerial photography not only advanced the cause of the geographer and geologist, it provided a detailed and literal description of the mountain terrain that could serve as an invaluable resource for the mountaineer. Subsequently, Washburn employed aerial photography and reconnaissance on nearly every expedition that he directed.

In the fall of 1929 Bradford Washburn followed a long-standing family tradition and enrolled at Harvard College, where he studied French history and literature. To those familiar with his passion for exploration, geography, photography, and mountain climbing, Washburn's choice seemed a bit odd. However, he would later declare "you must pursue those endeavors that make you most happy." The beauty of the French language and culture had taken hold of Washburn. Quite simply, Washburn believed he could pursue a number of interests at once: academic pursuits in the classroom, and adventure when time allowed.[61]

While at Harvard Washburn began a busy schedule of public lectures profusely illustrated with his personal collection of climbing photographs and movie footage. Proceeds from his lectures augmented his college and living expenses, and provided a source of funding for future expeditions. His speaking circuit quickly expanded. In 1930 he lectured with acclaimed outdoor photographer Burton Holmes in New York's Carnegie Hall, Symphony Hall in Boston, and Chicago's Orchestra Hall.[62]

Although such "performances" have become a financial mainstay for many of today's more notable mountaineers, outdoor photographers, and explorers, it was Washburn, along with a small group of other mountaineers, who forged a path other adventurers have since followed. In doing so, he secured a place as one of America's first professional mountaineers.

By the age of twenty, the young Harvard student had amassed an impressive list of credits, including numerous first ascents, the production of a number of maps, articles, and books, an impressive portfolio of striking mountain photography, and a thriving lecture circuit. It is little wonder that such accomplishments caught the attention of National Geographic Society president Gilbert Grosvenor, who invited Washburn to lecture at one of the Society's official gatherings in 1930. That year Washburn joined a distinguished list of Society presenters that included such celebrated explorers as Captain Robert A. Bartlett, Sir Wilfred Grenfell, Rear Admiral Richard E. Byrd, and Dr. Laurence Gould.[63] Washburn's first National Geographic Society lecture, entitled "Following a New Trail to Green Needle's Tip," was illustrated with his private stock of photographs. The breadth of the talk and the crisp photographs impressed the audience of seasoned explorers; the Society's president was equally taken with Washburn's presentation.[64] By the end of the evening Grosvenor had become a fan of the young mountaineer, and thus began a unique relationship between the Society and Washburn that continues to this day.[65]

In the summer of 1930, with the promise of bold adventure and new horizons, the Harvard student turned his ambitions, expertise, and boundless energy to the glacier-clad mountains, unknown landscapes, and unexplored regions of Alaska and Canada. Washburn believed that this remote north country held untold opportunities to test his skills, in an unknown landscape that had not been mapped, climbed, or photographed in any detail. For Washburn, climbing, photographing, and exploring would soon turn from avocation to profession, and would lay the foundation for his life's work.

2

Glaciers, Grosvenor, and Grand Explorations

"Challenge is the core and mainspring of all human activity. If there is an ocean, we cross it; if there's a disease, we cure it; if there is a wrong, we right it; if there is a record, we break it; and finally, if there's a mountain, we climb it." James Ramsey Ullman

The Pathfinders

By the summer of 1930 Bradford Washburn had completed his freshmen year at Harvard and was preparing for his first of many expeditions to Alaska and the Yukon. The mountains of southeast Alaska and British Columbia rise dramatically from sea level to heights in excess of eighteen thousand feet. Powerful tides, dense forests, thunderous Pacific storms, and one of the world's largest concentration of temperate glacial ice serve as a natural barrier to the vast alpine system that extends inland for hundreds of miles.[1] The region is entombed in thousands of square miles of glacial ice.[2] The mountains of Southeast Alaska are generally divided into three distinct networks known as the Coast Mountains, the Saint Elias Range, and the Wrangell Mountains.

The Wrangell Mountains span approximately one hundred miles in length and sixty miles in width. They are located between the Chitina River in the south, the Nabesna in the north, and the Saint Elias Range and Copper River in the east and west respectively. Several large peaks are found in this volcanic range, including Mount Blackburn (16,390 feet), Mount Sanford (16,237 feet), and Mount Wrangell (14,163 feet).[3]

The glaciers of the Alaska Coast Mountains compose one of North America's most extensive mountain networks and define the Alaskan boundary with British Columbia.[4] The glaciers in this region cover an area from the Canadian border in the south to the Fairweather Range in the north. The Juneau and Stikine Icefields comprise the majority of ice within this complex, covering an area in excess of 2,500 square miles.[5]

The Saint Elias Mountains run adjacent to the Coast Mountains, extending three hundred miles in length and ninety miles in width along the Alaska-Canadian border. This area ranges on the southeast from Cross Sound, Icy Strait, and Lynn Canal northward to the Bering and Taku Glaciers, and terminates at the White River.[6]

The Fairweather Range is situated within the Saint Elias Mountains, stretching northward from Cross Sound in the Gulf of Alaska to the Alsek River. A cluster of glaciers flows from the heart of this range, where mountains rise from sea level more dramatically than in any other mountain system on earth. In some cases peaks soar above 18,000 feet within a few miles of the coast. The principal peaks of the Fairweather Range include Mount Root (12,860 feet), Mount Crillon (12,700 feet), and Mount Watson (12,516 feet). The monarch of the range, Mount Fairweather (15,300 feet), dominates the landscape.[7]

The mainland of Alaska was unknown to the outside world well into the eighteenth century. In 1741, Vitus Bering, in command of Russia's Great Northern Expedition, sailed southeasterly from Kamchatka around the Aleutian Islands, then northeast, where the ship anchored off Alaska's southeast Panhandle. From this vantage point the expedition noted a massive snow-clad mountain towering high above the shore. Bering named the peak Mount St. Elias in honor of the feast day of St. Elias on the Orthodox Church calendar.[8]

The expedition's naturalist George Steller was charged with collecting, cataloging, and describing the area's natural history and ethnographic findings. However, Bering was less interested in this aspect of the expedition and more concerned with documenting the region's abundant and lucrative marine mammal population. He was even more concerned with their prompt and safe return to Russia, so Steller was permitted a mere five hours on nearby Kayak Island to collect and study specimens of both fauna and flora. Despite the short time made available to him, Steller documented the significant population of the much-coveted sea otter and made the first ethnographic studies of the region. His scientific work, the first systematic investigation of the region's resources, triggered a decades-long exploitation of the area's marine mammal populations.[9]

Russian merchants, government, and church all followed Bering's lead, and settlement of the region expanded in the decades following discovery.

Yet Russian dominance of geographic exploration of the region, mostly in the interest of resource extraction and economic development, would eventually be challenged by other nations. Celebrated British explorer Captain James Cook surveyed Alaska's coastline during his Pacific voyage in 1778, and noted the existence of an entire network of towering mountains, which he named the Fairweather Range. Less than a decade later, French explorer La Perouse, in search of the Northwest Passage, explored the waters and coastal areas of Yakutat Bay and later discovered and mapped Lituya Bay.[10] In 1787, while carrying out the first systematic survey of the region, English explorer George Dixon produced the first map of Yakutat Bay.[11]

Alejandro Malaspina, an Italian in the service of Spain who executed a more accurate survey of the bay, followed Dixon's exploration in 1792. Yakutat Bay was of particular interest to the Spaniards, as they believed that the still undiscovered link from the Pacific to the Atlantic, the "Strait of Anian" or Northwest Passage, lay in the immediate vicinity of the Bay.[12] Upon further investigation Malaspina found the bay to extend further inland than previously believed, yet his work was abruptly halted as the waters terminated in an immense network of ice known today as the Hubbard, Turner, and Miller glaciers.[13] Leaving a permanent footnote in the region's history of exploration, he named this area "Disenchantment Bay."[14]

Captain George Vancouver's Northwest Passage expedition of 1794 carried out the most extensive survey of southeast Alaska to that time. In doing so, Vancouver found no evidence of the Strait of Anian and noted in his diary that he had "removed every doubt, and set aside every opinion of a north-west passage."[15] It is interesting to note that early exploration (and significant geographic discovery) of this region, similar to that of the eastern and northern Canadian Arctic, found much of its impetus from the determination of many nations to discover and subsequently exploit for economic and political gain a navigable Northwest Passage.[16]

Numerous expeditions were dispatched to southeast Alaska throughout the nineteenth century, including the 1874 United States Coast Survey. Under the auspices of William Dall and Marcus Baker, the expedition conducted a detailed survey along Alaska's southeast coast, including Yakutat Bay. Dall carried out many observations of the area's geology and glaciers, and recalculated the height of Mt. St. Elias to be nineteen thousand five hundred feet, over one thousand feet higher than today's accepted height.[17] A subsequent triangulation completed by the Coast and Geodetic Survey found the correct height of St. Elias to be 18,100 feet and set Canada's Mt. Logan at above 19,000 feet.[18]

The pioneering naturalist John Muir explored the glaciers of southeast Alaska with Presbyterian minister S. Hall Young in the summer of 1879. On this and subsequent visits Muir was captivated and inspired by Alaska's natural beauty. He wrote numerous popular accounts of his Alaskan experiences, painting for the reader a landscape etched by glaciers, abundant wildlife, stands of ancient forests, and limitless wilderness. His romantic language and love of the wild came at a time when nineteenth-century American expansion was slowing and its frontier diminishing. For the armchair explorer and would-be adventure traveler, Muir offered images of a vast land, undiscovered, wild, and untainted, just as the American West had been just decades earlier. Muir so eloquently brought to life America's last frontier that his work soon served as a scientific catalyst for Alaska, extending the last remnants of American continental "Manifest Destiny" to this still relatively unknown region.[19]

Although Lieutenant C. E. S. Wood was the first European to discover Glacier Bay in 1877, it was Muir who popularized the Bay. By 1883 Muir inspired both tourist and scientific cruise ship excursions to Glacier Bay and the surrounding region. The number of scientific investigations increased dramatically in the coming years as tourism and science formed a unique partnership in one of the grandest laboratories on earth for the study of alpine glaciers. Indeed, Muir's powerful observational skills were surpassed only by his ability to describe the natural landscape. This "inductive method," which came easily to Muir when applied to geologic inquiry, had by this time become a fundamental component of scientific investigation.[20] While in Yosemite, contemplating the vital role glaciers played in the formation of the valley, Muir became fascinated with their role in shaping the mountain landscape.[21] His observations in Alaska served to confirm his conviction that glaciers had indeed been the powerful mechanisms responsible for the formation of the Yosemite Valley.[22] Muir's observational skills and uncanny ability to convey a dynamic landscape on paper spurred significant glacial research in Alaska throughout the closing decades of the nineteenth century.[23] "John Muir's greatest contribution," suggests historian Morgan Sherwood, "was the publicity he gave to the Far Northwest as a field for scientific and aesthetic investigation."[24]

Yet Muir's work was not the sole catalyst for such exploration. In the late nineteenth century, the United States government, most notably the Army and United States Geological Survey, founded in 1879, began a systematic survey of Alaska's resources. Growing interest in Alaska's mineral wealth, geography, geology, and the emerging discipline of glaciology, combined to fuel these efforts.[25]

William Blake conducted the first extensive scientific study of Alaska's glaciers along the Stikine River in 1863, nearly three decades after similar investigations had begun in Europe.[26] G. Frederick Wright explored and studied Glacier Bay in 1886 and was followed by two expeditions under the auspices of Professor Harry Reid to the region, in 1890 and 1892.[27] Reid was joined by a complement of students from Cleveland's Case School of Applied Science who conducted motion studies of Muir Glacier. Reid deployed the most modern scientific and photographic equipment available and developed standards and practices for further research on the mechanics of glacial flow and behavior.[28]

While Reid was investigating Glacier Bay, geologist Israel Russell led survey and scientific expeditions to the Mount St. Elias region in 1890 and 1891, under the auspices of the fledgling National Geographic Society and the USGS. Russell was directed by the Society to give "special attention" to the distribution of glaciers and to compile information "with reference to the age of the formations. . . and the type of structure of the range."[29] Moreover, the Society charged Russell with a reconnaissance of the largest area possible, from which he was to prepare a map of the region and attempt an ascent of Mount St. Elias. The result encompassed an area in excess of one thousand miles.[30] Although Russell failed to reach the mountain's summit, he did complete a rough survey of the peak (elevation 18,100 feet), photographed the mountain and surrounding glaciers, and obtained substantial glacial observations and ground-based photographs. He also wrote a detailed description of the Malaspina Glacier's unique characteristics as well as those of the Hubbard Glacier. Russell's data would serve as benchmark information with which subsequent observations could be compared.

Before the end of the nineteenth century, two noteworthy private expeditions also explored this region. In 1897 the Italian explorer, the Duke of Abruzzi, made the first ascent of Mount St. Elias. During the expedition he also documented the Malaspina Glacier's interesting composition, and speculated as to its source. Along with celebrated mountain photographer Vittoria Sella, Abruzzi took hundreds of photographs that illustrated the expedition's official account, including Sella's now famous large format black and white pictures. Sella, a pioneer in mountain photography, was one of Washburn's boyhood heroes and inspired him throughout his early photographic career. The two men (Sella and Washburn) would add significantly to the photographic record began by Russell just years before.[31]

In 1899 Edward H. Harriman, the American millionaire industrialist, privately financed the Harriman-Alaska Expedition, for which he secured the services of leading scientists, geologists, and naturalists such as William Dall, Grove Karl Gilbert, Henry Gannett of the USGS, and of course John Muir. Thus Harriman created a floating scientific laboratory whose accomplishments included a comprehensive photographic record and survey of the termini of numerous glaciers along Alaska's southeast coast. The expedition's contribution to science cannot be overstated. Information obtained by this floating "interdisciplinary institute" has today proven invaluable to further scientific investigation in that it provides a basis for subsequent research in areas such as climate studies, glaciology, and related fields.[32]

Muir's popular writings, coupled with the published reports of Russell, Abruzzi, and others, spurred a small cottage industry in Alaskan glacier photographs. In fact, widespread sale of glacier postcards from Southeast Alaska became a popular tourist craze. Many professional photographers were lured north and a significant collateral benefit of their work resides in their permanent record of the precise location and disposition of many of the glaciers of the region at the turn of the twentieth century.

By 1900 the general features and location of most of Alaska's coastal glaciers had been documented but a relatively small group of surveyors and topographers journeyed further into the region to measure and photograph the coastal glaciers. Their names now constitute some of the most distinguished early twentieth century geologists and field scientists, among them Otto Klotz (Canadian Topographic Survey), USGS topographers/geologists Stephen Capps, Ernest Leffingwell, Alfred Maddren, J.W. Bagley, Walter Mendenhall, John Mertie, and pioneer glaciologists Harry Fielding Reid and William Field, whose career spanned more that six decades. During the first two decades of the twentieth century, photography played an integral role in documenting and mapping the position and termini of many of Alaska's glaciers.

Among those celebrated scientists who quickly incorporated the camera into their fieldwork were Ralph Stockman Tarr of Cornell University and Lawrence Martin of the University of Wisconsin. The pair conducted extensive glacial surveys along Alaska's Panhandle from 1904 through 1912, when Tarr died; they took several thousand photographs over the course of their study. Their research encompassed a broad geographic region from Prince William Sound to Yakutat Bay, Valdez, to Cordova. Beginning in 1909, under the auspices of the National Geographic Society and the American Geographical Society, the two scientists concentrated their efforts in the Yakutat Bay and Prince William Sound region. Their findings, which included photographs and detailed survey data of the region's glaciers, were published in the classic text *Alaskan Glacier Studies,* a benchmark turn-of-the-century resource.[33]

Mount Fairweather

In 1926 renowned American glaciologist William Field a graduate in geology from Harvard College, organized his first of many photographic and survey expeditions to southeast Alaska. Field was particularly interested in Glacier Bay and Lituya Bay, where he recorded conditions and the termini of numerous glaciers.[34] This and subsequent research by Field in Alaska was a bridge from the pioneering work of the late nineteenth and early twentieth-century scientists to an emerging cadre of young and eager novice exploratory scientists. Upon his return to Harvard several years later, Field presented to the school's faculty and students a lecture accompanied by vivid photographs, describing his summer explorations.

In attendance that evening was the young Bradford Washburn. The mountain scenery, dramatic glaciers, and the little-explored region beyond the coastal ice absorbed the Harvard undergraduate. By the close of the presentation, Washburn was convinced of Alaska's enormous opportunity for geologic and geographic exploration and the lecture sparked an interest in southeast Alaska that would drive his desire to explore this region in the years to follow.[35]

Captivated with Alaska, Washburn raised the subject of an expedition to the region several months later with good friend Bob Morgan, a member of the team to make the first ascent of Canada's Mount Logan in 1925. On a winter's evening in January of 1930, the two men discussed several ideas for an expedition to the area. Over the course of several hours, they concentrated their attention on Mount Fairweather, the tallest unclimbed mountain in North America, and reexamined the unsuccessful attempt on the peak in 1926. As the discussion continued, Washburn became more intrigued with the challenge of making a first ascent in Alaska while at the same time capturing topographic and geological information that might be of benefit to the scientific community.

Bill Field's mesmerizing Alaskan photographs and the lure of the continent's tallest unclimbed mountain consumed Washburn's thoughts throughout the winter and spring of 1930.[36] Although Washburn was well aware of the many expeditions to the region, he later commented that the Fairweather region still provided a "big chance for exploration."[37] This romantic idea consumed the thoughts of the young Harvard student, and "having nothing better to do," Washburn spent many "enjoyable February evenings" counting up "probable costs of a trip to Alaska and listing foods and equipment."[38] The far north that William Field had introduced to Washburn would soon become a path to chart the uncharted, photograph the unknown, and climb the unclimbed.

Preliminary plans to climb Mount Fairweather during the winter of 1930 progressed so well that Washburn recruited six Harvard classmates to comprise what became known as the Harvard-Mount Fairweather Expedition.[39] Washburn planned carefully for his first foray onto Alaska's rugged peaks. He knew that many remote expeditions in this era of exploration experienced significant challenges with food preparation, distribution, and transportation. He was adamant that such logistical hurdles be eliminated "so that if we were beaten it would be by the mountain and not by our own under preparedness."[40] This point vividly illustrates Washburn's maturity and leadership abilities at the age of twenty. From this philosophy emerged the Washburn "food bag system" of preparation, whereby each day's food for the entire team was contained in its own food sack. This process eliminated the tedious and time-consuming labor of measuring and allocating stores of bulk food on the mountain. The bags were numbered for each day of the trip, guaranteeing the men an ample food supply "because the same amount was waiting untouched" in the next day's provisions.[41] Washburn incorporated this simple and efficient technique into many future expeditions. Its ease and efficiency soon caught the attention of other explorers and mountaineers who incorporated the scheme worldwide.[42]

Although the expedition's primary focus was to make the first successful climb of Mount Fairweather, Washburn included in his plans a number

"the treacherous ocean currents negated any plans of landing anywhere near to the Cape"

Members of the 1931 Fairweather Expedition aboard the "Typhoon," on their way to Lituya Bay. Left to right: Ken Olsen, Ralph Batchalder, Art Emmons, Gene Kraetzer, Bob Burns (pilot and boat owner), Washburn, Dick Hodges in front

Negative 57-302, copyright Bradford Washburn, courtesy Panopticon Gallery, Waltham, MA of relatively modest field research components. He was determined to document and photograph the mountain's geologic features and glacial systems for a preliminary survey map of the mountain's surrounding landscape.[43] Nevertheless, the primary purpose of the expedition remained the ascent of the tallest unclimbed peak in North America. The all-Harvard expedition headed north to the territory of Alaska on June 13, 1930, arriving in Juneau, Alaska four days later, seven months after the crash of the U.S. stock market.[44] Their equipment was transferred to a rented thirty-four foot gasoline powerboat, the *Typhoon,* on which the team would travel for a day and a half to their planned coastal base camp near Cape Fairweather.[45] However, the treacherous ocean currents negated any plans of landing anywhere near to the Cape. Washburn was forced to establish a base camp at Lituya Bay, the only protected waters in the vicinity, and the site of several cursory explorations.[46]

With their plans now altered, the team faced a long march to the base of the mountain over nearly twenty miles of virtually unexplored country. The added distance and subsequent time delays taxed the food and fuel supplies they had so carefully calculated and packed. Although a rough and dated map of the Lituya Bay area existed, the team was in relatively virgin country.[47] At nearly every turn they found opportunity to climb, survey, explore, and study in a region that noted Alaskan geologist Alfred H. Brooks had proclaimed "par excellence . . . in which to study glaciers."[48]

The men began their arduous ascent to the base of the mountain, placing camps along the lower moraine-strewn slopes of Fairweather. The unplanned march to the mountain challenged the team beyond their expectations. In two weeks they ferried over fifteen hundred pounds of supplies to the base of the mountain, straining under back-numbing packs that ranged in weight from forty-five to over one hundred pounds. Eventually they climbed to an altitude just short of seven thousand feet, where they encountered an impassable ice face that required a lengthy circumnavigation. Such a route, Washburn calculated, would have taxed the expedition's food to within just a few days of supply.[49]

"We had reached the limit," Washburn would later write, "where safety and sport give place to undue risk."[50] With obvious regret, and after much thought, Washburn realized that the "time had come for us to turn back," and preparations were made to begin the long and arduous trek back to

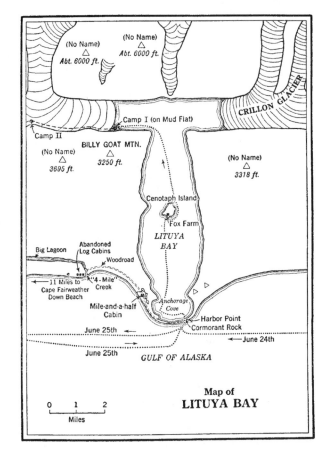

*"a preliminary ground-based survey from which a map of Fairweather's lower
slopes and potential climbing routes were eventually produced"*

Washburn's Fairweather Expedition map of Lituya Bay

Courtesy of Bradford Washburn

the Pacific coast." Washburn later confessed that his first foray among the
peaks of Alaska was a "great disappointment" and the Fairweather
expedition was a "bitter introduction to Alaska mountaineering." He did
however note that the "risks of so hurried a campaign would be great" to
continue.[51] Washburn consoled himself with the amount of scientific data
the group was able to compile, including weather records and geologic
samples.[52] In addition, he took hundreds of photographs and thousands
of feet of motion picture film of the region's glaciers and mountain
landscape. The team also carried out a preliminary ground-based survey

from which a map of Fairweather's lower slopes and potential climbing routes was eventually produced.[53]

By the summer of 1931, Washburn's skills as an outdoor photographer and mountaineer were in such demand that he was invited to make the first commercial film of an ascent of Mont Blanc for outdoor adventurer and lecturer Burton Holmes. While Washburn was filming in the Alps, two of America's best-known alpinists, Terris Moore and Allen Carpe', beat him to the prize, the first ascent of Mount Fairweather. Upon his return to the United States Washburn began working on a second expedition to Fairweather for the summer of 1932, when he planned to expand the cartographic and geologic work he had started in 1930.[54]

In order to bypass the landing at Cape Fairweather that had plagued the 1930 expedition, Washburn had the men and some equipment ferried by plane to a lake at the mountain's base. With that prescient decision, Washburn incorporated the airplane into the many tools of Alaskan mountaineering and geographic exploration, altering the nature and conduct of both endeavors from that time forward. Improvements in the airplane's structural and engine design during the First World War and the inter-war years made airplane use possible in such isolated regions and under unpredictable weather conditions.[55] From this point forward, Washburn's career was defined and often identified by his continued use of emerging technologies and the innovative incorporation of such technologies in remote geographic exploration and field science.

Mount Crillon: If at First You Don't Succeed . . .

Despite his planning, Washburn's second expedition to Fairweather fared no better than the first. During the flight, Washburn discovered that the lake on which he intended to land was still ice-covered from the long Alaskan winter. His original plan was to land at Lituya Bay and pick up the more than three thousand pounds of supplies cached there via boat from Juneau by the expedition's advance party. However, the Bay now became the expedition's base camp, and Washburn's hopes of surveying Fairweather were dashed before the expedition's work began.

Although such a diversion was a bitter pill to swallow, Washburn was able to execute an aerial reconnaissance of the region, and took scores of aerial photographs, capturing for the first time from the air the vast network of glaciers and geologic formations found far inland from the mountain's ocean location. The photographs would be added to the groundwork of topographers and geologists who had earlier explored the region by foot and packhorse.

Washburn refocused the expedition to concentrate on 12,728-foot Mount Crillon, whose summit dominates the sky high above Lituya Bay. Crillon was not only more accessible to the expedition, but also had the distinction of being the second tallest unclimbed mountain in the Fairweather Range. In fact, since the region directly surrounding the peak was virtually unknown, a clear path to the mountain had not been identified. The team, comprised of Walter Everett (who had climbed Mont Blanc with Washburn the previous summer), Harald Paumgarten, Richard Riley, Robert Monahan, and close friend Robert Bates, spent the remaining weeks exploring the slopes and glaciers adjacent to Lituya Bay, looking for a reasonable route to the summit. They spent considerable effort collecting geologic samples, photographing the landscape, and extending inland the topographic survey work of the U.S. Coast & Geodetic Survey in 1926, and the coastal aerial photographic survey carried out by the USGS and U.S. Navy. This latter expedition had produced over seven thousand photographs of the area, including the coastline of the Fairweather Range.[56] In addition to new survey stations, Washburn reoccupied several existing stations established by the U.S. Coast & Geodetic Survey just six years earlier. Dr. Hamilton Rice, director of Harvard's Institute for Geographic Exploration, was a significant supporter of the expedition, making fieldwork possible through the use of the Institute's survey equipment.[57]

Although the Crillon region had not been the expedition's original goal, Washburn completed an energetic plan of mountaineering, topographic surveys, geologic investigations, and aerial photography. By late summer of 1932 the team had spent nearly seventy days in and around Crillon, completing an extensive reconnaissance survey of Lituya Bay, Crillon Lake, and Crillon Glacier. Eventually, the mountain's slopes proved too challenging for Washburn and his team and Crillon's summit would have to wait. In fact, Washburn twice more attempted to climb the mountain and on each attempt incorporated a broader and more complex scheme to survey and photograph from the air a larger portion of the Fairweather

Range, in hopes of extending the previous ground-based survey data he had obtained. "To me the attraction of the Fairweather Range lay not only in climbing on its virgin mountain Peaks," Washburn would later write, "but also in the study of their geology and in delving into the unique secrets of their great glaciers."[58]

In the spring of 1933, Washburn earned his undergraduate (A.B.) degree from Harvard and enrolled for the following fall in the University's graduate geology program, one of the most eminent in the country. He returned to Crillon in 1933 and 1934 with expedition teams composed of students from both Harvard and Dartmouth College. Crillon Lake served as the expedition's base of operations. From here Washburn expanded his previous survey stations to more than a dozen, and calculated the position and altitude of each peak in the area.[59] Washburn's topographical work began to yield significant information about the region's unknown areas, peeling back the layers of the landscape in precise and extensive surveys.

Like Washburn's previous Alaskan expeditions, the 1933 Crillon expedition failed to reach the mountain's summit, although during the course of the summer the team made two attempts to reach the peak. The first was thwarted after an agonizing seventeen hours of climbing, when a fierce blizzard forced them to descend from an altitude of 11,500 feet. The team returned to the refuge of their high camp at 11:00 at night, for a few short hours of rest while the storm abated.

At 2:45 the next morning the clouds lifted from the summit and Washburn, along with Bob Bates and Walter Everett set out on a second attempt. Although Alaskan summers provide nearly twenty-four hours of daylight, bitter cold temperatures, high winds, and exhaustion dogged the men as they retraced their steps from the day before. By 7:00 in the morning the trio had reached the summit ridge, where the men took turns plowing a trail through deep new snow. An hour of backbreaking work found them only one hundred yards closer to their goal. The ridges dropped away on all sides to a twisted floor of ice and crevasses, and badly corniced ridges demanded extreme concentration.[60] The wind continued to build, often forcing the men to their knees. The cold brought their hands close to freezing in their ice-encrusted mittens. After a lunch of corned beef and chocolate at 9:30, the winds died down enough to allow the men a clearer view of their surroundings. To their delight they discovered that the mountain's slopes dropped away into thin air. Hopeful that the summit lay just beyond the broken clouds ahead, they mustered enough energy to cheer in unison, "It must be the summit," but as Washburn later reported via radio from the mountain to his contacts at the *New York Times*, "hardly had our cry of triumph been raised when out of the driving mist and snow a great spectre loomed before us." Crillon's summit was still five hundred feet above the team. The climb was "more treacherous than ever. We were dealing with climbing conditions far too delicate for weary legs." Although the summit was tantalizingly close, "better judgment told us to turn around while we had strength."[61]

Despite the fact that his Alaskan expeditions had yet to yield a successful summit bid, Washburn's topographic and photograph work were indispensable. He returned to Boston later that summer with the most comprehensive topographical, geological, and photographic record of the region to date.[62]

Under the auspices of the Geological Society of America and Harvard University's Institute for Geographic Exploration, Washburn returned to Crillon one final time in 1934, determined to expand the scope of his previous topographical and scientific fieldwork, and make yet another attempt to scale the peak.[63] Renowned American glaciologist Dr. James Goldthwait suggested an ambitious study to determine the flow rate and behavior of the Crillon Glacier. Goldthwait encouraged Washburn to select his son Richard, a recent graduate in geology from Dartmouth and a member of the 1933 Crillon team, to conduct the fieldwork.

As a member of Washburn's Crillon 1933 expedition, Goldthwait had conducted a series of bihourly movement observations of the South Crillon Glacier, using a "Tavistock" theodolite and glacier-motion markers. These observations, the most extensive carried out at that time, indicated significant fluctuations in glacial velocity with possible diurnal periodicity in flow.[64] As Washburn later reported in a 1935 edition of the *National Geographic Magazine*, Goldthwait's findings "dealt a death blow to the popular idea that a glacier moves slowly, steadily along, like an irresistible river of ice." The data, he continued, "stand as mute evidence that a glacier moves in waves or jerks."[65] However, as Goldthwait's methods and technology were relatively new to the field of glaciology, he cautioned that the data raised more questions than they answered. For this reason,

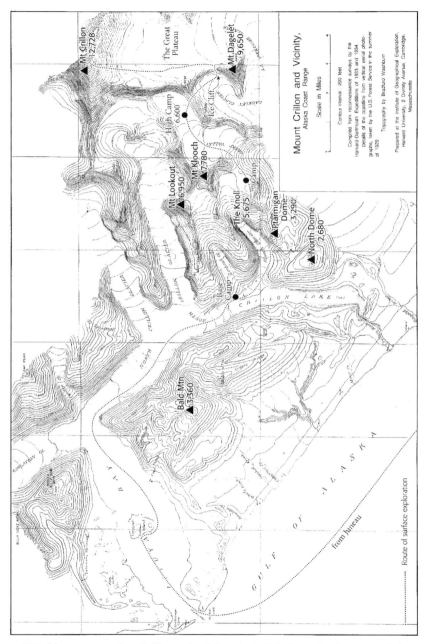

"Washburn returned to Crillon a final time in 1934, determined to expand the scope of his previous topographical and scientific fieldwork"

Washburn's 1934 Mount Crillon route

Courtesy of Bradford Washburn Collection

subsequent readings were undertaken the following year so that the technology and data collection could be verified.[66]

In the summer of 1934, more elaborate scientific and survey equipment was transported by plane to the base camp at Crillon Lake. A permanent survey station was built next to the glacier, where a cement pillar was placed as an accurate base for the Wild T-3 first-order theodolite, its first use in Alaska. Dr. Hamilton Rice, Director of Harvard's Institute for Geographic Exploration and primary champion of Washburn's photographic and glacial fieldwork, provided him with survey equipment and the Geology Department supplied geophysical blasting equipment to determine the depth of the glacier and the valley floor.[67]

The theodolite was used for continuous tracking of relatively minor movements in the glacier. The glacier marker consisted of a battery-powered lightbulb in a one-half inch brass tube dubbed the "glacier glider," on an eighteen-inch box placed on the ice.[68] A series of hourly and bihourly glacial observations showed that the rate of movement was irregular, "varying from zero up to a maximum of nearly 6 centimeters an hour," as Goldthwait and Washburn would later report. Weather records kept throughout the same period revealed a significant correlation between ambient temperature and the rate of movement. The glacier "flows faster during warm, sunny weather than when the sky is overcast," with the slowest movement occurring "during a cold rainstorm," the two men recorded in the expedition's official scientific account. They also found four general periods throughout the day when glacial motion intensified: "shortly after midnight; around eight o'clock in the morning; around noontime; later in the afternoon."[69]

Moreover, Washburn and Goldthwait identified a number of factors that could affect the rate and time of flow, resulting in a pattern of irregular and even spasmodic movement.[70] Although this evidence seemed to correlate neatly with ambient temperature, humidity, and day/night patterns, Washburn recommended additional research to support these findings. In 1936, Washburn secured funding from the Geological Society of America's Penrose Bequest, as well as technical and equipment support from Hamilton Rice, to place in the field a team of three men (Russell Dow, David Brink, and Benjamin Twiss) to reoccupy the 1934 Crillon survey stations and conduct a more detailed set of observations. Their data supported that of Goldthwait and Washburn, indicating very irregular and even "jerky accelerations" of Crillon Glacier.[71] As in 1934, the data revealed acceleration in ice flow during four specific times throughout the day, with a peak movement of twenty millimeters during a single fifteen-minute period. These findings supported numerous observations made on other Alaskan glaciers as well as those in Europe.[72]

During his Alaskan expeditions, Washburn incorporated a number of now-familiar scientific exercises including geologic sampling, aerial photography, air transport, topographical fieldwork, weather readings, and glacial observations. In 1934 he introduced the use of geophysical measurements in Alaskan glacier studies by obtaining seismic profiles of both Crillon Lake and Crillon Glacier. The technique was first employed by German geologist Hans Mothes from 1926-1929 on the Aletchgletscher and Hintereisferner in the Alps.[73] Washburn and Goldthwait were most interested in the precise depth and deposits, as well as the previous location of the glacier. Through seismic soundings of Crillon Lake, they found the U-shaped contour of the lakebed to be consistent with similar discoveries in other glaciated valleys.[74] Goldthwait's geophysical work was made possible by a rather generous stockpile of "40 percent DuPont nitroglycerine dynamite," enough explosive to generate sufficient seismic waves needed for such a study.[75]

The work of Goldthwait was also made possible by grants from Harvard's Milton Fund and the influential Harvard Committee on Geophysics. The Committee played a significant role in furthering geophysical research in the United States as a conduit for multidisciplinary work in an academic framework.[76] As a graduate student in Harvard's geology program, Washburn was quite familiar with the institution's prominent geophysics and geology faculty, and was aware that his interdisciplinary fieldwork was consistent with the Committee's interests.[77] As a result, he obtained not only financial resources for his work but technical assistance as well. Harvard faculty advisors to the Crillon expedition included several eminent geologists, including Dr. Kirtley Mather, Chair of Harvard's Committee on Geophysics, Professor Reginald Daly, and seismologist Dr. L. Don Leet.[78] Their participation and considerable support of a twenty-four year old explorer-scientist underscores the importance the committee placed on interdisciplinary expeditionary science. Moreover, the expedition's seismic work was of particular interest to the Committee, which supported such work throughout the 1930s, by more eminent explorers than Washburn.[79] Indeed, the Committee financed similar research during Admiral Byrd's first Antarctic expedition (1928-1930), and provided additional funding for seismographic investigations of the Antarctic ice sheet during Byrd's subsequent Antarctic work.[80]

The use of seismic techniques to study glaciers was a relatively new yet powerful tool for the emerging field of glaciology. Before 1934, few published accounts existed, although such techniques were employed by private industry in exploring for oil and mineral deposits.[81] Perhaps this is why Goldthwait suggested careful analysis of this new application. However, he believed that the "unearthing" of such innovations "is an encouraging indication" that such a method "may some day yield definite answers."[82]

During his Crillon expeditions, in particular the 1934 field season, Washburn introduced aircraft in support of scientific and geographic exploration and the transport of both men and equipment to and from remote regions. However, of particular interest and significance was the airplane's use in the relatively young yet burgeoning fields of aerial photography and photogrammetry.[83]

The 1934 Harvard-Dartmouth Mount Crillon Expedition traveled from Boston by train via Vancouver to Seattle, which they reached on June 2. The team consisted of David Putnam, Russell Dow, Adams Carter, Waldo Holcombe, Howard "Hal" Kellogg, Henry "Bem" Woods, Edward "Ted" Streeter, A. Lincoln "Linc" Washburn (no relation), Robert Styx, and Dick Goldthwait. From Seattle the team secured passage on the steamer "Alaska," and repacked baggage and supplies. Washburn even managed to fit in a bit of fun and relaxation. His diary for June 12 documents the evening's activities: "The party lasted until *4:15 A.M.*—a record lateness for me—I never saw so much beer go down so few throats in all my life! I drank a whole bottle of *MILK* and nearly disrupted the party!"

Washburn departed for Juneau the following day and arrived to meet his team there on the sixteenth. From here the team planned to ferry equipment to the Crillon Lake camp by boat and by air with pioneer Alaskan bush pilot Bob Ellis. On the twenty-second, Washburn boarded a Lockheed Vega seaplane equipped with pontoons to transport equipment from Juneau to Crillon Lake. The plane also was used to airdrop supplies and scientific equipment for eventual use by the team along Crillon's upper slopes.

"We had a most wonderfully beautiful plane-ride of all my life," he wrote that evening, "All Icy Strait was beautiful and clear with silvery seas of clouds to the west and north and the whole Fairweather Range rising silhouetted against the pale evening sky."[84] In just over an hour Crillon Lake came in to view, "it was a grand feeling to see the old glacier again" Washburn confessed, "It all looks so much like home."[85]

In preparation for the team's ascent and fieldwork, the following day Washburn began airdrops of equipment along the upper slopes of Crillon.

> We loaded the plane just level with 31 boxes and tents! The mechanic and I rode in the rear of the Vega and we took off the door and left it at the bay. We were so full that I had to crouch with my knees against my chin and hold a box from falling on top of me as we started to taxi toward the ocean to take off. We tried once with no success. I was pretty worried that we might have to take two trips. Then we taxied way back behind the island and gave her full throttle again. It took nearly 3 miles of taxiing before we finally got off the water just above Anchorage Cove! We swung up the bay in a gentle arc, climbed up the Crillon glacier, over Crillon Lake and over the La Perouse Glacier making Altitude. [86]

Large numbered boxes, painted orange for easy identification in the vast sea of ice, were strategically dropped in predesignated areas without parachutes. Washburn tossed each load out the plane's main door, allowing for a "terrific drift due to our speed and altitude of at least 1,000 feet above the snow field." They kept a detailed list of each box's contents, and a map indicating the "last known position" of each box, to facilitate recovery. According to Washburn's calculations, his aerial supply technique completed in one day what a full complement of climbers would take as much as two weeks to accomplish afoot.[87]

The expedition methodically moved up the mountain as the days passed. Long hours establishing a route to the summit, surveying, photographing, and searching for the orange supply boxes filled the days. Evenings were spent repairing equipment and enjoying the spoils of Washburn's use of air transport to supply such a remote camp. The men had almost all the luxuries one could want at such a place: a radio transmitter, operated by David Putnam, provided two-way communication with the outside world; dinner feasts were topped off with raspberry tarts; and Viennese waltzes played on the team's "Victrola" set the proper mood for dining.

On the morning of July 12, 1934, Washburn and Goldthwait began the aerial photographic reconnaissance. The photographic survey was underwritten by the Penrose Research Fund of the Geological Society of America, whose leaders were particularly interested in obtaining aerial photographs of the unique banding characteristics of the Malaspina Glacier. Grantland Rice donated additional financial support to the project, making possible an expansion of the reconnaissance to include the peaks and glaciers of the St. Elias Range.[88]

As the plane ascended to ten thousand feet, Washburn removed the door, and placed in his lap a large Fairchild aerial camera. With a hemp rope about his waist tied off to the plane's internal frame, Washburn leaned out from the door into the roar of Arctic winds and photographed Lituya Bay, Yakutat Glacier, and the receding Nunatak Glacier. His photographs revealed that the Nunatak's ice front was nearly six miles further inland than Tarr and Martin's coastal surveys twenty-five years earlier, an average rate of retreat approaching one quarter-mile per year.[89] The Nunatak had, to this time, experienced numerous recessions from its maximum advance during the eighteenth century, which were documented at the turn of the twentieth by Gilbert as well as Tarr and Martin.[90] Indeed, the latter had found significant recessions of the Nunatak from 1895-1909, followed by a two-year advance. The advance was short-lived, as the glacier once again receded between 1911 and 1913.[91]

The Nunatak glacier had not been explored since Tarr and Martin, and now Washburn had documented its surface for the first time from the air, providing researchers a scientifically significant perspective of the entire area.[92] These calculations and observations, later supported by those of Maynard Miller, a Harvard alumnus, in 1946-1947, further amplified the historic record of glacial surges and recessions.[93]

The flight exceeded even Washburn's expectations. However, the trip did not come without its problems. Exposure to the raw elements at nearly three vertical miles above the mass of ice took its toll on photographer and crew. With the plane's door removed, "It was terribly cold at 14,000 feet," Washburn recorded in his diary that evening, "and I had lost all sensation in my knees." In addition to the cold, other perils faced the team. "We ran out of gas in our tank halfway across the [Malaspina]," Washburn later declared, "almost exactly where we did last year—and glided about 20-30 seconds before the other feed-line got functioning—these are always rather nerve-wracking waits especially in a sea-plane over an icefield 30 miles from the nearest water."[94]

From the Nunatak Glacier the plane headed towards Hubbard Glacier, the largest tidewater glacier in North America.[95] From this vantage point, Washburn noted that the "Turner, Haenke, Varigated . . . seem to be essentially where they were 30 years ago."[96] Washburn's work added detail only available through aerial photography to the ground-based work of Russell (1890-1891), Gilbert (1899) and Tarr and Martin (1905-1913).

Washburn's aerial photographs were so concentrated on this region that they provided a wonderful perspective of Alaska's glacial landscape as an integrated and interdependent network of geologic processes. As the eminent glaciologist William Field observed, survey teams could not obtain such details because of the "difficulty in making observations at higher levels," a domain left to those hearty "mountaineering or surveying parties" who struggled desperately to "extend their activities" above the snow line.[97]

Moreover, scientists could now study and map these glacial networks as part of the total ice system of which they were a part. Glacial characteristics such as crevasses, annual bands, and moraines could be seen in a new dimension, part of the larger mountain-glacier system. Field noted that the airplane, in the employment of a skilled photographer, "made possible an expansion in the scope of glacier studies in Alaska."[98] Quite simply, Washburn was the first to implement these techniques in Alaska on such a grand scale.

A primary objective of 1934 aerial reconnaissance (as well as the shorter and less extensive 1933 survey) was to secure more detailed aerial photos of the dynamic processes evident on the surface of the region's glaciers, in particular the complex folded medial moraines of the Malaspina Glacier. Washburn succeeded in capturing wonderfully detailed images of the bands and loop moraines from a maximum altitude of sixteen thousand feet. He also photographed the unique forest growth that tenuously sprouts from the stagnant, moraine-covered terminal ice of the glacier. The "end of the glacier is covered by trees . . . but not so widely spread and only a fringe at the coast," he later noted. [99] Washburn carried out a series of detailed photographic studies of the "surficial phenomena of the glacier in an attempt to solve from the air the problem of their origin."[100] The severe temperatures and flying conditions failed to daunt his enthusiasm as he realized the significance of his work. "What a marvelous view to get an idea of the vast extent of the glaciers there in the Pleistocene," he would later recall."[101]

The Malaspina Glacier had been the subject of a number of scientific investigations before Washburn's photographic survey. Located in the Yakutat Bay region, the Malaspina is categorized as a "piedmont glacier," an impressive expanse of ice created by the convergence of several tributary glaciers, of which the Seward Glacier and Agassiz are most extensive.[102] While exploring the Yakutat Bay region in 1874, Dall and Baker had made note of the glacier, but were not able to study in detail its unique surface characteristics. They had returned in 1880 and documented its impressive low-lying ice plateau, to which they gave the name Malaspina, in honor of the Italian explorer.[103] Ten years later, Israel Russell placed the glaciers of the St. Elias Range within two distinct groups. He categorized the first group as alpine glaciers, or "ice-streams" similar to the "type found in Switzerland," and the second as "piedmont glaciers."[104] Russell found that the formation of massive ice plateaus, such as the Malaspina, occurred "where alpine glaciers leave rugged defiles through which they flow and expand and unite on an adjacent plain."[105] He compared this type of glacier to "a vast lake of ice" and named this previously unrecognized ice system a piedmont glacier.[106]

As a result of this particular convergence and interaction of ice streams and the subsequent debris deposited from such a union of ice, referred to as the Seward-Malaspina Complex, the Malaspina's surface is covered with extensive medial moraines. The glacier also exhibits darkened bands of debris. Known as "annual bands," these were described by Tarr and Martin as "long, sinuous lines of scroll-like moraine, forming a black tracing in the expanse of clear white ice." However, they failed to identify the band's origin, admitting that the phenomenon was "difficult to understand."[107] Russell had suggested the bands were the result of variation in ice flow, whereas Tarr and Martin hypothesized their origin to be the product of rock and avalanche ice that had fallen onto the upper reaches of the glacier, subsequently spreading out across its surface over time.[108]

Washburn's photographs and subsequent study led him to propose a number of theories as to the origin and behavior of both folded moraines and annual banding. He theorized that the Malaspina's contorted moraines were a result of the "spasmodic variations in volume of the many tributary glaciers" feeding into it.[109] In this sense, Washburn and Russell were in agreement. However, the cause of these variations was not yet known. Ralph Tarr suggested that the observable variation in ice flow and glacial advances throughout the Yakutat Bay region was created by "avalanching during earthquake shaking," the result of which is a magnificent force capable of moving great volumes of ice. This proposal formed the basis of his Earthquake Advance Theory.[110] Tarr dismissed other theories such as climactic variations and snowfall accumulations (or mass-balance), noting that only a "very notable addition to the reservoirs could bring about so spasmodic and so great a forward movement."[111]

Washburn supported Tarr's assertion, arguing that his survey of the Malaspina reinforced the notion that contorted moraines were a result of the pressure exerted on the debris by great volumes of ice triggered by large regional earthquakes. Through his graduate studies and devoted readings in this area, Washburn found "completely acceptable . . . this 'earthquake advance theory'" responsible for "the patterning of Alaskan moraines."[112] However, this theory was deemed suspect by subsequent researchers, including Austin Post and Maynard Miller. Three decades later Miller argued that earthquakes are "but a supplemental and generally minor factor" in glacial advances, and the primary catalyst was a result of "meteorological causes."[113]

Although Washburn supported the theory, he did leave sufficient room for additional interpretations. In 1935 he wrote, "Either this [Earthquake Theory] or some complex climatic change may be the cause" for the variations in the ice flow.[114] This issue would long remain uncertain.[115] Regardless of the underlying fundamental causes for the spasmodic glacial flow of the Malaspina's tributaries, Washburn's aerial photographs clearly portrayed the entire Malaspina network, complete with its complex sequence of tributaries converging into one massive ice lobe at its terminus.

Although Dall, Russell, Tarr and Martin had studied and photographed from the ground the Malaspina's glacial surface and unique valley terminus, Washburn's ability to capture such images from the air afforded a visual understanding of the interaction and interdependence of the entire Malaspina-Seward glacial complex. Today many theories are offered to explain the "flow instabilities" that produce folded and contorted moraines. These features are commonly associated with surging glaciers.

Washburn was also interested in photographing and studying the annual bands found along the surface of other glaciers. From such work he advanced not only descriptions of the phenomenon, but also provided some thoughts on their development. The annual banding of many of the world's steepest mountain glaciers was a topic of debate during the late nineteenth and early twentieth century. Russell noted, as did Tarr and Martin, that annual banding was clearly evident on Alaskan glaciers, yet their origin was not fully understood. Subsequent research would show that the bands, now known as "ogives," develop only within glacial icefalls, yet not all icefalls generate ogives.[116]

There are two distinct forms of ogives. "Forbes bands," named for the Scottish geologist, who first described them, are characterized by alternating light and dark bands or "waves".[117] Topographic waves evident on the surface of a glacier just below an icefall are known as "wave ogives" and, as Robert Sharp points out, "consist of a series of transverse swells and swales."[118] Like Forbes bands, wave ogives are created by glacial ice flowing over and through an icefall, each pair representing one year's advance of the glacier.[119] Although both types of ogives are created within icefalls, their formation is dependent upon two very different and distinct mechanisms.

King and Lewis showed that Forbes bands are created by the accumulation above, and subsequent passage through, the icefall of debris-laden ice in summer months and snow in winter months. As the dark summer bands and lighter winter snow bands slowly move through and are compressed by the icefall, they emerge as alternating narrow sets of bands.[120] Indeed, Forbes envisioned the bands to be the "true annual rings of the glacier, like those of a tree."[121] Washburn's aerial photographs of the Malaspina and adjacent glaciers, as well as surveys carried out in Europe of the Mer de Glace, vividly portrayed the Forbes band phenomenon on a grand scale. A significant portion of glacial flow above and below the icefall, in particular, can be seen in these photographs, allowing for detailed and enhanced study of glacial banding. In addition, Washburn's photographs provided sufficient information for him to speculate on the creation and dynamics of both Forbes bands and wave ogives, although the latter term had not yet been developed. He understood that the formation of both types of bands was contingent upon ice flow through an icefall.[122]

Washburn's photographs captured the dynamics of ice behavior, allowing for detailed study of the ice movement immediately before, passing through, and after its flow through an icefall. He found that relatively smooth ice above the icefall abruptly ended and fragmented into shattered blocks, which then flowed through and over the brink of the icefall. At the foot of the fall, ice blocks lay jumbled on the glacier's surface where they were annually melted down by the process of ablation. The result was a sea of valleys and troughs that became evident as the glacier advanced. "In place of every ridge," Washburn noted, "a band of white remains, and in the spot once occupied by every hollow lies a dirt-band."[123] Thus, in addition to alternating light and dark bands, topographic waves or wave ogives are also evident.

Washburn surmised that annual seasonal variation from year to year was responsible for significant ablation of ice blocks at the foot of the icefall during the summer months, thus creating "hollows" in which debris (Forbes bands) accumulates. Moreover, a combination of colder temperatures and snow accumulation during winter months "leads to the formation of a wave of ice instead of a hollow." Washburn's description is not unlike the "swell and swale" description of wave ogives advanced in later years by eminent American glaciologist Robert Sharp.

A similar process was proposed by Nye in the 1950s and subsequently supported by Vallon's research findings on the Mer de Glace.[124] However, Nye found that wave ogives were indeed a result of seasonal mass-balance fluctuations above the icefall and the deformation of the ice as it passed through the fall. In the falls, Nye found that large vertical blocks of ice experienced considerable horizontal stretching that increased surface exposure to summer sun, resulting in increased ablation and the creation of troughs in a wave ogive system.[125] Washburn noted and photographed the deformation and plasticity of glacial ice, particularly on the Malaspina Glacier in 1934. However, he did not attribute the mechanics of ice deformation in the icefall as a contributing factor in wave ogive generation.

Washburn's aerial photographs and ground surveys conducted throughout the Mount Crillon area captured dynamic geologic processes at work on a grand scale. He also proposed mechanisms responsible for the creation of glaciological features, some of which are still supported many decades later. In 1986 glaciologist E. D. Waddington noted that although Washburn "did not attempt to formulate the principle mathematically," his aerial photographs provided crucial information that allowed him to theorize "that the annual mass-balance cycle could cause wave ogives."[126]

In analyzing Washburn's researches in southeast Alaska, it is tempting if not compelling to draw comparisons with the work of John Muir. Each contributed uniquely to contemporary understanding of the natural world, yet neither was generally considered a "scientist" by his contemporaries, who were engaged in increasingly stratified scientific disciplines. Each approached the investigation of the natural world in a more interdisciplinary fashion, looking for the interconnectedness of the processes that underlie the study of the natural world.[127] Each man, whether by pen, sketchbook, or modern technologies, afforded a new vision of the land, and new avenues for the appreciation and further study of the mountain landscape.

Washburn's Alaskan expeditions (Mount Fairweather in 1930 and Mount Crillon in 1932 and 1933) failed to reach the summit of either mountain. However, in the summer of 1934, Washburn's Crillon team established depots along the mountain's slopes with the support of aerial supply flights, and aerial surveys were used to identify a practical climbing route to the summit. Washburn would employ this technique on all of his subsequent Alaskan expeditions.[128]

During the early part of July, 1934, the team made progress moving up the mountain, in hopes of placing a party within striking distance of the summit when the weather and busy fieldwork schedule allowed. On July 19, the team set out from their high camp at eight thousand feet for Crillon's summit. Washburn's lengthy and dramatic diary entry, written four days later, captures the toil, drama, and elation of that day. "Off for the South Col and points North!!!, south, west, and east at exactly *2 A.M.*" he began:

> When we left camp we planned to have a try at roping the cliff [one of the many obstacles the team would need to navigate on their way to the summit] and then, if plans fail, to make a trip to False Dagelet [a nearby lesser peak] for movies. In fact, the original plan had been to try False Dag [Dagelet] and never try the cliff at all on account of loose snow from this last storm, but the weather was so *perfect* and the night so clear and cold and the crust so hard that when we reached the South Col at 3:10 AM., we decided at once to have a whole-hearted stab at the cliff. We packed up (after changing to ski boots in grey of dawn) 200 willow wands, all the rations, 1 box of still film, 900 feet of "fixed rope," 3 rappel pickets, crampons and a few other necessities such as a shovel for cornice excavation. Then we skied to the base of the Cliff over the most divine snow imaginable—a hard crust with about 2 millionths of an inch of soft, fluffy frost surface. It was a curious sensation to just *fly* through the almost darkness and not have *any* idea of the contours of the snow ahead—all we knew was that it was safe to take it straight!—and we did. The cliff looked more formidable than ever; all studded with buttresses of rock that had never been there at all last year. But, although the snow slopes themselves were badly scarred by avalanches, not a single one had recently crossed the shrund. The cornice was *vast*—we started with the first clear dawn at 4 A.M., I with the determination that this climb was to decide the fate of the whole expedition's success or failure and that I must do my utmost in leading to try and break *some* way through the top. Bem went with me. Abner and Hal followed close behind. Wok and Ted awaited instructions below. Bem carried the fixed rope, Hal and Ad each had another rope plus the shovel and the three pickets. That was all we took, except for three bars of chocolate and some lemon drops, planning to be back at the col for lunch.
>
>   The schrund was our first surprise. The avalanche trough that had looked so easy several days ago, turned out to be a veritable terror of thin blue ice that we couldn't cross at all without a fixed rope from above. A short try convinced me of this and we retired a bit to the lower lip of the crack and looked about. The left side looked better, so we traversed a bit,

cut across a place where avalanches had filled the trough and then Bem belayed me and I climbed ahead. The lip of the schrund was almost vertical ice and it meant chipping both foot and handholds. At 4:30, I'd at last succeeded in stretching my foot around the corner and into the avalanche-chute—Zeus, what a feeling of comfort after that sheer wall of ice! Bem followed after a belay and then we simply *rushed* up the chute. He let me out full rope (20 meters) and then I belayed the rope and he pulled himself up it. All went perfectly. 2/3 way to the rocks he stopped and threw a fixed rope to Abner, belayed it and brought him and Hall up to us. Then we went ahead, Bem with the rope tied to his belt, till we reached the first rock ledge and the others followed again. We took another fixed rope to Bem's belt and continued upward without hesitation, this time up the steep *rocks*, always to the right of last year's route parallel to it.

The rocks were very steep in places, but we scarcely had a moment of doubt as to the best route and just roared ahead to the end of the new rope. This was fixed to another ledge 2/3 of the way to the top. Sunrise on Dagelet and the sea of clouds over the ocean was flooded with light—and the shadows of the great peaks with the curious "western darkness" above them. Crillon had appeared over the ridge to our left. We were at last as high as the lower lip of the Plateau and going strong. To our left we suddenly saw one of *last year's rappel pickets still standing* at a rather cock-eyed angle in the snow between two rock ledges. Well I remember what a relief it was to reach the Gibraltar on each damned trip! Now, however, we were on a narrow rib or buttress completely safe from avalanches that would course down the gullies to our right and left and never come at all near us—we'd believed it impossible last year, and maybe it was when covered deep with new snow.

After fixing this second rope we had no more and continued as fast as possible to the top of the buttress where a fine rock gave us a corking view of the cornice. Two bits of delicate rock only held us up for a few minutes. At 6:20 we reached the ledge with our hearts pounding like sledge-hammers. Above us, the edges of the plateau sharply cut the pale blue sky of early morning. To our left rose Crillon, crystal-like and defiant and sparkling, to our right towered the massive summit of Dagelet, its peak bathed in the full rays of the morning sun. Behind us the sea of clouds stretched endlessly to the horizon. *The cornice was swell*; the slope between it and us was *short* and *easy*. I gasped for joy. We'd made it! Moreover, we'd made a record ascent! 5 minutes of easy belayed climbing through perfect hard snow brought us to a sort of grotto beneath the cornice and, after twenty minutes of careful excavating, we were ready to make a new try for the Plateau.

I clambered on Bem's shoulders, tottering as I tried to get an axe-hold in the slope above a tiny gap in the overhanging snow. But I could find no firm spot into which to jam my axe, and I had to descend to my original place beside him and scratch my head for another solution. I chopped the handholds in the vertical snow above us and then jammed my axe in above them for a handhold to steady us as we slowly rose again in our little tumbler's act. This time we were more secure and I jammed my axe deeply into the hard snow several feet back from the edge of the cornice. The sun caught me full in the face. The ranges behind Glacier Bay burst into view. The Plateau glittered before me once more. I jammed the ice-axe to the very head, warned Bem to brace himself and, with a last little shove on his shoulder, I clambered out into the mystic county that Walt, Bob, and I left a year ago expecting never to return. What a feeling! It was inexpressibly marvelous to be there on the great plateau once more, face to face with the grandest old hill of them all! Bem followed quickly on my fixed rope after handing up my crampons, that I'd taken off to stand on his shoulders. We wasted no time. Abner and Hal were hot on our heels. The cornice work had given them time to catch up to us.

A council of war changed plans quickly. The crust on the plateau was solid and smooth. It was 6:45 in the morning and such a change at Crillon could not be overlooked. Ad and I were the logical ones for the attack. We *must* get *someone* up that old hill this year or bust. Then the new climbers showed their stuff. They buckled down to work and started to excavate a deep trench through the cornice to safen the uphill route (with the shovel). We yelled to Wok and Ted and they rushed to the South Col for more supplies. They were to act as the support party and follow us across the Plateau with the food and willow wands. Not a cloud was in the sky and there was scarcely a *breath* of wind. We could talk clearly to the men 600 feet below us at the bottom of the cliff! The assault now began in earnest.

We were totally unprepared, but the beautiful day and the presence of a large support party following close on our heels made possible climbing that would otherwise have been totally out of the question.

Ad and I took all the chocolate and lemon drops and I borrowed Bem's goggles. Then we started for Crillon at top speed. As we rushed across the Plateau, all glittering in the brilliant early sun, we planned our route of attack on the summit cone. The great snowfield seemed to melt away beneath us as we dashed ahead, our only thought was on that icy final pyramid that rose above us, ever neared and ever higher it seemed. At 8:15 we rested a few moments at 9600 feet at the foot of the summit slope. Then we started upward, Ad leading, I following to save myself for any difficulties that might arise higher up. All went perfectly. Details are useless! The slope was in utterly perfect shape, hard as rock and except for one wide crack at 10, 500 feet, quite free of all avalanche danger. We hurried by these in less than ten minutes, but avalanches must come down there very rarely to judge from the appearances. The slope above here steepened rapidly and by *9:20* we'd reached the upper lip of the great barrier crack that we'd seen from the plane. That plane trip saved us a long detour for I had the whole route perfectly imprinted on my mind. The grade lessened, cracks followed each other faster, but always covered deep with firm snow: the walking was harder—thick semi-windpacked snow that broke through ankle deep. Ad led us with a superb pace—slow, steady, short steps—the kind that get one up fast. The summit cone now rose in a staggering mass of blue ice, white snow and frost feathers to our left. The route that we'd chosen directly up the ridge looked possible, but we were not yet sure of it. An alternative lay to the left with a traverse about the summit cone 300 feet below the top and the final ascent of the west ridge. This we planned to avoid unless necessary, as the traverse to it was very steep and there was obvious danger of starting an avalanche in these loose snow conditions.

We made the ridge at 10:35—a good 23 minutes ahead of my predicted time from the top of the cliff and phenomenal time at that for a walk of 4 miles at least and a vertical climb of 3100 feet! We never rested, but kept relentlessly ahead, always fearing a change in the weather and not wishing to risk the loss of the top by lingering anywhere too long. The breaking became stiffer. The powder on top became considerably deeper (1 foot or so) but Ad kept nobly on. Here and there a bulge of blue ice under the snow warned us that Crillon was in much the same shape as when we tried it a year ago. At 11:00 we had traversed under the two bulbous gendarmes of frost feathers that lie between the col and the summit and were resting in a deep grotto, studded with a myriad fantastic frost feathers beneath its sheltered, overhanging southern wall. A tiny outcrop of granite here showed us that the whole peak is solid rock despite its icy appearance from this side. It was bitterly cold with a north wind. Powder snow sifted swirling by us. The wind hummed through the frost feathers and blew little eddies of them down our necks. Clouds were rolling in one endless ceiling to the north. Fairweather's peak had disappeared. We must hurry fast and not waste a moment.

The hardest part of the climb still lay before us. We could never tell how long it would take. Crillon was a tough customer to the last inch. We hastily ate a bar of chocolate, our next-to-last, munched a few fruit drops and put on our crampons. Ad's hands were so cold that I had to put his on for him. I had no parka. That was at the bottom of the cliff. My ski jacket had always been warm enough before and this time it was to get the acid test. I pulled my light snow-hat darn tight over my ears (my beret was also in Wok's sack coming up) and we started off through knee-deep powder, I now in the lead. Below us on the plateau, now all in the hot morning sun, we could see four tiny specks approaching the bass of the mass of Crillon. They were far behind us and the walking must be bad with the morning thaw. The sun looked hot down there! Circling the base of our second gendarme, we crossed a narrow bridge of snow on a steeply inclined bridge of ice across a deep green crack that acts as a sort of moat or shrund about the summit pyramid. The col between the gendarme and the peak was smooth, hard and safe. The wind hit us with a blast, leaden heavy with cutting snow and frost-feather. The clouds dropped lower. Mist swirled just above us, ripped off the peak by frigid wind.

For the first time we could look down on the other side of Crillon. The Johns Hopkins Glacier wormed its tortuous way below Glacier Bay, a mass of jagged ice-pinnacles . . . vast bottomless slope of jagged rock and ice and snow.

The summit cone now rose only 200 feet above us to the left. Its lower end was abrupt and vertical for a dozen feet. A short delicate traverse above the precipice was necessary before we could actually start the ridge itself.

Powder snow a foot deep covered lower layers of the blue ice. The snow must first be brushed aside before steps could be chopped. This I did leaning over while Ad belayed me from our last tiny col. Ten minutes work and we were on the ridge. Here the work was slow and steady. The danger would have been great without the greatest care—its whole crest was buried under an 8" coating of light powder and frost-feathers. The *actual* crest of the ridge was not where it seemed to be and was a good foot further to the left on the south side—the wind had built up a fake crest of treacherous frost and powder. Every time I brushed the layer away, first with the axe, then with my hand, to lay bare the smooth ice below, a swirl of nasty, cold snow blew up in my face, swirled down my neck and speckled my goggles! We progressed by *inches*, Ad constantly belaying, I slowly cutting steps, first balanced on one foot, then on the other. Ten minutes above the col the others disappeared behind a ledge below us, well on their way up from the plateau. Then the cold mist closed in on us. All we could see was swirling snow and a narrow knife-like ridge here rising before us and melting out of sight in the fog. But it wasn't long and we knew it. We kept steadily on; Crillon was to lose this time—she was doing her best to stop us, but she'd started too late.

At 12:20 the grade ahead seemed to lessen. A spectral ridge of white appeared from the clouds to our right. We must be nearing our goal. The steps could now be further apart. My left leg no longer swung in free air between footholds, nor did I lean precariously any more against the icy ridge. I planted my axe securely for the last time. Ad came to my side from the narrow ridge below. I pointed ahead and he grinned—"Oh if Bob Bates and Walt Everett and Harold Paumgarten could be with us now!" We both thought the same thing at the same moment. Then, too exhausted from the strain of the ridge to make a dash for it, we slowly plodded a hundred feet up a gently rolling surface of deep feathery snow. At 12:29:50 by my trusty Ingersoll (which I'm sure was at least a half-hour off at the time) we planted our axes in the peak of Crillon and shook hands till our wrists ached!

The stay on the top was short. Sheltered as we were by an up-draft of the wind, it was clear that the storm was increasing rather than diminishing. We took a couple of jubilant pictures with Ad's little camera—mine was somewhere on the slope at least a thousand feet below us! Then we started the descent after only ten minutes of the grandest exultation that two men have ever had!"[129]

Back at high camp the following morning, Washburn discovered that the lens of the camera he had used on summit day was loose. "The pictures yesterday were such a wild and complete flop," he wrote, "that I determined that we better do something to make up for our loss." Although Carter and Washburn had secured summit photographs with Carter's small pocket camera, Washburn was eager to capture the view with his larger format and more accurate camera. "The only solution was to try Crillon again and do it immediately," he proclaimed "and to bring along the movie camera and all the still cameras . . . this would ensure my reputation at least of bringing back good movies of wherever we've been."[130] With Washburn's desire for a quality photographic record of the peak, good weather, and willing teammates, the larger party headed for Crillon's summit once again the following morning just past midnight, loaded down with no less than thirty-five pounds of camera equipment.[131]

"we planted our axes in the peak of Crillon and shook hands till our wrists ached"
Washburn and Ad Carter on the summit of Mount Crillon
Negative 57-1899, copyright Bradford Washburn, courtesy Panopticon Gallery, Waltham, MA

At 12:35 A.M. on July 21, the team set out to reclimb Mount Crillon—without Bem Woods, who was nursing badly blistered feet and struggling with fatigue. Taking advantage of the fixed ropes and the steps chiseled into the slopes by Washburn and Carter the day before, the team moved quickly up the mountain. In contrast to the cold and blowing weather previously encountered by the men, Washburn noted that at 12,300 feet "*it was so hot that we could scarcely walk!*"[132] Just over ten hours after leaving camp, at 10:45 A.M., the men reached the cloudless summit of Crillon. "The view was utterly magnificent," Washburn later wrote, "Saint Elias, Fairweather, Logan, Lucania—all stood out clear and sharp to the north."[133]

Cenotaph Island, where previous Washburn expeditions had stopped on their way to Fairweather and Crillon, was like a "sapphire set deep in the lovely waters of Lituya Bay" from the summit. "How many have been the times that I've strolled the rocky shores of that island looking longingly and hopefully at the spot where we now triumphantly stood," Washburn recalled. The team unfurled the American flag and the Harvard school banner, and lashed them to a ski pole, to celebrate the expedition's two ascents. The men left the summit at 12:00 noon and arrived at their base camp at 5:00 P.M., an extended but exhilarating finish to one of Alaska's great mountaineering achievements.[134]

Among Washburn's many innovations in Alaskan expeditionary science and mountaineering was the use of radio communication, similar to that used by Admiral Byrd on his first Antarctic expedition in 1929-1930.[135] Byrd enlisted noted radio pioneer Lloyd Berkner to install communication equipment on his four planes similar to that devised by Berkner for Amelia Earhart's transatlantic flight.[136] Byrd's entire expedition stayed in close radio contact, and Byrd became "convinced of the value of radio to the safety and success" of the expedition.[137] Breakthroughs in radio technology had made such communication a viable and indeed critical tool in remote scientific exploration.

Washburn's team relied on "portable," twenty-pound, 56-megacycle frequency radiotelephones and a five meter high antenna for intercamp communications. The radio later played a vital role in coordinating the numerous glacial, cartographic and geologic projects Washburn directed: "It is truly *marvelous* to be able to hear detailed reports by voice from the high camp while things are going on."[138] Since the team was situated in areas that did not always afford line-of-sight communication, Washburn found that the team's ability to communicate in such fragmented and adverse terrain greatly improved his ability to carry out numerous projects at the same time.[139] He relied also on the radiotelephone to conduct the tedious aerial supply efforts, coordinating ground-to-air communication in support of multiple team members' supply needs throughout the Crillon expedition. Moreover, the use of a short-wave radio allowed for continued communication with Juneau and as far south as the continental United States.[140] Washburn declared the radio to be "the most vitally important factor in the success" of the Crillon expedition.[141]

Washburn and Grosvenor

Of Washburn's early accomplishments in Alaska, perhaps the most significant and innovative was his uncanny skill at taking oblique and vertical aerial photographs, and in applying them toward highly accurate maps. Although Washburn's systematic aerial photographs of remote regions ushered in a new era in Alaskan field exploration, the use of limited aerial photography had been employed in Alaska and other remote regions before the 1930s.[142] Before the turn of the twentieth century, the United States Coast and Geodetic Survey and other surveyors employed ground-based photographs to complement their work along the U.S.-Canadian International Boundary.[143] Using the technique pioneeered by Gilbert in 1899, C. W. Wright incorporated panoramic photographs in topographic surveys in Alaska in 1904.[144] J. W. Bagley, a USGS topographic engineer, introduced to Alaska the use of the camera in support of plane-table field survey work prior to the First World War.[145] R. H. Sargent, also with the USGS, in cooperation with the United States Navy, employed aerial photography to survey Alaska's Inside Passage just before Washburn's arrival in the region,[146] just as Admiral Byrd's Antarctic expeditions obtained significant vertical and oblique aerial photographs from which survey maps of the Antarctic were later produced.[147]

Although aerial photography was selectively employed by the nineteenth century from balloon and kite platforms, the advent of the fixed-wing airplane expanded the number of opportunities now available to the photographer and explorer.[148] Further technical refinements to the airplane, and to photographic film and equipment, allowed for the increased application of aerial reconnaissance and photography of troop movements and battlefield conditions throughout Europe during World War I. As geographer Arthur Robinson points out, during the first half of the twentieth century "nothing had exerted so great an influence on geographic cartography as has the occurrence of two world wars."[149]

Technical advances in photography and aircraft engineering during the interwar years were adopted by private industry, and later found domestic applications.[150] As evidenced by both Byrd and Washburn, such advances became a vital component of geographic and scientific exploration. Historian Ronald Doel points out that the photographic efforts associated with expeditionary science provided a powerful tool to detect and explain natural phenomena, and lured potential patrons, through tangible "dividends" of their patronage at work, to subsidize future endeavors.[151] Indeed, if a landscape photograph possessed such power, an aerial photograph would have even more redeeming aesthetic and scientific value.

Photographs such as those taken by Washburn not only illustrated geographic features and geological processes, they afforded an "aerial dimension" that dramatically portrayed a dynamic landscape. Washburn captured Alaska's vast ice-laden mountains in a visually compelling fashion, stirring the romantic yearnings of many an armchair explorer. Washburn capitalized on his talent by securing outlets for his images in popular magazines, journals, and books throughout the United States and abroad.

Washburn focused his energy on capturing the highest quality large-format mountain photographs possible, because this format highlighted and underscored the drama of the terrain and captured the detail of the landscape.[152] Washburn was determined to capture the natural landscape on its own terms, without regard to the difficulties in doing so. "When people climb big mountains," he would later recall, "there are always excuses why the photos didn't come out." Washburn invited, even sought the challenge, and found it "fascinating . . . to take large-format pictures in difficult circumstances and somehow or other make them come out."[153] The early master of large-format mountain photography was the celebrated Italian photographer Vittorio Sella, whose mantra, "big scenery should be photographed with big negatives," Washburn incorporated into his own style.[154]

Washburn's large-format techniques brought out the dramatic relief and vivid geologic patterns far better than previous Alaskan photographic surveys carried out by the United States Navy, USGS, and other state or federal branches, who had been concerned mostly with broad geographic data and international boundary issues. The photographic record Washburn amassed throughout the 1930s became a valuable benchmark and blueprint for those field scientists in Alaska who introduced large-scale glaciological research in the decades to come.[155]

In August of 1934, the Crillon expedition came to an end, and Washburn had accomplished his mountaineering, cartographic, geologic, and photographic goals. Impressed by his achievement, the *National Geographic Magazine* purchased the rights to Washburn's official expedition account. However, the Society's magazine publisher Gilbert Grosvenor was interested in the story only if the Society had sole rights to the expedition's account and Washburn's sweeping photographs. Grosvenor recognized early on that the superior quality of Washburn's work satisfied the society's rigid standards for publication. He was impressed with both the aesthetic quality and scientific value of the photographs, and was prepared to bet on their broad appeal to the public. So we can understand Grosvenor's frustration on discovering that Washburn had sold a few advance expedition photographs to the *New York Times*. "The value of your material to us," he scolded, "is very much lessened if you have arranged for the widespread publication of it elsewhere."[156]

Washburn explained his motives to Grosvenor, stating "every cent of the costs of the expedition this year has been made from lecturing or selling photographs." He apologized for the necessity of selling the pictures, and declared that he would not have done so if "I had thought that so few pictures would make a difference to the *Geographic* article."[157] Although Washburn's Harvard education was paid for in part by his wealthy uncle, he needed additional financial support to cover many outstanding expedition bills. Indeed, having liquidated a personal life insurance policy to fund the 1933 Crillon expedition, Washburn found himself in a tenuous financial situation. He confided to Grosvenor that he was "up against the problem of making ends meet as well as studying." He also cited the significant research advice and financial support given him by Harvard's

Committee on Geophysics and the Penrose Foundation, but found it extremely difficult to secure significant funding "for an expedition into unknown country, which is led by an unknown explorer."[158]

Despite these difficulties, Washburn's first feature article for the Society, "The Conquest of Mount Crillon" was published in the *National Geographic Magazine* in March of 1935. The article brought the second-year Harvard graduate student instant recognition from the Society, as well as from the Geological Society of America and Harvard's Institute for Geographical Exploration. Moreover, both Washburn and Crillon team member Dick Goldthwait were invited to lecture at the Royal Geographical Society of London on the scientific and geographic accomplishments of the Crillon expeditions.

With such recognition, however, came criticism. In a business where patrons are few and far between, press, image, and headlines translate either into financial support or empty promises. Young Washburn was now perceived by some as competition for the limited resources necessary to underwrite remote exploration.

Father Bernard Hubbard, the "glacier priest," was one such critic. The veteran Alaskan explorer and geologist publicly denounced Washburn's Crillon expedition, minimizing its accomplishments and significance, describing Mount Crillon as a "lousy little mountain, one that we would take in stride on our way to something else."[159] Hubbard's motives were somewhat unclear, but Washburn wrote them off to professional and academic jealousy. He suggested to Grosvenor that his Crillon article and photographs were "raising enough comment to start him [Hubbard] off on the warpath."[160]

As Washburn was hard at work in the summer of 1934 on Mount Crillon, Hubbard, also under the auspices of *the National Geographic Society*, had been exploring and mapping the volcanoes of the Alaskan Peninsula. While the Society published Washburn's work as a full-length, lavishly illustrated article, Hubbard's expedition account received far less coverage.[161]

Hubbard also claimed that members of Washburn's expedition were "laid out" with injuries in a Juneau hospital following the expedition, and noted in an interview that he was "proud that no injury has ever come to any" of his [Hubbard's] expedition teams.[162] Although one Crillon team member did suffer the loss of a finger, Hubbard's claims were inflated.[163] Grosvenor played the middle ground, soliciting Washburn's reaction to Hubbard's public volley. Washburn began a written assault by branding Hubbard a more "Frank Buck type explorer than anything else." Washburn's policy on such public debate, he shared with Grosvenor, was to "praise other scientists and explorers when they have done admirable work and to keep quiet when they haven't." Washburn was not interested in having a public debate with Hubbard in the newspapers. "The faker and publicity hound," Washburn wrote, "usually seems to get put in their place in due time – he is nothing more than an out and out headline hunter."[164] He asked Grosvenor to "judge for yourself from my pictures and my article as to whether he [Hubbard] could 'take in stride' [such difficulties as Crillon presented] on the way to the four-thousand foot hills of the Aleutians" which Hubbard had described in his expedition account.[165]

Despite Hubbard's public criticism, Washburn's accomplishments in Alaska were celebrated in both scientific and expedition circles. As for the National Geographic Society, they had added to their ranks a new explorer, proven by the hardship of remote scientific fieldwork. Although his career was still very young, his promise was such that this young Bostonian could well develop into one of their most celebrated explorers. The skills and abilities of the young man placed him well along the path pioneered by such renowned American scientist-explorers as Israel Russell, Grove Karl Gilbert, William Dall, Ralph Tarr and Lawrence Martin, and, at that time, Admiral Richard Byrd.

Washburn had proven more than capable of delivering an exotic photographic product consistent with the Society's ever-evolving emphasis on captivating photography that underscored a rich, lively text. As scholars Catherine Lutz and Jane Collins point out, "The *Geographic* sought, on one hand, to be a potent force in exploration and scientific research . . . and on the other to win the attention of large masses of people"[166] placing the Society in an unique position to underwrite and disperse scientific knowledge. This allowed the "*Geographic* to speak with the voice of scientific authority."[167]

Support for official Society expeditions depended upon many factors, including the professional accomplishments and capabilities of the leader,

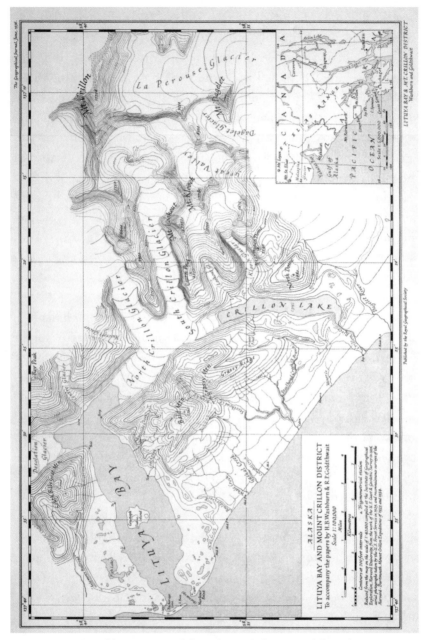

*"Washburn's accomplishments in Alaska were celebrated
in both scientific and expedition circles"*

Washburn-Goldthwait map of Lituya Bay and Mount Crillon District

Courtesy of Bradford Washburn Collection

the expedition team, and the potential to capture, in text and in photographs, the "romantic exploration" of remote and mysterious geographic regions.[168] Grosvenor was determined to meet the public's demand "for something that stirs the imagination."[169] Having positioned the *Society* to make the photograph a centerpiece of its work, he eventually succeeded in making photography its principal conveyor of geographic information. For this reason, Grosvenor was continually searching out new explorers who could contribute to the magazine's appeal through this format.[170]

Washburn's Alaskan photography certainly fit Grosvenor's formula. Since the First World War, the Society had been interested in aerial photography and exploration made possible by the use of aircraft.[171] In addition to supporting Admiral Byrd's 1928-1930 aerial photographic reconnaissance of Antarctica, in 1934-1935 the *Society* sponsored a portion of Captain Albert Stevens' stratosphere flights and aerial photographic surveys from high altitude balloons.[172] As Lutz and Collins point out, throughout the 1920s and 1930s the Society adopted a "straight photography" format that captured a "literal transcription" of the landscape, relegating the "presence" of the photographer secondary to the reader's interpretation of the image. Washburn's photographs fit this philosophy well, affording a bird's eye view of sprawling and dynamic landscapes, and allowing the reader to absorb vast expanses of mountain terrain, busy in detail and gripping in aesthetic value.[173]

The 1935 NGS Yukon Expedition

Just months after the Crillon expedition, Washburn seized upon the Society's interests in such endeavors. He knew that, despite his youth, he had proven himself worthy of future expeditions: "All of us here at the National Geographic Society," wrote Grosvenor, "are much impressed by your ability and success in achieving what you set out to accomplish."[174] The explorer quickly proposed to Grosvenor an ambitious expedition "to the east and north of the Saint Elias Range in the Yukon Territory," in country "which has never been explored by anyone."[175]

In 1913, the International Boundary Commission had surveyed from a distance Mounts Hubbard and Alverstone, two prominent peaks that delineated the boundary between the Yukon and southeast Alaska.

However, the survey teams did not explore or survey in great detail the terrain immediately surrounding the peaks.[176] The region west of Kluane Lake, traversing the 141st meridian to the Alsek River and further west of Yakutat Bay, remained virtually unknown. The *Society's* renowned field scientists Tarr and Martin described this area as "still largely unexplored," with "an intricate system of through glaciers filling valleys and passes."[177] Washburn's objectives included a detailed mapping of this region's landscape by air and overland exploration.[178]

Washburn's Yukon-Alaska proposal was no doubt appealing to Grosvenor, since as early as the 1890s the *Society* had invested significant financial resources in support of geographical exploration in this region. The young explorer brilliantly played this appealing angle. Washburn wrote to Grosvenor in early November of 1934 about an expedition "which has been proposed to me by one of the members of the two Crillon expeditions." The expedition, Washburn explained, would explore "to the east and north of the Saint Elias Range in the Yukon Territory," and is composed of "a large area of mountainous glaciated country which has never been explored by anyone." Washburn reminded Grosvenor of the "extensive experience" his team now possessed in the use of "radio, camping and airplane-photographic work." He underscored the need for such an expedition to "explore and map this last totally unknown corner of Northern Canada, which is really physiographically Alaska." Such an expedition, Washburn promised, "would bring back an immense wealth of knowledge from a glacial, topographic and geologic character. I believe an expedition would be able to justify itself many times in the data it could gather from an area known to contain the largest glaciers in the world." In conclusion, Washburn reminded Grosvenor, "the other side of the same range of mountains was explored" by Tarr and Martin's "National Geographic Society expeditions some twenty-five years ago." Washburn's proposal would provide a necessary supplement to the Society's earliest sponsored field explorations. He argued such an expedition would powerfully "associate the Society with the opening up of this magnificent country," and with the "popular science of glacial investigation."[179]

Washburn submitted his plan to Grosvenor on November 13, 1934, proposing a detailed exploration of the St. Elias Region, and a summit attempt on either Mount Lucania or Mount Vancouver, two of the tallest unclimbed mountains in North America. Grosvenor notified Washburn just two days later that the Society had approved his proposal and had awarded the team five thousand dollars "to conduct exploration under your leadership, as outlined in your letters of November 6 and 13."[180] Washburn quickly assembled his team, securing the assistance of Crillon expedition members Ad Carter and Bob Bates as well as veteran Alaskan guide, mountaineer, and sourdough Andy Taylor.[181] Other members of the team included Hartness Beardley, Ome Daiber, and Jack Haydon.

Through the remaining days of 1934 and into the first two months of 1935, Washburn and the team members purchased, packed, and finally shipped the expedition's food, equipment, and supplies to the Yukon Territory via the Panama Canal.[182] The expedition was scheduled to begin in February of 1935, and the team planned to travel by train, ship, and airplane to their base of operation in Carcross, Yukon Territory. From here, Washburn planned a sequence of aerial photographic and reconnaissance flights. The town would also become the team's base camp for their now publicly stated goal of traversing the Wrangell-St. Elias Range, completing the expedition by reaching Yakutat Bay and the Pacific Ocean.

"Yours is the first expedition we have entrusted to a man as young as yourself"

Washburn with his Fairchild F-8 Camera and Pilot Bob Randall during the Yukon Expedition

Negative 86318, copyright Bradford Washburn, courtesy Panopticon Gallery, Waltham, MA

Before the team's departure, Grosvenor offered "a few lines of caution" to the young explorer. Striking closer to fatherly advice than a cursory note of concern, Grosvenor wrote: "Yours is the first expedition we have entrusted to a man as young as yourself and your remarkable record . . . might very naturally lead you to be a little over-confident and take risks . . . that an older man might not venture to take."[183] He "emphatically" instructed Washburn to "take no chances in flying or in mountain climbing or in surveying" which may "imperil your life or the life of any member" of the team.[184]

The degree to which Grosvenor supported Washburn is evident in the letter's final sentence: "Remember that the mountains will be there next season, also the National Geographic Society, and there will be opportunities to return."[185] Indeed, his concern for Washburn and the expedition exceeded that of the Society's obvious interests in a successful campaign. Grosvenor was personally involved in the endeavor, and even wrote in advance of the expedition to representatives of Pan American Airways, the company contracted to provide air support to the expedition. Grosvenor outlined his expectations of the airline, trusting they would "take care" that Washburn be provided "SAFE" accommodation as he "will be exploring a very difficult region where inadequate or poorly equipped planes will bring disaster."[186]

The team reached Carcross, Yukon Territory, sixty miles north of Skagway, on February 25, 1935, just over three months after receiving financial support from the Society. Tons of fuel, food, camp equipment, movie and still cameras, survey and mapping equipment, sledges, and sled dogs were transported to this remote outpost. The following day Washburn, Andy Taylor, and pilot Everett Wasson set out on the first of several aerial reconnaissance flights into the heart of the St. Elias Range. Not long after the plane reached the virgin peaks, Washburn discovered and photographed "an immense glacier . . . finding its source right beside [Mounts] Alverstone and Hubbard and going all the way to the Alsek River." He measured it at nearly fifty miles in length, and named his first discovery Lowell Glacier in honor of Harvard's president A. Laurence Lowell, who had taken great interest in Washburn's work.[187] The Lowell Glacier, approximately 150 miles west of Carcross, was selected as the team's base camp. Washburn's aerial reconnaissance discovered that the glacier provided access into the St. Elias Range and offered the most practicable pathway through the mountains to the Pacific Ocean. Washburn's plan for the first traverse of the range depended entirely on decision.

Investigating the boundary peaks of Mounts Hubbard and Alverstone from the air, Washburn found the Hubbard Glacier to extend further into the St. Elias Range than had previously been documented. The Hubbard had been studied and photographed by Russell in 1890, Gilbert in 1899, and several Canadian Boundary survey teams in the late 1800s, as well as by Tarr and Martin in the early twentieth century.[188] "In the absence of more thorough survey," Tarr and Martin noted in a 1914 publication, "we cannot be certain of the length of the Hubbard Glacier." However, the glacier was generally accepted to be between thirty and fifty miles in length from tidewater to its hitherto unknown source deep within the St. Elias Range.[189] Although "no one has yet explored this region" in great detail, Tarr and Martin believed the Hubbard's origin lay in the vast expanse of glacial tributaries "of various sizes from Mount Hubbard, Mount Vancouver, and in the mountains beyond."[190]

Washburn's aerial survey of the Hubbard revealed that Tarr and Martin had been accurate in their now decades-old assessment. In a telegram from Carcross to the Society, Washburn noted that the Hubbard Glacier passed unobstructed from Yakutat Bay "all the way *through to [Mount] Logan in a ten-mile wide valley!*" and calculated its length to be nearly seventy miles, and "probably the largest glacier on the continent." The Society prepared a press release just days later, noting a "new demonstration of the amazing part that airplanes can play in exploring unknown patches of territory that are still left in the world."[191] It is now well documented that the Hubbard is the longest valley glacier in North America, more than ninety miles in length.[192] Throughout the expedition, Washburn's team made use of both telegrams and high frequency radios to provide progress reports to the Society. Grosvenor was able to keep the newspapers abreast of the expedition's progress. This type of public relations also built anticipation for a final account in the *National Geographic Magazine*.

In one telegram to Grosvenor, Washburn reported a previously unexplored landscape spanning an area over one thousand square miles. "The trip was accomplished at an altitude of slightly over 18,000 feet on a Fairchild Monoplane and took seven hours" roundtrip. "The door was removed from the plane for photographic purposes. The warmest temperature experience was five below zero," he continued, but the "flight commenced at 26 below zero in the morning." Washburn's narrative captures the day's drama and discoveries:

After flying across the maze of mountains between Carcross and the Alsek Valley we flew over three great unexplored glaciers south of Mt. Hubbard which the expedition is planning to map during the next two months on its journey toward Yakutat Bay from the Yukon. Circling to make photographs over the glacial waste south of Hubbard we flew west once more nearly over the corner of Yakutat Bay to determine whether it will be possible to cross the range to the Pacific side on foot while making our map. We believe that we have discovered both a safe and feasible route although it involves some 80 miles of dog sledging from our present base. Turning north we followed the course of the gigantic Hubbard Glacier for 50 miles to Mt. Logan. There we swung westward again crossing the vast expanse of the upper Seward Glacier and obtaining the first photographs ever taken of Mts. Cook, Vancouver, Logan and St. Elias from this angle. At this point we attained our maximum altitude of nearly 19,000 feet and had to descend on account of lack of oxygen and the intense cold. Almost brushing our wing tips on King Peak we passed over the Ogilvie Glacier up which the historic ascent of that great peak was made in 1925. We had hoped to be able to return by way of Kluane Lake and Mt. Lucania but here we encountered such a heavy northeast gale that we were scarcely able to make any progress at all in that direction.

After ten minutes of fruitlessly bucking this wind we descended to warmer and less turbulent air at 12,000 feet and made our way back to the base camp east of Mt. Hubbard where a landing was made at about one thirty in the afternoon. After lunch there we took a short flight to Kluane for our dog team which was carried 50 miles to camp in the airplane. We took off again reaching Carcross just after sunset. [Bob] Bates acted as recorder while I took the photographs. The [f]aultless piloting of [Bob] Randall and the perfect operation of our Fairchild camera and plane made possible a flight which with another that we plan for the near future is one of the most important features of our expedition. The number of glaciers and peaks which we have seen and photographed on our first two flights is almost inconceivable. These mountains represent the last stronghold of the great ice age on the North American continent; and I believe that we are successfully obtaining a photographic record of peaks and glaciers whose immense size and number have been dreamed of by the early explorers of the Yukon.[193]

Subsequent photographic flights, flown at altitudes over seventeen thousand feet without oxygen, uncovered four new glaciers and a previously unknown mountain range. Noting that 1935 marked the silver jubilee of the British Monarchy and Canada's status as a Commonwealth nation, Washburn named two of the more prominent peaks within the range Mount King George and Mount Queen Mary.[194] Washburn found the Logan, Seward, and Hubbard Glaciers to be interconnected, forming one of the largest expanses of glacial ice in North America. He was intrigued by the discovery of a towering ice-encrusted mountain with "terrific cliffs," which he named East Hubbard.

John Kennedy's Mountain

One of the more interesting discoveries of the 1935 Yukon Expedition was the Himalayan-like peak christened East Hubbard by Washburn in the spring of that year. The mountain's dramatic cliffs, etched slopes, and grand presence intrigued the explorer. In 1965 the Canadian Government renamed the peak Mount Kennedy—in honor of the slain American President.[195] Washburn's connection to the peak ran deep. John F. Kennedy had been a long-time friend and served on the Board of Trustees of the Boston Museum of Science, the institution Washburn led as Director from 1939 to 1980. To Washburn it was only natural that an expedition be formed to photograph, survey, and make the first ascent of the mountain.

Building upon the interest generated by the announcement, Washburn proposed to the National Geographic Society a comprehensive survey expedition of the mountain, along with a detailed study of Mounts Hubbard and Alverstone, the two original international boundary peaks. The expedition was set for the spring of 1965, almost exactly thirty years after he had discovered the mountain. It was quickly planned as an expedition of two phases, jointly sponsored by the Society, Washburn's

"The mountain's dramatic cliffs, etched slopes,
and grand presence intrigued the explorer"

The 1935 Yukon Expedition beneath their discovery of East Hubbard. The mountain
was later renamed Mount Kennedy in honor of President John F. Kennedy

Negative 57-68426, copyright Bradford Washburn,
courtesy Panopticon Gallery, Waltham, MA

Museum of Science, the University of New Brunswick in Canada, and
Michigan State University. In classic Washburn style, the expedition became
a complex mosaic of aerial photography, ground-based surveys, airplane
and helicopter landings, aerial resupply, international cooperation and
coordination, and of course mountaineering. [196]

From March through the end of May 1965, scientists, surveyors,
explorers, mountaineers, and photographers attacked the Mount Kennedy
region. The Yukon Flying Service, the Royal Canadian Air Force, and the
Alaska National Guard, with Klondike Helicopters providing critical
transportation, provided aerial support throughout the spring of 1965.

Detailed vertical aerial photographs were taken from altitudes ranging from 30,000 feet to a high of 60,000 feet, and were key components of the later map of the area.[197]

Ground control surveys, directed by Dr. Gottfried Konecny of the University of New Brunswick, were accomplished from mid-April through mid-May, spanning thirty-one days. The subsequent map of Mounts Hubbard, Alverstone, and Kennedy was the result of a large-scale and complex effort.[198] The completion of the mountain survey signaled to Washburn a closing of the circle that had begun in the winter of 1935. Yet the 1965 expedition also drew together the lines that would join the spirit of two brothers atop one of Canada's most remote peaks.

Writing in summer of 1965, New York Senator Robert Kennedy declared, "When the Canadian Government announced last winter that it would name this mountain after President Kennedy, it occurred almost simultaneously to my brother Edward and to me that we should climb it."[199] Although the younger Kennedy was not able to make the climb, a determined Bobby Kennedy let it be known that he would take part in the expedition.

Although primarily focused on the challenges of surveying in a remote region, Washburn met the news of the Senator's interests with more than a little trepidation. Washburn was concerned with the Senator's lack of mountaineering experience, the associated liabilities of having a novice participate in an expedition to such a remote region, and the political pressure to accommodate the Senator's time constraints. Washburn's initial response to the National Geographic was *No.* Negotiations with the Society, who supported the Senator's inclusion, continued for some time, threatening to delay the expedition. The Society was faced with a troublesome choice. How could they omit the President's brother from such an expedition? It is always good to have friends in high places, and the Society wished to keep the Senator happy while assuring Washburn that in no way would Kennedy's participation interfere with the expedition. "It is agreed that Senator Kennedy's opportunity is a one-shot deal," wrote *NGS Magazine* assistant editor Newman Busted, and guaranteed that the NGS will not "further delay the climb on Mount Kennedy because of his [Kennedy's] inability for weather or any other reasons to climb the mountain early in the week of March 22."[200]

On March 17, the Society's press release announced establishment of the expedition's advance camp at the base of Mount Kennedy. Mention of the Senator's participation was not included in the release, but it was noted that the team would survey, photograph, and explore the peak, as well as attempt "the first ascent of Mount Kennedy," led by "James A. Whittaker of Seattle, member of the victorious American Mount Everest Expedition."[201]

Robert Kennedy, Whittaker, James Craig of Canada, and NGS photographer William Allard arrived at base camp by helicopter from Whitehorse, Yukon Territory, on March 22. The following day the team, which now included Barry Prather, Dee Molina, George Sinner, and William Prather, began their climb along Cathedral Glacier to an upper camp where they spent a wind-tossed night at over 13,000 feet. Both Kennedy and Whittaker captured the climb in their subsequent article for the Society, in which they shared the joys of a first ascent and the celebration of a bond between two brothers.[202]

Perfect weather greeted the men the following day, and they set off along the north face of the summit pyramid. The team climbed all morning, till the summit came into sight just before 1:00.[203] Leading the team, Whittaker crested the last ridge and waited for the Senator to join him, "It's all yours Bob," Whittaker said. The Senator paused for a moment and then broke trail the last remaining feet toward the summit. Whittaker later wrote:

> Then Bob walked up to the summit, and he stood there about five seconds, ten seconds, and reached back over his shoulder, just the way I had reached back for my American flag on top of Everest. I remember thinking of that when he reached back, without looking. He groped for it, felt it, and pulled out the pole around which was wrapped the Kennedy flag and streamer. He jammed in into the snow.

After a few moments of silence, the Senator made the sign of the cross and as Whittaker recalled, "It was his brother's peak, and he stood there a long time."[204] Before leaving the summit, the Senator knelt and placed a number of family keepsakes in the snow, which he had carried with him throughout the trip. The *National Geographic Magazine* article describes the event as follows:

"I climbed Mount Kennedy for compelling personal reasons"

Senator Robert Kennedy on the summit of Mount Kennedy with William Allard. Kennedy stands behind the Kennedy coat of arms

Courtesy of Dee Molenaar

Mementos of a President lie on the mountain named in his honor. Senator Kennedy carried up John F. Kennedy's Inaugural Medallion, Address, and three PT-boat 109 tie clasps. The Senator's children, who adored their uncle, asked their father to bring the objects back. He did—all except one tie clasp, which was left in a hole in the snow."[205]

Before leaving the summit, the party obtained survey data of Mounts Hubbard and Kennedy that would later play a critical role in establishing the mountain's exact altitude and position.[206]

"I climbed Mount Kennedy for compelling personal reasons," the Senator later commented. And although he achieved a grand personal fulfillment, Robert Kennedy was also moved by the sheer experience of climbing and adventure.[207] "There was the mountain itself," he wrote, "and there was the knowledge that we had helped bring this remote part of the world closer to all of us." Kennedy's brief expedition account, in particular the last two short paragraphs, provides some insight into his emotions toward the death of the nation's president and his brother:

President Kennedy loved the outdoors. He loved adventure. He admired courage more than any other human quality, and he was President of the United States, which is frequently and accurately called the loneliest job in the world. So I am sure he would be pleased that this lonely, beautiful mountain in the Yukon bears his name, and that in this way, at least, he has joined the fraternity of those who live outdoors, battle the elements, and climb mountains.[208]

In 1968 the National Geographic Society published Washburn's map entitled "The Massif of Mount Hubbard, Mount Alverstone, and Mount Kennedy." The map was met with accolades from the scientific and geographic community. The Board of Trustees of the National Geographic Society awarded Washburn the prestigious F.L. Burr Prize for "extraordinary achievements and contributions to geographical knowledge through your exploration of the Yukon Territory of Canada, the discovery in 1935 and subsequent naming of Mt. Kennedy and the subsequent mapping of the Mt. Kennedy, Mt. Hubbard, and Mt. Alverstone area in 1965."[209]

Through Uncharted Ice

Washburn's 1935 aerial reconnaissance, photographs, and discoveries helped to guide his ground team through the massive ice-puzzle of the St. Elias. At the conclusion of each reconnaissance flight, he returned to Carcross and developed the photographs, which were labeled, logged, and placed into photo books so the men could later use them to navigate their way through the mountains to the Pacific. Washburn attributed the expedition's success to these aerial photographs: "Without that book," Washburn noted, "we would have been *utterly lost*."[210] Clearly the most important component of the expedition was the "photographic record of peaks and glaciers whose immense size . . . [had] never been dreamed of."[211]

By late March the aerial photographic surveys were complete, and Washburn permanently joined the rest of the team on Lowell Glacier as they moved steadily toward the heart of the St. Elias Range through the month of April. The men collected geologic samples, took moving and still photographs, and carried out Washburn's ambitious ground survey. Most the their time however was spent transporting by dog team the expedition's considerable stores of food and equipment into the unknown glacial network, slowly weaving their way up and over the mountain passes toward the Pacific Ocean.

On May 1, 1935, the team occupied the highest survey station (12,200 feet) in Canada to date.[212] "After a short rest at the beginning of the shelf, or plateau, at 11,000 feet," Washburn wrote, "we pushed ahead into a hard wind. It was a slow fight. It took us an hour and three-quarters to make the two and half miles that put us abreast of Mount Alverstone." After a brief lunch stop, Washburn began taking survey measurements "on some snow-covered rocks and started what was one of the most frigid surveys I've ever attempted."[213] Washburn's diary entry for that day notes the value of enduring cold and wind. "We located loads of new peaks, though the actual top of Mount Logan was in clouds. We were working from the highest survey station ever occupied in the Yukon Territory of Canada." As the weather worsened, the men retreated 2,700 feet to the safety and comfort of their high camp, where Washburn reflected on the "single most important day of this expedition's survey program."[214]

The expedition continued surveying, photographing, and negotiating crevasse-lined glaciers and avalanche-laden peaks. Day in and day out, the men encouraged their dogs to haul four-hundred pound sleds from camp to camp, testing the men and the animals. "The sled must have turned over a thousand times in the nine miles" from one camp to the next, Washburn wrote. After such days the men took comfort in Washburn's uncanny expedition planning. "Supper was fantastic," he noted on May 3, "Cold tomato juice, bear-meat hamburgers, creamed corn, thick mushroom soup, and to cap it off, a juicy fig pudding."[215]

On May 8 the team began their final push to Yakutat, although their efforts were hampered by bad weather and decaying conditions on the glacier from the warmth of the season. "We sledged six hundred pounds as far as we could pull it over terrible, brittle crust in a blazing sun," he noted on May 9. Although the going was tough, the men took courage from the promise of expedition's end, now sharpened by the salt-filled scent of the distant ocean. Departing from his standard fact-filled entries, Washburn allowed himself to be carried away by the promise of what lay ahead: "At last we sniffed a real sea smell, borne on the gentle wings of a soft, southerly breeze."[216]

Thick clouds, heavy wet snows, wind, and warm temperatures plagued the team's survey work and hampered any considerable progress. Washburn's disgust was apparent on May 12: "There just doesn't seem to be any end to this filthy weather, which, as expected, gets worse and worse as we near the coast." The expedition's "waterproof" tents were "leaking like old sieves." Water, pooled on the tent floor, made the men miserably wet and their clothing heavy and uncomfortable. "I am from New England," Washburn confessed in a diary entry, "but honest to god, I have never seen such a hell's kitchen for weather in my life." [217]

On May 14 the men held a "vital council of war" in which they discussed the worsening travel conditions that would now prevent the entire team from blazing the trail to Yakutat. It was decided that the men would stay together until May 20, when the team would split into two. Washburn, Taylor, Ad Carter, and Ome Daiber would traverse the remaining portion of the St. Elias Range to Yakutat with about thirty days of food. Jack Haydon would remain with the Yakutat team for a while, to transport Washburn's supplies as far as possible toward Yakutat. The rest of the team would head for Bates Lake, where they would be picked up by seaplane. Along the way Washburn continued his work, as conditions allowed, conducting "clean up survey work on dozens of tiny peaks." [218]

On May 19 "Jack {Haydon} hitched the dogs onto his empty sledge," Washburn recalled, "and after fond and almost tearful farewells we bade him and all the dogs goodbye." Haydon later joined the other men further down the Lowell Glacier for their trek to the Alsek River and Bates Lake. As for Washburn and company, they turned their attention to Yakutat Bay and the promise of a cooked meal, hot shower, and a roof above their heads at the region's fish cannery. [219]

Rain, wind, snow, and slush hampered every step made by the four men. A three-day snowstorm buried the team in one hundred inches of heavy wet snow; they sat tent-bound just ten miles from the ocean. On May 23, when the sky cleared, the team began its last push to the coast. Washburn's diary entry for May 24 captures the difficulty the men had from that point on. "It would take a year to write down half of what's happened since daybreak today." Washburn and Taylor departed their last glacier camp at 4:30 in the morning. Ad Carter and Harty Beardsley accompanied the two men, but would return to the camp to be picked up later once Washburn could make the proper arrangements. The route to the ocean was lined with immense "smooth and unclimbable" cliffs, waterfalls and brooks soaked the two to their skin, and they were repeatedly barraged by "little snow avalanches and rocks as big as a fist." As the men neared the coast and the Nunatak Fiord where they were now camped, the "bombardment became worse," Washburn wrote, "as the sun rose higher and higher, melting more debris free from the slopes above us."[220]

Washburn led the four-man team through a maze of rock, ice, snow, and water to tidewater, dubbing the final descent "Hell's Half Mile." Later in the day, as Beardsley and Carter returned to the camp along the Art Lewis Glacier, Washburn and Taylor surveyed the fiord's icepack for a safe paddle to Yakutat Bay and civilization. "We've been camped in snow and ice for eighty days, and it's a thrill to be on dry land at last." However, the day's challenges plagued the two men. Again Washburn provided a window into the nearly three months of physical and emotional strain placed on the men. "As I was getting gear arranged and Andy was cooking a can of roast beef hash," Washburn noted, "I asked 'Andy, were you scared this afternoon?' His reply: 'During the last half hour, the shit was right up in the back of my throat!' I have heard of people being scared shitless, but never before had I heard anything like Andy's memorable response."[221]

The following day the men pushed off in the inflatable two-man raft they had hauled across the ice for the entire expedition. Navigating through open leads in the fiord's icepack, they made steady progress. Danger was still evident everywhere they looked, as the glacier continuously shed its ice front. Chunks of ice "ranging in size from a small peanut to a two-story office building—falling off the top, bursting out of the middle, or exploding up from beneath the water with terrific tidal waves" played havoc with man and raft.[222]

They paddled continuously away from the glacier and toward the cannery at Yakutat. The smells and sounds of the ocean and its wildlife filled their senses for the first time in almost three months. They camped that evening on a sandy beach "with real trees and a freshwater brook," Washburn noted, "Pure Heaven!" On May 26 they decided to forgo a more direct route in front of Hubbard Glacier to Yakutat Bay because of the large and ominous icebergs that continually rained down from the glacier's oceanfront terminus. A detour took them down Russell Fiord and an eventual portage to Yakutat. The route was slush and mud, along inclined slopes of forty degrees or more, with Taylor's pack weighing at least fifty pounds and Washburn's exceeding ninety. "After all," Washburn later wrote, "he's sixty years old and I'm not quite twenty-five." The going was difficult. They bushwhacked their way to within six miles of Yakutat Bay, carrying the raft all the way, as it was still needed to negotiate the final segment to the cannery.[223]

On May 28 they continued to battle hollows, bogs, and brush, picking up old footpaths and then losing them in the dense overgrowth of the coast. Early in the evening they stumbled upon what Washburn called a "real footpath" and followed it to a clearing where they discovered a "wonderful little white cottage with green blinds, right in front of us on a wee island less than a mile away." Inflating the raft once again, Taylor and Washburn negotiated the small distance across to the refuge. Fresh water, a fire, coffee and the swells of the Pacific Ocean were a welcome comfort, "it's thrilling," Washburn declared, "to have a sheet-iron roof over our heads."[224]

The following day provided clear and calm weather, perfect for their final push to Yakutat. The vast Malaspina Glacier and Mount St. Elias lay in all their grandeur before them. At 2:45 in the afternoon, Washburn and Taylor paddled past their final obstacle and sighted the cannery at Yakutat; civilization was within a few paddle strokes. A group of children curiously watched as the men came ashore. "When they asked where on earth we'd come from," Washburn later wrote, "our unexpected response was 'from Carcross, Yukon, Canada.'" Washburn's last diary was quite simple and anticlimactic: "The great St. Elias Range has been officially crossed!"[225]

Soon after arriving, Washburn and Taylor arranged for the rest of the team members to be picked up at various locations. Bob Bates and company were brought from Bates Lake (no connection). Ad Carter and Beardsley arrived at the cannery by boat later that day. Washburn soon busied himself sending telegrams to friends, family, and Gilbert Grosvenor at the National Geographic Society. Congratulatory telegrams came flooding into the tiny radio shack of Libby and Company's cannery throughout the day. As Washburn recalled, one particular message caught the attention of the radioman. "All of a sudden the radio operator shoved back his chair and cried out 'Jesus Christ, this message is from the King! (of England)'" The telegram, signed by the British foreign secretary, read "The King commands me to express to you the sincere appreciation of the compliment which the National Geographic Society Yukon Expedition have paid to his Majesty and to the Queen in naming two newly discovered peaks after their majesties in commemoration of his silver jubilee. The King congratulates the expedition on their important achievement effecting the first crossing of the Saint Elias Range from Yukon to Alaska."[226]

On June 7 Washburn and pilot Frank Barr from nearby Atlin arrived at Bates Lake—landing in a small opening in the ice. The men were ferried over to adjacent Dezadeash Lake in two relays, from which they hiked to the small community of Champagne on a well-established trail. From there the men traveled by truck to Whitehorse and eventually on to Carcross by train where they would leave the North for the East Coast and the comfort of their families.

In the meantime, Washburn's communiqués to Grosvenor were met with celebration and accolades. Grosvenor telegraphed his "Heartiest congratulations" to Washburn, "and to every member of your courageous and resourceful group. Your successful accomplishment of extremely difficult explorations as originally planned, " he praised, "reflects greatest credit on every individual in your party."[227] Washburn could not think of a better way to place an exclamation point on the expedition than to have Grosvenor praise the work of this young and daring group, all college men apart from sourdough Andy Taylor.

The days immediately following were spent gathering equipment and making plans for the return home. Washburn traveled from Whitehorse to Ketchikan, and then on to Prince Rupert by airplane, and finally took passage east on the Canadian National Railroad. Jasper, Winnipeg, Edmonton all lay on his route to Minneapolis and Chicago. On June 13 he caught an early flight to Boston, arriving home later that evening to the welcome of family and friends. At the age of twenty-five, having celebrated his birthday just days before on June 7, Washburn led his young team to one of the most extraordinary expedition feats of the decade. The seven-man force, with a robust team of sled dogs, managed thousands of pounds of equipment and food, coordination of aerial supply, extensive survey work, exhaustive photographic surveys, ground surveys, and months of backbreaking man-sledging, for a total of 89 days. The expedition endured the hazards of some of the most rugged terrain in North America. Publishing the expedition's account and publicizing its accomplishments soon became the focus of Washburn's energy, and Grosvenor assured the young explorer that this extraordinary journey would receive its fair share of recognition and publicity.

Before the expedition, Washburn believed a successful traverse through the St. Elias Range "would be some stunt if we could pull it off." Just week's after the expedition came to a close, the Society issued a three-page *Geographic News Bulletin,* in which the Washburn expedition was praised. The article underscored the Society's critical role in unraveling the mysteries of five thousand square miles of previously unknown terrain. Holding true to its continued interest in the use of aerial photography and transportation in geographic exploration, the Society highlighted the benefits of their extensive use throughout the expedition. "Airplane Facilitates Exploration," one *National Geographic Bulletin* subheading declared, noting that Washburn had "high praise of the airplane in connection with the expedition." Indeed, the *Bulletin* continued, "Photographs taken from the plane . . . were used to lay out the ground route and saved many days of difficult travel" in addition to recording previously unknown mountains, glaciers, and terrain.[228] Washburn soon delivered to the Society an eagerly awaited story with its impressive series of discoveries.

In 1938, Washburn extended westward his 1935 photographic survey of the St. Elias Range under the auspices of the Society and Harvard's Institute for Geographic Exploration. The Institute's independently wealthy Director, Dr. Hamilton Rice, personally donated five thousand dollars to "complete the aerial photographic survey of the glaciers in the Chugach Range," and the continued work in the Wrangell Mountains.[229] Washburn was particularly interested in obtaining detailed aerial photographs of the Miles, Childs and Bering glaciers. The Bering was rumored at the time to be one of the largest glaciers on the continent. Indeed, subsequent surveys would prove it the largest and longest glacier in North America.[230]

Washburn's photographic surveys of the 1930s are of particular interest to geologists and glaciologists who continue to research these features. For example, continued retreat of the Bering Glacier has been interrupted by several surges during the twentieth century. In an article analyzing these movements, glaciologists Bruce Molnia and Austin Post illustrated their discussion with many of Washburn's 1938 photos of the glacier because they "provided the first complete look at the area," one against which subsequent movement could be measured.[231] Thousands of square miles of unmapped country were photographed during the 1938 expedition, and Washburn discovered what is now known as the Bagley Ice Field, one of the largest in North America, named in honor of Harvard colleague and pioneer Alaskan surveyor Colonel James Bagley.[232]

Immediately following the Yukon Expedition, Washburn spent the winter of 1935-1936 working on a detailed map of the Wrangell-St. Elias region. Using his field survey data and oblique aerial photographs, Washburn developed the map with the assistance of the nation's leading mapmakers, including Dr. Erwin Raisz of the National Geographic Society and Harvard University. The resulting map, which represented a coordinated application of Washburn's work, was sent to Albert Bumstead, the Society's chief cartographer, for inclusion in a new-large scale map of Canada.[233] Grosvenor had planned for a special June 1936 "Canada" issue of the magazine, featuring an article by Lawrence Burpee entitled "Canada's Awakening North."

However, Washburn's compelling written account of geographic discovery, complete with crisp and dramatic photographs and maps of hitherto unknown regions, took center stage.[234] Grosvenor's investment in the young explorer had paid significant dividends for the Society, and solidified a special relationship between the two men. Even before the Yukon Expedition, Grosvenor had offered Washburn a position at the Society. "My highest ambition," Washburn responded, "has always been to work for the society."[235] The lure of working for Grosvenor was great, and such a position would allow Washburn the freedom and flexibility to develop and lead future Geographic expeditions. Indeed, he confided in Grosvenor his fear of someday relinquishing his newly developed niche within the field science and exploration community: "God forbid that I should ever become a 'hard-boiled scientist,'" he declared.[236] Clearly, Washburn had no interest in laboratory science, peopled with white-coated, bespeckled academics. Washburn was much more at home in the tradition of John Wesley Powell and Grove Karl Gilbert, preferring the multiple roles of expeditionary scientist, field geographer, and most of all, explorer. He was happy to alternate between the field and the darkroom or cartography lab, where analysis was a part of the cycle of investigation, not the sole focus of his work and attention.

Yet in November 1935, as a result of the Yukon Expedition, Washburn accepted an invitation from Hamilton Rice to join Harvard's Institute for Geographical Exploration as an instructor. This was "a grand job," he confessed to Grosvenor, and one that "I sincerely hope will give me many chances to write for the *National Geographic Magazine*."[237] Indeed, the position was ideal for Washburn. The institute, founded in 1930, was entirely funded by Dr. Hamilton Rice, a medical doctor who had studied surveying at the Royal Geographical Society. A strong proponent of aerial mapping, Rice played an integral role in advancing the still-fledgling discipline of photogrammetry.[238] Although Harvard President Lowell cared little for the development of "institutes," which he believed had the potential to create fiefdoms within academe, Rice offered substantial funding for a new interdisciplinary cooperative, a popular approach in the U.S. scientific community in the 1920s and 1930s.[239]

The Institute's mission reflected Rice's belief that geography and geographical exploration should take a more important role in scientific investigations, primarily in the training of students in the collection of geographical field data. Rice directed his Institute toward a "quantitative" geography, emphasizing aerial photography, topographical surveying, and the "technical development of portable wireless apparatus for communication in the field."[240] As Washburn had studied aerial photography and surveying under both Rice and Captain Albert Stevens prior to the Yukon Expedition, it is easy to see the influence both men had on his work and the significant degree to which he incorporated so many of the institute's technical "directives" into his fieldwork.

Hamilton Rice had forged unique partnerships with industry, securing agreements with the Fairchild Aviation Company and Eastman Kodak, both supporting field exploration. The Fairchild Company publicized its support for the Institute by publishing an "information" pamphlet about the Institute's work. One such pamphlet highlighted Washburn's photographic images, using one of his glacier photographs to grace the document's cover. Among the institute's outstanding faculty,

"Fundamentals of the various subjects are taught by . . . Dr. Hamilton Rice {Harvard University}, Professor Erwin Raisz, and Mr. Bradford Washburn, all of whom are men of considerable practical experience."[241]

A Path Now Chosen

If the 1930 Mount Fairweather and 1932-34 Mount Crillon expeditions served as Washburn's introduction to large-scale scientific exploration, the Yukon Expedition became the foundation on which he would build an international reputation as explorer, geographer, mountaineer, cartographer, and photographer. Indeed, the National Geographic Society placed him among its most celebrated explorers, declaring that the quality of Washburn's photographs "resemble those of the Antarctic taken by the Byrd Expedition."[242] Washburn firmly established the airplane, aerial photographic techniques, and radio communications as viable and integral parts of Alaskan scientific exploration. His interdisciplinary framework for scientific investigation and exploration was recognized and celebrated internationally when he received the Cuthbert Peak Award of the Royal Geographical Society of London for his pioneering exploration during the 1935 Yukon Expedition. He received many other accolades from abroad, including that of Lord Tweedsmuir (John Buchan), Governor General of Canada, who declared, "how extraordinarily good this type of young American is!—pioneering in the Mount St. Elias range in Alaska."[243]

In June of 1935, just as the Yukon Expedition was ending, glaciologist Walter Wood, under the auspices of the American Geographical Society, used many of Washburn's field techniques during his own expeditions in the glaciated mountains of the Yukon Territory. Like Washburn, Wood was particular interested in obtaining and using aerial oblique photographs to produce topographic maps.[244] All in all, 1935 signaled a new era in Alaskan exploration that witnessed the continued introduction of emerging technologies and application, such as photogrammetry, and innovative techniques in field science.[245]

It was not until the end of World War II, a full decade after Washburn's Alaska expeditions, that large-scale, multi-year glacier studies were again undertaken in Alaska. Most notable were those of Maynard Miller and William Latady, directed by William Field, the same William Field who had introduced Washburn to the glaciers and mountains of Alaska nearly

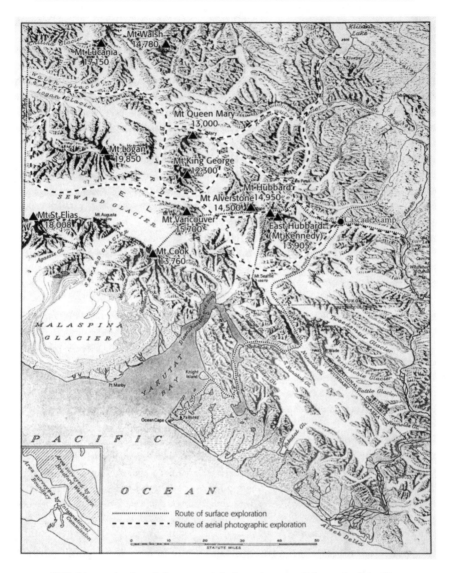

"Washburn developed the map with the assistance of the nation's leading mapmakers, including Dr. Erwin Raisz"

Map of the Yukon Expedition, edited by Washburn and Raisz

Courtesy of Bradford Washburn Collection

two decades earlier. In 1948 Field established the ambitious Juneau Ice Field Research Project or JIRP, under the auspices of the American Geographical Society.[246] In the hands of a few young intrepid explorers, technology now provided a pathway for intensive scientific studies of previously unexplored regions of Alaska. At the age of twenty-five, Washburn had established himself as one of the founding fathers of this new age.

Although Bradford Washburn's many geographic discoveries, survey work, and first ascents all are important in terms of Alaska exploration, they are eclipsed by the significance of the thousands of aerial photographs he obtained. This contribution to geology is immeasurable, because the photographs are as scientifically and aesthetically valuable today as they were over six decades ago. Washburn's artistry, coupled with his academic training in geology and geography, made it possible for Washburn to identify and photograph from the air fundamental principles in geology, geomorphology, and glacial dynamics. These photographs have been used in hundreds of academic texts, journals, technical manuals, and popular writings. They continue to provide classroom instructors with a powerful tool to identify and interpret glacial features, and they supply the trained geologist with illustrations of complex research problems and investigations. For example, a photograph of the Woodworth Glacier, Alaska, shows glaciofluvial fans, eskers, evasion modes, subglacial floors, and proglacial lakes, leading American glaciologist Robert Sharp in 1988 to declare the image a "veritable textbook of glacial features."[247] Indeed, Washburn believes his photographs to be "the real scientific contribution" of his exploration, "illustrating fundamental principles of glacial geology,"[248] and glaciologist Bruce Molnia has found the photographs an invaluable tool to identify changes spanning as much as sixty-five years.[249]

As an example of the degree to which Washburn's expertise was not only celebrated, but also sought after, by the mid 1930s he was courted by some of the most prominent explorers and businessmen of the period. Because of his extensive use of radio communications in aerial logistics and photography, Washburn was invited by his publisher George Putnam in 1936 to interview for the position of navigator on Amelia Earhart's ill-fated round-the world flight scheduled for the following year. Putnam, Earhart's husband, believed Washburn's experience in Alaska would be of benefit to her. After spending a weekend with the two discussing the expedition in great detail, Washburn withdrew his name because Earhart, in Washburn's opinion, lacked "adequate radio coverage for the Pacific legs of the flight."[250]

Several subsequent Washburn expeditions to Alaska during the decade focused more upon the mountaineering challenge than the gathering of scientific and cartographic information. Nevertheless, they did incorporate some components of field research, adding to the geographic understanding of the region. Of note are the first ascent climbs on Mount Lucania (17,150 feet) in 1937, Mount Sanford (16,250 feet), and Mount Marcus Baker (13,250 feet) in 1938, all of which added to Washburn's mountaineering prowess.[251]

The Boston press had followed each of Washburn's Alaskan exploits closely, providing to the public a detailed account of his expeditions and accomplishments in far-off northern North America. He rose to a prominent "Boston's son" status, and in 1938 was offered the vacant position of director of the New England Museum of Natural History (now the Museum of Science in Boston). The museum, founded in 1864 and one of the oldest natural history museums in the world, was a financially beleaguered and rather static institution.[252] In its annual report for the year 1978-1979, in which Washburn shared his thoughts about the museum's past challenges, he noted that in 1938 there were about twelve staff, a budget of nearly $45,000, and an operating deficit of approximately $15,000. Clearly, the museum was in desperate shape.[253] Museum president John K. Howard considered Washburn a man of boundless energy, fortitude, and ability to lead the museum forward. By chance, the two men were on a flight from Boston to Philadelphia in the winter of 1938. Howard confided in Washburn that the museum was having a tough time finding a suitable director; two candidates had just turned down the job. Washburn, on his way to lecture in Philadelphia, shared with Howard his intention to seek advice on how to assist Dr. Rice in his efforts to save the Institute from Harvard's antagonists.[254] According to Washburn, Howard "turned to me and said, 'You're exactly the kind of fellow I'm looking for!!'" Later that evening, as Washburn readied himself to speak, he received a telegram from Howard: "I meant what I said on the plane this morning," it read, "I want you to accept the position of Director of the New England Museum of Natural History. See you as soon as you return to Boston."[255]

Upon his return, Washburn dined with Howard and Museum trustees Ludlow Griscom and Wendell Endicott. Washburn later noted: "I told them that I didn't have the slightest idea about how to run a museum, nor did I have any experience in fund-raising." The latter point Washburn underscored to the three men, noting that the museum was in need of significant financial resources. Not to fear, Howard assured him, fund-raising would not be in his job description. By evening's end, the men were successful in convincing Washburn that he should take the job. He officially assumed his responsibilities on March 1, 1939. "As for K. Howard's promise that I'd not be responsible for the fund-raising at the Museum" he later wrote, "I've done almost nothing but raise money ever since I was appointed Director!!"[256]

The relationship between Washburn and the museum was symbiotic. The additional income (three thousand dollars per year) supplemented his proceeds from public lectures, and the museum benefited by its association with Washburn and the guaranteed celebrity of his expeditions. From that time forward, Washburn's every success and honor generated the public recognition the museum so desperately needed. Eventually, this relationship, which lasted over forty years, resulted in tens of millions of dollars in private and corporate support for the museum, and transformed the once aging institution into a vibrant, twenty-first-century, interactive, Museum of Science.[257]

As the 1930s ended, Bradford Washburn, Harvard graduate, explorer, and now museum director, solidified his place in American exploration circles. His ability to organize and obtain significant financial support for scientific expeditions in remote regions of North America was well documented. He had learned well from his mentors, Hamilton Rice and Captain Albert Stevens, the techniques of aerial photography and photogrammetry. He had also transformed himself from a Harvard graduate student into an instructor, working alongside some of the most respected explorers and field scientists in the nation. Washburn's continued relationship with the National Geographic Society supplied the needed funding to pursue his interests and afforded the Society the benefit of his accomplishments. Thus his work was given broad distribution throughout the country and within very influential circles. At the age of twenty-eight Washburn had become one of America's most celebrated explorers, and his career had just begun.

Washburn assumed the Museum's directorship with the same energy and dedication he showed in the field.[258] One of Washburn's first tasks was to oversee the hiring of a personal secretary. He selected a bright and strikingly good-looking Smith College graduate, Barbara Teel Polk. "I was given a battle-ax of an old secretary," he later noted, "so I hired Barbara Teel Polk to replace her . . . and we were married on April 27, 1940."[259] The couple spent their summer honeymoon on the slopes of Southeast Alaska's Mount Bertha, an unclimbed peak 10,182 feet tall. With no mountaineering experience to speak of, she scaled the peak in fine fashion and became the first woman in nearly thirty years to reach the summit of an Alaskan peak.[260] After the birth of their first child, Dorothy, on March 7, 1941, the couple returned to Alaska the following summer, where they made the first ascent of Mt. Hayes (13,740 feet) in the Alaska Range.[261]

Washburn occupied his first years at the museum touring and studying other museums in the United States, as he developed a master plan to revitalize the old New England institution. However, his efforts were cut short in late 1941 by America's entry into the Second World War. Along with many other distinguished mountaineers and polar explorers, Washburn was called upon to serve the United States in the development of cold-weather equipment for U.S. troops preparing to fight in the world's remote mountain and Arctic regions. Their collective expertise would become the cornerstone of U.S. efforts rapidly to prepare and protect American soldiers in these little-understood environments.

3

The War Years

"Although there is scarcely a man in any branch of our services who does not feel that some of his equipment was far from perfect, you will not find one in ten thousand who would prefer to renounce all of his American food and equipment in exchange for that issued by any other of the warring powers. The United States equipped its fighting men better than any other country in the world." Bradford Washburn

Lessons Learned and Forgotten

At the onset of World War II, the United States was ill-prepared to engage in a global conflict. The world's remote and inhospitable regions presented military planners with the daunting task of providing to their troops clothing and equipment capable of protecting them in extreme and diverse environments such as deserts, rain forests, and Polar Regions.[1]

Before World War II, the United States military was relatively unprepared for cold weather warfare, regardless of the known challenges and dangers experienced in past conflicts by soldiers from the U.S. and many other countries. [2]   Despite this knowledge, the United States did not place a great degree of importance on this issue before the war. For example, cold-weather injuries (frostbite, hypothermia, and death) were experienced by the armies of Alexander of Macedon and later by Greek soldiers fighting in Armenia during the third and fourth centuries B.C.[3] General George Washington's troops at Valley Forge suffered terribly from inadequate clothing and exposure to the damp and cold winter conditions along the Eastern Seaboard.[4] Similarly, Napoleon's Grand Army suffered temperatures as low as minus 30 degrees Celsius while in retreat from Russia to France in 1812-1813. Larrey, Napoleon's field surgeon, documented the torment of the retreat, noting inadequate shelter, food supplies, and lack of any adequate winter clothing at all. French soldiers were "freezing during every bivouac," Larrey observed, causing them to lose "equilibrium and fall into the snow-filled ditches alongside the Russian roads." Here, the men experienced "painful stiffness . . . followed by paralysis . . . prior to death which followed quickly." He estimated that of the nearly eighty thousand troops who began the retreat, just over half reached the Russian border, and of these a fraction returned safely to France.[5]

Injury and death associated with cold weather also was reported during the Crimean War of 1854-1856, in the twentieth century during the Russo-Japanese War, in the Balkan War of 1912-1914, and in World War I.[6] A striking number of British troops fell prey to frostbite in World War I from inadequate cold-weather footwear; over one hundred thousand cases of frostbite and "trench foot" were reported. The British military appeared to have learned little from their experiences during the Crimean War.[7] In contrast, United States Expeditionary Forces in Europe luckily experienced significantly less frostbite and trench foot injury (approximately two thousand documented cases), partly because of the Americans' relatively short participation, and partly because U.S. soldiers had better protective clothing.[8] However, later U.S. research and development efforts were curtailed, and limited emphasis was placed on enhancements to cold-weather equipment and logistics.

With the outbreak of the Second World War, however, the United States became increasingly uneasy about its capacity to wage a global war. In addition to inadequate stockpiles of munitions and the basic equipment needed to sustain a competitive military force, the United States recognized significant deficiencies in its ability to develop, procure, and disseminate cold-weather clothing and equipment. As a preamble to the global warfare of World War II, in the winter of 1939 Russia invaded Finland. The "Winter War," as it came to be known, brought to the forefront the importance of a well-equipped army capable of carrying out extended military campaigns in harsh environmental conditions.[9]

In late 1939, the Soviet Union had become convinced that a German invasion of Russia, via Finland, was inevitable. The Russian government sought to annex a forty-five-mile "buffer zone" of Finnish border country on which such an invasion would be met, and where, as one Russian official declared, "the main battle would be fought."[10] Citing their stated neutrality in the unfolding war (as did Norway and Sweden), the Finns refused to negotiate with the Russians on the creation of such a zone. On November 26, 1939, nearly one million Russian troops crossed the Russia/Finland border and were met by a mere three hundred thousand Finnish soldiers, eighty percent of whom were reserve forces.[11]

The initial battle was a classic David and Goliath confrontation. Vast columns of Russian troops, aircraft, and scores of mechanized vehicles poured across the border. Yet the outnumbered Finnish army relied on knowledge of their country and their ability to negotiate the snow-covered terrain. The Finns, clad in white parkas and traveling quietly and quickly on skis, conducted an efficient Arctic version of guerrilla warfare. This countered the Soviet advance; which was hindered by an inability to drive their mechanized columns through deep snow and rough terrain. The Russians were forced to consolidate their resources along the region's limited road system, making them relatively easy prey. "If an approaching armored enemy column could be halted," historian Barry Gregory noted, "Finnish troops moving swiftly across the wilderness could strike at the flanks and rear" of the force.[12]

In addition to difficulties with the Finn's unconventional approach to warfare, Arctic temperatures reaching as low as minus forty degrees Celsius overwhelmed the Russian army. Russian troops were equipped only with standard summer-weight underwear, socks, and lightweight trousers, which afforded little protection from the cold. Moreover, Soviet tents, designed for warmer climates, did not provide sufficient insulation against the Arctic environment. As a result, untold numbers of soldiers lost toes and fingers from frostbite, and many simply froze to death.[13] The Soviet troubles were compounded by their reliance on mechanized support for transportation and firepower. The inability of this equipment to function at extreme temperatures made it virtually useless. Motor oil and other lubricants froze, batteries died, fuel lines cracked, and engines stopped running. The Soviet war-machine sat idle at times, an easy target for the elusive Finnish sharpshooters who darted in and out of surrounding forests, picking off cold and hungry Russian troops. In contrast, the Finns relied on skis to move about the terrain and employed a layered system of dressing that optimized body heat. The typical Finnish trooper wore heavy underwear, a wool sweater and trousers, and a field jacket over which a white parka served as effective camouflage.[14]

Despite the gallant efforts of the Finnish army, the Soviet's overwhelming force numbers in the spring of 1940 defeated what remained of the resistance. However, the Finnish troops had embarrassed a furious Stalin, who raged to Nikita Khrushchev that even though "many bridges have been destroyed . . . many trains have been crippled" the Finns fight on with "only their skis." It infuriated the Russians that these skirmishes continued, resulting in a high loss of life compared with relatively small numbers lost by the Finns.[15] The Soviet debacle in Finland demonstrated that the military might of even the greatest nations could not withstand the forces of nature for which they were not prepared. With this realization, United States military leaders endorsed plans for research and development of cold-weather equipment, in hopes of avoiding the mistakes made by their Russian counterparts.[16]

Historically, U.S. interest in developing and deploying military cold-weather gear was minimal. For the most part, it had been limited to providing troops warm clothing for stationary garrisons in locations such as the North Atlantic and Alaska. The United States Army had experience in Alaska after its purchase from Russia in 1867. Continued boundary disputes between the United States and Canada and the discovery of gold in 1897 resulted in a permanent U.S. military presence in the region.[17] During the first three decades of the twentieth century, military responsibility in the territory ranged from building and maintaining road systems to the construction and operation of vital communication links known as WAMCATS (Washington-Alaska Military Communications and Telegraph System) between Alaska and the continental United States.[18] Although the U.S. military had non-combat-related experience in harsh, remote, and cold regions, equipment, clothing and living conditions were simply not adequate for large-scale winter warfare.[19]

Generally, U.S. military planning was based on a defensive strategy developed before World War II and the Russian invasion of Finland. It was built upon the premise that future military engagements would take place near or within the continental United States or in relatively mild climates. As a result, little substantive research and development had been carried out on Arctic, mountain, or desert clothing and equipment.[20]

Indeed, during the First World War, existing cold-weather equipment was far from ideal. In Alaska, these deficiencies were augmented by indigenous materials and layering techniques. Extensive use had been made of moose-hide moccasins, horsehide gauntlets, mittens, pants, parkas made from duck, and muskrat fur caps that needed, according to military regulations, to be "thoroughly dressed with butter or oleomargarine, and cleaned with sawdust."[21] Such materials supplied a rather small and relatively stationary garrison, consistent with the army's plans of limited troop movement and deployment in harsh environments.[22] However, in the late 1930s, there was a meeting of Alaskan military officers, concerned with the state of military equipment. Their discussions resulted in specific recommendations related to new items of winter equipage that laid a foundation for future research and development.[23]

Although enhancements were made to the soldier's winter wardrobe by 1940, Alaskan troops were still afforded only limited protection from the elements. Burlap boot socks, dried-grass insoles, and "Eskimo" mukluks fashioned out of reindeer skin and fitted with soles constructed from "rawhide made from bearded seal" constituted regulation footwear. At the time of the United States' entry into World War II, the military's standard cold-weather manual included only a cursory description of winter equipment and a superficial discussion of preventive measures for warding off cold-related injury.[24]

It was obvious to military planners that America's resources were inadequate for a global conflict. William House, celebrated American mountaineer and special military consultant for cold-weather equipment, found the U.S. situation to be "desperately lacking" because the United States had "neither equipment nor tactical understanding to function in extreme conditions." House contended that "lessons on cold weather problems learned in the First World War were forgotten and were not available when the need arose."[25]

In the waning months of 1941, the United States was precariously situated between two inevitable theaters of war. Hitler's Germany continued its onslaught across the European continent, setting the stage for U.S involvement across the Atlantic. Simultaneously, the war of words and threats of economic isolation and retaliation between the United States and the Empire of Japan signaled the impending conflict that would soon erupt in the Pacific.[26] As the geopolitical environment deteriorated, U.S. Secretary of War Henry Stimson summoned the combined expertise of members of the American Alpine Club, the National Ski Patrol, and scores of civilian cold-weather experts to assist in a complete review of Arctic and mountaineering equipage. Stimson knew well the tactical advantages Italian and German Mountain troops had enjoyed in World War I, and was determined to train and supply U.S. troops adequately for such an environment.[27]

The U.S. military established a subsection in the Clothing and Equipment Branch within the supply division of the Quartermaster Corps, which soon began an ambitious program to evaluate the military's capability to anticipate needs.[28] As American mountaineer and explorer Robert Bates later recalled, he was recruited to assist in planning, designing and developing "completely new functional equipment for the Army's prospective mountain divisions." According to Bates, the branch was to consider the needs of troops in "Iceland and Greenland and for such requirements in Arctic and cold weather warfare as might develop."[29] He found the task most challenging, as "no one knew how to design this type of material or . . . why there were people who could tell you manufacturing costs but no experts to tell you the [clothing] specs."[30]

The Clothing and Equipment Branch was eventually renamed the Special Forces Section and divided into four specific research areas: mountain, Arctic, jungle, and desert warfare.[31] At the same time Simon Buckner, commander of the Alaska Defense Command, was increasingly concerned with the lack of adequate clothing and equipment for the simple day-to-day functions of Alaskan troops. As Bates later noted, General Buckner convinced the quartermaster to investigate "simple items" for use by troops in Alaska, "such as big coats, boots, parkas and sweaters." According to Bates, Buckner's efforts proved the catalyst for research and development of a full range of mountain and Arctic gear.[32]

The "Cold War" on the Home Front

On December 7, 1941, the United States was catapulted into the Second World War when the Japanese Imperial Air Force dealt a swift and devastating blow to the U.S. Pacific Fleet at Pearl Harbor, Hawaii. Just four days later, Germany and Italy declared war on the United States.[33] With war raging across both oceans, efforts were intensified to procure adequate cold-weather equipment. However, the United States was not the only nation in need of winter clothing. German troops stationed in Russia during the winter of 1941-1942 had little in the way of adequate equipment and clothing. To underscore this point, one need only consider the fate of the members of a single German Panzer division, inadequately clothed during a January cold snap, who suffered nearly eight hundred cases of frostbite per day.[34]

Aware of the valuable expertise in mountain equipment that still existed in Europe (even though most had been forgotten in the interwar years), the U.S. government enlisted the services of H. Adams Carter, a member of Washburn's successful Crillon expedition, a veteran U.S. mountaineer, foreign language expert, and future editor of the *American Alpine Journal,* to serve as a civilian advisor to the military's G-3 Division (Operations and Training). Carter's work included the translation and interpretation of scores of European documents pertaining to mountain warfare tactics and equipage. Carter also interviewed former mountain troops living in the United States who "gave valuable first-hand information."[35]

With these modest efforts underway, the U.S. military turned to the collective expertise of leading authorities in cold-region exploration and survival. Washburn would soon be included in a group to develop a comprehensive research and development program capable of meeting the fighting man's needs in both mountain and cold weather environments. Robert Bates and Colonel L. O. Grice, chief of the Standardized Branch of the QMC, assembled a most impressive board of advisors who were to pay close attention to the "practicability of the development, manufacturing, transport and dissemination of equipment to the field."[36]

Polar explorers Vilhjalmur Stefansson and Sir Hubert Wilkins were called upon for their expertise in polar travel and survival. Outdoorsman and clothing manufacturer Leon Leonwood Bean (founder of L. L. Bean Inc.) reviewed the military's production of all outdoor equipment, but was particularly interested in the development of adequate footwear.[37] Bradford Washburn, whose experience leading expeditions to remote regions of Alaska and Canada was recognized, served as an expert consultant to the U.S. Army Air Force.

Throughout the winter and spring of 1941-1942, the Quartermaster Corps engaged in a massive effort to evaluate the effectiveness, functionality, and durability of existing winter equipment and clothing. The QMC's advisors brought to this work personal expertise and biases, advocating for equipment and clothing designs each considered most effective. Time constraints, limited production capability, and the scarcity of many materials created a challenging and dynamic forum for discussion.[38] "When you add personal prejudices and idiosyncrasies with the added problem of military requirements," stated William House, "you create a field for discussion even more than usually conducive to difference of opinion."[39] Debate ranged from the type of boot one could use in an Arctic setting to the most versatile outer garments suitable for mountain warfare.

An example of the diverse opinions of, and the problems encountered by, the QMC group is evident in the spirited discussion during the development of a basic outer layer of cold-weather clothing. Stefansson had long advocated to polar explorers the notion that one must adapt to the Arctic environment by employing clothing and hunting strategies widely used by the Eskimos.[40] He advocated strongly for the use of igloos rather than tents, and natural furs in place of manufactured materials. He suggested the calculated slaughter of tens of thousands of caribou by military aircraft so that superior cold weather clothing could be fashioned from their hide.[41]

Stefansson's idea was quickly overruled by Bean, who called the killing of so many animals and the manufacturing of hides impractical on such a grand scale, and the QMC spared one of the continent's northern ungulate populations.[42] The large supply of winter equipment the U.S. would need to outfit its soldiers eliminated from consideration the use of most traditional furs. The military instead concentrated its research and development efforts on substitutes, such as synthetic garments made of pile, and looked for innovative means to design and produce hundreds of new items.[43]

The United States faced a rather daunting task of outfitting an entire army for warfare in literally any part of the globe. As mountaineer William House later explained, many questions were asked in preparation for future research and development initiatives: "Would American troops be involved in the mountains of Greenland or Iceland, the Pyrenees, Norway, the Alps, the Caucasus, even the Himalayas?" House recalled that the planners struggled to conceive of a "single mountaineering kit which would be usable in any mountain range" in the world.[44] In addition, the nature of warfare dictated that a soldier's equipment and clothing be as lightweight as possible, so newly developed gear needed to be versatile and lightweight while providing sufficient protection in a harsh and still poorly understood environment. Washburn's air and land expeditions to the remote mountain regions of Alaska and Canada in the decade before the war made him uniquely qualified to help develop appropriate equipment and clothing for both air and ground forces.

Each branch of the military had its own set of clothing and equipment needs. Washburn contributed his unique expertise to a number of areas, including cold-weather survival, the use of planes in remote and frigid environments, and knowledge of cold-weather clothing strategies. Early on in his duties he came to appreciate that the airman's needs were far different from those of the ground forces. "It was not unusual for our fliers, whether based in England or in China," he would later recall, "in summer or in winter, to run into Arctic conditions less than an hour after takeoff."[45]

Until 1941, the U.S. military did not fully appreciate the different needs of its servicemen and therefore operated a modest centralized research and development program. Washburn argued against such a structure, advocating for a separate Army Air Force research and development program. Only then, Washburn believed, would the military fully appreciate and address fundamental differences between the requirements of the air and ground forces, involving the "simple, yet frequently unappreciated fact that the flier does his fighting sitting still."[46] Hence, the primary concern in developing clothing for the Army Air Force was to use materials that could adequately insulate a stationary flyer. Yet the reality of warfare mandated that such clothing be as versatile as possible, since the Air Force was equally concerned with protecting the flyer shot down in northern regions or during winter months. Conversely, as Washburn noted, once on the ground, the airmen would need clothing capable of achieving "the proper balance between insulation and ventilation."[47]

General Simon Buckner of the Alaskan Defense Command shared Washburn's concerns, stating that a "compromise must be made between extreme of comfort and the extreme of mobility." He further noted that "troops equipped with every comfort will be tied to one spot," while those "outfitted for the maximum mobility are likely to freeze to death."[48]

Therefore, in the spring of 1941, the United States military found itself pressed on multiple fronts to develop, procure, and deliver adequate clothing and equipment to its troops. These needs were complex, demanding a balance between adequate protection from extremely low temperatures at high altitudes and substantial versatility for ground-based combat and survival.

During the early days of the war, Army Air Corps crews detested their equipment, citing its lack of insulating qualities, impractical maneuverability in the cockpit due to its bulky design, and an overall lack of consideration given to the flyers' needs. So inadequate was the situation that airmen stationed in Alaska preferred civilian clothing and QMC mountain-troop equipment over those items issued to them by the Army Air Force.[49] Washburn's preliminary study of the situation identified a number of serious problems that he attributed to insufficient direction and ineffective research programs on the part of the QMC. In January 1942, he informed Robert Lovett, Assistant Secretary of War for Air, that there existed an immediate need for emergency equipment specifically developed for the Air Corps. Lovett dispatched Washburn to Wright Field, Ohio, where most of the QMC's equipment was under development. After a thorough review, Washburn concluded that the basic items available to a downed flyer were "extremely heavy, impractical and a lavish waste of critical materials."[50]

Despite Washburn's bold claims, officials at Wright Field defended the equipment, citing the military's urgent need to develop equipment and clothing sufficient to protect airmen and infantry stationed from the tropics to the Arctic. Washburn argued that the clothing requirements of the two environments were so diverse that no one strategy could be employed.[51] He was so alarmed by the lack of adequate AAF equipment that he suggested to Lovett the creation of a comprehensive testing program to include food rations, clothing, and emergency gear. However, Colonel Chidlaw of the military's Material Division found such a program "only mildly" interesting.[52] This general lack of response to such a critical problem by those in charge at Wright Field was not new. In 1932, Major General Kilner, Office of Assistant Secretary of War, declared that there existed "very extended and bitter criticism" of AAF clothing. However, Brigadier General Pratt had defended the QMC's supply of equipment, stating that it was "difficult to obtain a satisfactory solution or uniform consensus of opinion." At the outbreak of war ten years later, such a consensus was just as elusive.[53]

Throughout the spring of 1942, lack of coordination and internal disagreements plagued the military's efforts. The result was a change in their approach, a move toward specialized equipment for the different theaters of war, to include jungle, desert, mountain, and arctic environments. Distinct branches, including mountain and Arctic units, were eventually established within a new "Special Forces Section" of the Army. Robert Bates was selected to direct the QMC's Arctic program. The Army Air Force, frustrated with its inadequate equipment, reoriented its efforts as well.

With research and development efforts now on a more solid foundation, the QMC and AAF developed and selected for testing over one hundred items of equipment, clothing, and food rations, addressing the needs of both air and ground forces. The manufacturing of these prototypes for field-testing was carried out by private industry. In response to the war effort, U.S. factories, which President Roosevelt had declared the great "arsenal of Democracy," retooled and restructured their work force to accommodate the needs of war, and began work on a multitude of military contracts. For instance, the Mishawaka Rubber and Woolen Manufacturing Company produced felt boot liners that were placed in leather mukluks developed by the Rasmussen Shoe Co. of Westboro, Massachusetts. The Experimental Mountain-Ski Boot of G. H. Bass & Co. had nails, manufactured by the Asa Osborn Co. of Boston, driven into them to enhance traction on snow and ice. The Indiana Hoosier Tarpaulin & Canvas Goods Co. produced the Horizontal Ridge Tent, while the Atlantic Parachute Company made the Logan Tent. Anti Chap Lipstick was developed for military use by the Chap Stick Company, and Ashaway Line & Tine Company of Rhode Island manufactured the Signal Panel, Alpaca Lined Overcoat and the Nylon Mountaineering Rope. Socks, vests, and underwear made from paper products were also developed for testing.[54]

The QMC's Mountain and Winter Warfare Board conducted numerous field tests on clothing and equipment during the winter of 1942. As prototype equipment and clothing became available, the QMC believed it to be "imperative that the items be subjected to harsh usage in severe cold to establish their quality and practicability before procurement for the winter 1942-3."[55] In a meeting with Colonel L. O. Grice of the QMC, Washburn suggested that such an expedition involve several branches of the military, so that research and development programs could be coordinated. Assistant Secretary Lovett approved the joint field test, which marked the first cooperative effort between the two branches in the development of cold-weather equipment. Lovett selected Bradford Washburn as the AAF's representative to the expedition.[56]

In late spring of 1942, American mountaineer Captain Robert Bates, (Arctic Unit of the Special Forces Section, and a member of Washburn's Crillon and Yukon Expeditions), mountaineer and glaciologist Walter Wood, and Brad Washburn began the challenging work of developing the expedition.[57] The most pressing problem was the selection of a suitable environment in which a rigorous test of winter equipment could be executed during the summer months. Dr. Terris Moore, Expert Consultant to the QMC, noted the difficult decision facing the military:

> Where can we find natural out-of-doors temperatures of at least 20 to 25 below zero Fahrenheit, dependably during the coming summer, on the North American continent . . . reasonably accessible, where we can work on prototypes . . . to manufacture late this summer and early fall, for issue to mountain troops and Arctic troops in time for the winter of 1942-43?[58]

Although the military had identified a number of test sites, including Mount Logan in Canada and Mount Rainier in Washington State, Colonel Grice called upon the expertise of the American Alpine Club (AAC) to review the situation and recommend a suitable location.[59] After considerable discussion, Mount McKinley, Alaska, was selected as the ideal test site where "heavy snowfall, storms and temperatures to minus 20 degrees Fahrenheit might be found" even during summer months. The mountain's location close to Ladd Air Field in Fairbanks also "offered easier accessibility and greater speed in reaching higher test altitudes than other locations under consideration."[60]

In early May 1942, official approval for an expedition to be carried out inside Mount McKinley National Park was secured through National Park Superintendent Newton B. Drury. Lt. Colonel Frank Marchman was placed in command of the newly formed U.S. Army Alaskan Test

Expedition. Robert Bates served as second in command, and Bradford Washburn was selected to accompany the expedition and assess the performance of the QMC equipment under consideration by the Air Force, and to test new AAF equipment and clothing.[61] Later that month, the Army Air Force began transport of expedition personnel and over six thousand pounds of test equipment from Minneapolis to the expedition's staging area at Ladd Field in Fairbanks, Alaska.

The expedition comprised seventeen members representing several branches of the military, including the Quartermaster Corps, Army Air Forces, Army Ground Forces (Mountain Infantry), Medical Corps, Signal Corps, and representatives of the American Alpine Club. The Canadian Army and Royal Air Force also joined the expedition.[62] Walter Wood, a mountaineer and glaciologist serving as an expert consultant to the QMC, directed the expedition's aerial supply program from Ladd Field to Mount McKinley. Although the men would travel by rail from Fairbanks to McKinley Park, air cargo planes would drop a significant portion of the test equipment to the troops on the mountain.[63]

Washburn and Wood were first to arrive at Ladd Field for an aerial photographic reconnaissance of the mountain. Although Washburn already was familiar with the mountain, having conducted the first large-scale aerial photographic survey of McKinley in 1936 for the National Geographic Society, the two men surveyed the mountain at the end of May to assess the route on which the expedition would travel.[64] However, plans for additional flights and indeed the entire expedition were routinely jeopardized as a result of the Japanese hostilities in the Aleutians. Washburn was alarmed at the absence of defense preparations at the air field, noting that the "glittering roof of Ladd Field's huge hangar has not been camouflaged at all and can be seen clearly from 50 miles away!"[65] He ominously wrote that if the "Japs are successful in their bid for SW Alaska (Aleutians) our job may be nipped in the bud."[66]

Wood began transporting equipment and food along McKinley's slopes, and on June 9, the first contingent of the expedition departed from Ladd Field by rail, reaching McKinley Park that evening. From the train depot at the Park, Superintendent Frank Been transported the team by car and truck to Camp Eielson, where the expedition began the arduous eighteen-mile hike to the base of the mountain. Been noted that the "men had *"the men simply depended upon their equipment for survival"*

Washburn testing AAF Sheepskin Flying Suite during the 1942 Mount McKinley expedition

Courtesy of Bradford Washburn Collection

difficulty" as they "were soft" and were "carrying heavy packs" across difficult terrain.[67] Their physical condition would soon change, since the men were about to spend the better part of the summer climbing, skiing, and traversing the slopes of North America's tallest mountain.

A small base camp was established at the 7,600-foot McGonagall Pass, on the edge of the Muldrow Glacier. Here, the men diligently documented the performance of their equipment, which was certainly put through a rigorous test throughout the several days' march to the base of the mountain. Team members made detailed notes as to the functionality, durability, and overall usefulness of such items as socks, boots, mosquito head nets, frame packs, and tents. As time was of the utmost importance, this information was sent by radio to Ladd Field in Fairbanks, and relayed to research and development installations throughout the country, including Wright Field. This rapid communication allowed design modifications in both equipment and clothing to be considered rapidly.

Conditions on the lower Muldrow Glacier at the outset of the expedition were dismal, with rain and warm temperatures turning the glacial ice into streams of slush and running water. Yet such conditions were perfect for a rigorous test of the equipment. "Men let themselves be soaked to the skin to prove the value of water repellent materials," Robert Bates would later recall, while other men "allowed themselves to shiver to learn the minimum temperature" at which the clothing would lose its effectiveness.[68] Although such information attained at low altitude was useful, the military was eager also to test the integrity and effectiveness of the equipment under extreme conditions.[69] So from early to mid July, Washburn, Bates, Terris Moore, and Einar Nilsson, another civilian consultant to the QMC, established several camps along the mountain's upper slopes. The team eventually established a camp at 17,500 feet on the Harper Glacier, christening it the "High Test Area."

Other expedition members soon joined the four mountaineers at the high camp. Field tests of winter gear were conducted in a stark yet effective manner: the men simply depended upon their equipment for survival. Failure of any item to perform under such conditions could prove fatal. The "High Test Area" was established so that equipment could be tested under extreme conditions (from sixteen to eighteen thousand feet) for a prolonged period. There was a great deal of concern in the AAF about U.S. capabilities to supply mountain troops effectively. Indeed, many of the supplies dropped at the high camp veered drastically off course as result of miscalculating the air speed of the plane and the drag of the parachute. However, with the lessons learned from the McKinley expedition and elsewhere, such problems would be corrected for future operations in the European Theater of war.[70]

Although war raged around the globe, this team of mountaineers could not resist a summit attempt. McKinley remained a much-coveted prize. As Terris Moore later wrote, this group of men marked the first climbing party on McKinley on which "more than one member had . . . technical alpine experience. . . . The earliest climbers had no experience at all."[71] The opportunity was not lost on Washburn, who considered the conquest of McKinley alluring. Yet he was content to spend his "days and nights" on the Harper Glacier, "as it's full with ghosts—Belmore Browne, Hudson Stuck, and Harry Karstens—every serac, each steep grade, every rock and every plateau brings back stories of the pioneers" who tried decades before to climb the mountain. Colonel Marchman, the expedition's military commander, was well aware of the caliber of mountaineers situated below the summit. On July 23, he contacted Washburn via radio from the Muldrow Glacier base camp and declared that they should "try the top as soon as possible."[72]

Needing little encouragement, Washburn, Bates, Moore and Nilsson set off for the summit just before noon and reached the top of North America at 4:00 p.m., the third such team to do so.[73] Their place in mountaineering history was not lost on the small party. Washburn savored the addition of McKinley to his long list of mountaineering credentials, confessing that his "ambition of many years has been granted."[74] Yet the men quickly regained sight of their main purpose. Looking out from the summit to the green lowland 20,320 feet below, Robert Bates contemplated the "whole continent of people beyond" who "were united in the struggle for victory . . . and in imminent danger of invasion."[75] The team returned to the high camp later that evening and spent several more days evaluating the performance of their equipment. With this final work now complete, the men descended the mountain, rejoined the expedition at the base camp on the Muldrow Glacier, and then hiked the long trail back to the Park road. Bates noted that the men were weighed down under heavy loads that included "samples [of equipment] showing strain and wear, or failure of material and design . . . things that must quickly be corrected in Washington."[76]

"The Mess at Wright"

Washburn criticized the majority of AAF equipment he tested on McKinley, recommending against further use of most items, including bulky over-garments made of shearling wool.[77] Immediately following the expedition, he traveled to Ladd Field in Fairbanks, and shared his concerns with military officials. While he was at Ladd, he also interviewed a number of airmen, who underscored the significant problems with AAF issued equipment and clothing. This of course supported Washburn's findings. The men "refused to use the flying clothing given them," he noted; "nothing seems to be satisfactory."[78] The men were so disillusioned with their equipment that Washburn persuaded General Buckner to allow him access to flyers in the Aleutians for an evaluation of their AAF equipment and clothing. On August 16, just one month before the birth of his second child, Teddy, Washburn arrived in Umnak, a mere four miles from Japanese forces, and found AAF personnel echoing the concerns of those at Ladd Field. The men were in desperate need of sufficient emergency equipment, and had absolute disdain for their cold-weather clothing. "The feeling of everyone is that [the use of] fleece-lined flying clothing must be stopped at once," since it restricted movement in close quarters and tended to overheat the men after minimal exertion.[79]

Returning to the States, Washburn completed an official report on the McKinley expedition with bold recommendations. A "big change {is needed} in the personnel working in clothing if we are ever to expect results," he wrote.[80] Washburn perceived the situation to be so critical that he decided to fill the report with "factual, well proven *HELL FIRE!*" and headed "straight to [Commanding General, U.S. Army Air Forces] General [H.H., Hap] Arnold's office with the whole thing" in hopes of finding "fearless officials who can and will really set this thing moving."[81] Washburn assumed responsibility for correcting the situation, since the "men in the field seem to suffer in silence until someone comes along to make an investigation."[82]

Washburn's "Hell Fire" report included a review of problems at Wright Field, including the lack of a coordinated research and development program, inadequately trained staff, and a tendency to ignore complaints related to cold-weather equipment and clothing by men in the field and experts alike.[83] His critique was based on significant experience in coordinating and outfitting expeditions in remote Arctic environments, the very reason he had been recruited by the AAF in the first place.

Paul Manson, Civilian Chief of the Clothing Branch at Wright Field, took exception to the report. He viewed Washburn's condemnation of AAF equipment as a direct and crushing criticism of his leadership. When the two faced off over the subject, Washburn considered it to be a real "row," from which "I came out on top!" Manson was incensed because, as Washburn notes, "he realizes that I am gunning for him, and the report must go out, pronto, before he can double cross me."[84] However others, including Polar explorer Sir Hubert Wilkins, supported Washburn's findings. At a subsequent meeting to review AAF equipment, Washburn noted that Wilkins "did not realize it was Manson's stuff and every so often he'd say 'that's useless' and toss a pair of Manson's pet boots onto the floor."[85]

Although Washburn's review was supported by a number of cold-weather experts, he believed leaders in research and development programs at Wright Field had attempted to cover up the situation. "They have stalled my report," Washburn wrote, "and are trying to do things of all sorts so that it will be incorrect when it finally gets through." Indeed, officials at Wright Field appeared to have no intention of releasing a report with such harsh criticisms, declaring the critique to be "interpretative." The "Army boys are clearly trying to cover up what they realize to be a rotten mess," Washburn declared, since he had disrupted their "life of quiet incompetence."[86] In a later meeting with Wright Field's chief of Material Command, Brigadier General Arthur Vanaman, several commercial airline pilots and various equipment experts found few redeeming qualities in the AAF equipment. One pilot declared, "Wright Field has made no real clothing development progress since World War I." According to Washburn, Manson was "flattened" by such a public declaration.[87]

Shortly afterward Colonel Mills, Acting Head of the Equipment Laboratory at Wright Field, reviewed the report and, according to Washburn, believed it to be accurate. However, he refused to endorse or sign the document since it would be a "straight admission of incompetence." As Washburn later recalled, Mills attempted to end the conversation, stating that Washburn "could not appreciate the Army viewpoint" and declared, "we must stick together." Washburn was infuriated with Mills's statement, likening such actions to that of "skunks" who "try to keep close to each other for protection."[88] Yet he felt a "certain feeling of pride and triumph" with Mills' admission of "incompetence," which "completely vindicated" his report.[89]

Yet Washburn realized that such "vindication" did little to secure adequate AAF equipment. Indeed, the situation was far more critical than he had first believed, because in his opinion, a number of high-ranking Air Force officials now dismissed the equipment problems for obvious self-serving reasons. Of the Army Air Force's preparedness to outfit flyers for the winter of 1942-43, Washburn noted that "there is no clothing and no emergency gear . . . and a real crisis exists." "While we have stalled," he wrote, the Quartermaster Corps had transformed their Mount McKinley expedition research recommendations into "new and better items," which the AAF was now forced to adopt in order "to clothe the Air Corps this winter."[90]

Frustrated with the lack of progress at Wright Field, Washburn resigned and briefed General Arnold on the situation. Aware that his report now had become a sensitive military document, Washburn smuggled a copy of it past Wright Field guards in a rolled-up daily newspaper, and gave a copy to Arnold when the two met.[91] Washburn shared with Arnold his belief that the AAF was in dire need of a separate, expanded, and well-staffed AAF clothing program at Wright Field on a par with that of the QMC's Ground Forces program. Acting on Washburn's report, Arnold dismissed Manson, Washburn's chief antagonist, and implemented a number of additional changes. According to Washburn, despite Arnold's efforts, problems persisted in both equipment development and personnel issues at Wright Field.[92] Though frustrated with the AAF's research and development efforts, Washburn conducted a number of cold weather equipment investigations along the newly constructed Alaska-Canadian Highway for the Alaskan Defense Command through the winter and spring of 1943.

The Smoking Gun

During this time, reports of severe frostbite to the hands and feet of United States airmen in combat over Europe made their way home. The stories lent credence to Washburn's continued condemnation of Wright Field's leadership and overall direction. In February of 1943, Lieutenant Colonel Loyal Davis (stepfather to first lady Nancy Reagan), Senior Military Consultant, Neurological Surgery, identified fourteen cases of severe frostbite among members of the 8th Bomber Command (European Theater of Operations) over the course of a ten-day medical visit. In a stinging condemnation of AAF clothing, Davis attributed the direct cause of hand and foot frostbite to the failure of equipment, in particular the "tightly fitting gloves and boots" responsible for "constricting fingers and toes." He reported numerous instances in which "men have not worn adequate clothing so that the entire body becomes chilled," and identified a general lack of proper training in the use of their equipment. At the close of the 1942 McKinley expedition, Washburn had predicted these shortcomings. Davis also found problems with the "structural features" of the bombers, making it possible for "cold air" to flow through the frame and machine gun turrets, to "strike the gunners at high velocity."[93] Davis suggested, as had Washburn, that clothing and equipment recommendations be obtained from men in combat who could "prescribe

. . . proper flight equipment." He also proposed that electric suits worn by AAF crewmembers be wired in such a way as to avoid the break in the electrical circuit when a glove was removed, that caused the complete shutdown of the entire suit. [94]

Continued investigation by Davis of the Eighth Air Force in the spring and summer of 1943 revealed another ninety-three cases of frostbite, involving eighty-six patients. He took detailed photographs of the airmen's blackened and gangrened fingers, amputated digits and blistered toes. These photographs would not only serve as supplemental information for Davis's medical report, but would provide Washburn with tangible and subsequently damning evidence of the AAF's inefficient clothing programs. [95] Davis presented his findings to General Grow, Chief Surgeon of the Eighth Air Force, who dismissed Davis's broad equipment concerns. Davis's later attempts to discuss his findings were repeatedly ignored by Grow's staff. "It was obvious that Grow had indoctrinated his medical officers," Davis would write. [96]

Davis became increasingly frustrated with AAF officials, who he believed were endangering the welfare of United States airmen. His claims, as well as those made almost simultaneously by Washburn, were supported by additional injury statistics. From the onset of air operations in Europe through the end of 1943, over half of AAF-reported injuries were due to high-altitude cold and frostbite. Sixty-four percent of these injuries occurred in waist, tail and ball turret gunners who were exposed to winds in excess of two hundred miles per hour, in which they had to remove their bulky and tight-fitting gloves to fire machine guns or reload ammunition. At least half of all of these injuries were attributed to inadequate equipment, failure of equipment to perform, or the removal of equipment during combat. [97] Reiterating Davis's assertion that Air Force personnel required training in the use of their equipment, Dr. Michael DeBakey, who would later become one the nation's leading heart surgeons, wrote that American airmen had "not been adequately trained in the prevention of cold injury," and therefore, "most did not know how to protect themselves against the dangers of cold." [98]

In August of 1943, Davis discussed with General Arnold the troubling incidents of high altitude-frostbite he had discovered. Arnold ordered him to report his findings to Major General Norman Kirk, Surgeon General of the United States. Later that month Davis outlined the number, severity, and causes of the injuries reported to date, along with photographic documentation. Grow, also present at the briefing, "objected strenuously to any implications" that the AAF was not adequately addressing the airmen's needs. Davis fired back, claiming that "he [Grow] had placed every kind of obstruction in the way" of correcting the situation.[99] Davis continued his condemnation, accusing Grow of misstatements and a deliberate cover-up of the facts. Davis felt somewhat vindicated by the positive response from Arnold, that translated into some progress, both in research on human physiological response to cold, and in clothing and equipment development. He still believed, however, that the AAF harbored a number of individuals and processes in need of elimination or drastic restructuring.[100]

Unknown to Davis, Washburn and Henry Field, the AAF Civilian Consultant also concerned with the clothing situation, decided covertly to take issues into their own hands. They prepared an anonymous document for President Roosevelt entitled "Report on A.A.F. Materiel Center, Wright Field," in which problems related to Wright Field were outlined.[101] "It is reported" the two men wrote, "that the direction and initiative . . . of emergency and flying equipment are inadequate" and "clever 'whitewashing'" of the facts and replacement of personnel had "little real benefit," in correcting the situation. The two authors cited a lack of attention to the "importance of a high standard of safety . . . lack of competent and experienced personnel for research," and the desperate need for enhanced communication with "our Air Forces in the theaters of war." Washburn and Field recommended a complete investigation of personnel in Wright Field's Material Command and, if such allegations were to be verified, suggested "incompetent or obstructionist personnel should be transferred or removed."[102] Roosevelt's personal secretary Miss Grace Tully, an acquaintance of Field, placed the report on the President's desk on August 30 1943. As far as anyone can tell, Tully did not reveal the document's source. On the same day, Davis shared his photographic "evidence" with Surgeon General Kirk.[103]

Just two days after Tully placed the report on the President's desk, Washburn was summoned to the Office of the Air Inspector General, Captain Beeghly, on September 1, to discuss the situation at Wright Field,

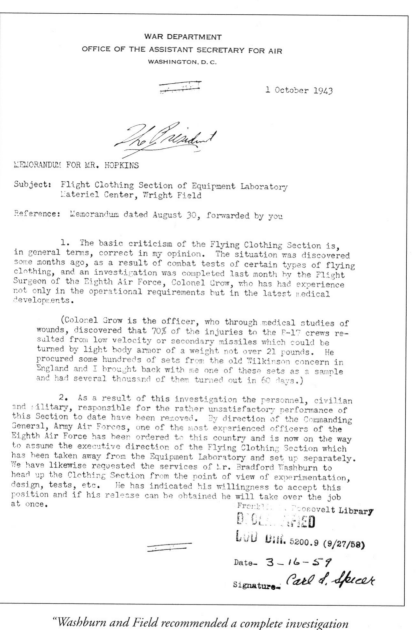

WAR DEPARTMENT
OFFICE OF THE ASSISTANT SECRETARY FOR AIR
WASHINGTON, D. C.

1 October 1943

The President

MEMORANDUM FOR MR. HOPKINS

Subject: Flight Clothing Section of Equipment Laboratory
Materiel Center, Wright Field

Reference: Memorandum dated August 30, forwarded by you

1. The basic criticism of the Flying Clothing Section is,
in general terms, correct in my opinion. The situation was discovered
some months ago, as a result of combat tests of certain types of flying
clothing, and an investigation was completed last month by the Flight
Surgeon of the Eighth Air Force, Colonel Grow, who has had experience
not only in the operational requirements but in the latest medical
developments.

(Colonel Grow is the officer, who through medical studies of
wounds, discovered that 70% of the injuries to the B-17 crews resulted from low velocity or secondary missiles which could be
turned by light body armor of a weight not over 21 pounds. He
procured some hundreds of sets from the old Wilkinson concern in
England and I brought back with me one of these sets as a sample
and had several thousand of them turned out in 60 days.)

2. As a result of this investigation the personnel, civilian
and military, responsible for the rather unsatisfactory performance of
this Section to date have been removed. By direction of the Commanding
General, Army Air Forces, one of the most experienced officers of the
Eighth Air Force has been ordered to this country and is now on the way
to assume the executive direction of the Flying Clothing Section which
has been taken away from the Equipment Laboratory and set up separately.
We have likewise requested the services of Mr. Bradford Washburn to
head up the Clothing Section from the point of view of experimentation,
design, tests, etc. He has indicated his willingness to accept this
position and if his release can be obtained he will take over the job
at once.

Franklin D. Roosevelt Library

DECLASSIFIED

DOD Dir. 5200.9 (9/27/58)

Date- 3-16-59

Signature- *Carl J. Spicer*

"Washburn and Field recommended a complete investigation
of personnel within Wright Field's Material Command"

Memorandum from Harry Hopkins to President Roosevelt
vindicating Washburn and Field

Courtesy of Franklin Delano Roosevelt Library

3. Those portions of the Equipment Laboratory relating to materiel other than flight clothing are represented by the investigators to be functioning with efficiency. The major function of the Equipment Laboratory relates to the procurement of items other than aircraft. These items include cameras, towing winches, engine covers, engine work stands, special fire extinguishers, and the thousands of items required for aircraft operation.

4. With respect to emergency equipment, Colonel Grow has been the individual in the Eighth Air Force responsible for the rescue and emergency equipment. The new system inaugurated last month provides for the prompt battle test and improvement of all such gear.

(Colonel Grow's considerable success with rescue equipment and procedure is dramatically indicated by the fact that following a raid some months ago, 120 men landed in the Channel and North Sea and 118 of them were picked up safely. A few weeks later on a similar mission crews of 12 B-17's were picked up in the Eastern approaches of the Channel and 116 were safely rescued by the RAF Sea-Air Rescue Service.)

5. Headquarters, Army Air Forces, advises me that the steps necessary to clean up the unsatisfactory situation with respect to flying clothing and equipment have been taken and I believe that the combination of new civilian technicians and experienced combat users of the equipment should assure the satisfactory conduct of this Section in the future.

ROBERT A. LOVETT
Assistant Secretary of War for Air

now a major topic of discussion throughout the ranks. Washburn reiterated to Beeghly, who could not have known that Washburn and Field had prepared the covert document for FDR, his long-held belief that emergency and cold weather equipment for AAF personnel was desperately inadequate. Change, Washburn hoped, would soon permeate the ranks. On September 10, the AAF created the Emergency Rescue Branch under the command of Lieutenant Colonel C. B. Whitehead. "Half the battle for a cleanup of Wright Field has been won," Washburn later declared.[104]

General Arnold returned to the States in early September from a fact-finding mission to several AAF operations abroad where, according to Washburn, "he saw a lot of men who had their hands frozen on account of rotten gloves in England." As Washburn later recalled, General Arnold convened a meeting of Wright Field staff and "gave them hell." As a result of the meeting, Washburn's adversary Major General Grow requested a complete QMC winter suit, developed by Washburn and others for ground troops, so that AAF personnel could test its effectiveness for consideration in England.[105]

"Half the battle for a cleanup of Wright Field has been won"

Cover memorandum from President Roosevelt to Harry Hopkins, attached to the Washburn-Field report

Courtesy of Franklin Delano Roosevelt Library

THE WHITE HOUSE

WASHINGTON

September 28, 1943

1943

MEMORANDUM FOR

HARRY HOPKINS: x4117

The enclosed comes from a civilian source, in no way connected with the Air Corps. You might like to take it up with Hap Arnold.

F.D.R.

Unsigned memorandum, dated 8/30/43 – "Report on A.A.F. Materiel Center, Wright Field.

×

Even though Grow committed to a review of new QMC equipment, he was not much interested in acquiring or developing many new items, since the AAF still had significant supplies of their own equipment ready for distribution. General Buckner of the Alaska Defense Command attempted to requisition some of the "new" QMC clothing for Alaskan flyers, but his request was denied. "Buckner was furious," noted Washburn, "that [they] are not going to let his men get our new stuff till the old junk is used up!"[106]

To Washburn, absolute reorganization at Wright Field seemed improbable. "It's depressing to the limit," he admitted, "but what in the hell can we do about it. . . . They've got such high political pressure."[107]

A fortuitous meeting between Loyal Davis and Henry Field, in which Davis shared his "frostbite" photos, soon eclipsed whatever power the authorities at Wright Field enjoyed. Field invited Washburn to his Georgetown home to visit with Davis. Here, Davis gave Washburn the photos, which he declared were "the grizzliest pictures of frostbitten hands I've ever seen."[108] Washburn delivered the pictures to Robert Lovett, Assistant Secretary of War for Air, suggesting the entire problem was a "result of . . . filthy incompetence at Wright Field."[109] According to

Washburn, Lovett "was really bothered and shocked" by the photographs.[110] On September 28, Lovett received from the White House a copy of Washburn's anonymous report. A short, terse note from Roosevelt to Harry Hopkins was attached: "The enclosed comes from a civilian source, in no way connected with the Air Corps. You might like to take it up with Hap Arnold."[111] Washburn was now working with the QMC and therefore protected from direct implication. His gamble had begun to pay dividends, and the turning point in the entire affair was soon to arrive.

House of Cards

Lovett immediately began a personal investigation into the report's allegations, and prepared for the White House a two-page review critical of the AAF equipment and clothing efforts. This memorandum was a blistering condemnation of Wright Field, in which he called the criticisms anonymously leveled by Washburn, Field, and Davis "correct in my opinion." Lovett revealed that such problems had been discovered months earlier by AAF Flight Surgeon General Grow, whose "investigation [on the inadequate AAF clothing] was completed last month."[112] Indeed, Grow had been informed of the problems in the 8th Bomber Group by Davis, yet chose to ignore the seriousness of the situation. It was only after Surgeon General Kirk placed stock in Davis's report that Grow was forced to acknowledge the problem. Since he dared not challenge Lovett on the subject, he no doubt convinced him that he had taken proactive measures to correct the problem.

Lovett indicated that personnel "responsible for the rather unsatisfactory performance of this section to date have been removed" and a total reorganization of the Flying Clothing Section was underway.[113] The restructure included the separation of the Flying Section from the Equipment Laboratory, and the appointment of Lieutenant Colonel A. Pharo Gagge as Head of the now autonomous section.[114] To expedite the needed changes, Lovett selected Washburn to lead the "Clothing Section from the point of view of experimentation, testing, etc."[115] Washburn felt vindicated, as indeed he had been. He reveled in the "triumphant end of a battle . . . starting since I left the Aleutians."[116] His return to Wright Field would be a rather interesting turn of events. "God knows what awaits me," Washburn wrote, "It's a far cry from 13 months ago when I left – now I'm going back as a Special Assistant to the Commanding General [Major General Charles Branshaw, Material Command]."[117]

Washburn's later effectiveness at Wright Field would have been minimal at best, had he not been given the latitude and authority to make the necessary changes. He felt strongly that an infusion of fresh staff was needed at the Material Command, to whom he would entrust the operation of research and development. Washburn argued for "new able experienced men" who were "fearless" and whom he could "trust." Agreeing with him, General Branshaw drafted a recruitment letter for such personnel, stating:

> There is no other place in the Army where such huge quantities of costly and intricately important material are entrusted to the care of so few young men. In addition to this, there is no other position of responsibility held by any group of men where failure of only one part of the clothing of a single individual can cause so much disastrous results.[118]

Washburn encountered many hurdles in revitalizing the Wright Field clothing program. Designing protective clothing for AAF flyers involved the consideration of many competing patterns, to provide comfort, style, and articulation of garments in both the sitting and standing position. However, in the winter of 1943-1944, demands on design and functionality were intensified by a considerable increase in high-altitude bombing missions undertaken over Europe.[119] Incidents of cold injuries increased dramatically from 1942 through the winter of 1944 as a result of expanded aerial bombardment that required men to spend longer periods of time in the air, and to fly more missions.[120]

Although efforts were now underway to correct AAF equipment problems, the lag time in adopting new designs and the production of such items was still substantial. Change at Wright Field first occurred with the restructure of a number of clothing units and procedures. A complicated organization of departments was responsible for development, testing, or production, and this interfered with procurement and distribution of the equipment. Historian Edward Purtee points out that the structure at Wright Field mandated the requisition and eventual procurement of clothing "so far ahead of the time when the equipment would be available that the equipment was frequently outmoded before it arrived."[121]

"Unconventional Methods"

The new Clothing Branch initiated many design changes, but the substantial number of "old" clothing and equipment already in production delayed procurement of the newer items. Washburn's predecessors had invested considerable financial and human resources in the development of the now substandard equipment and clothing. The military was stuck with thousands of items it was legally bound to purchase from private manufacturers, and later delivered to the various theaters of combat. Meanwhile, the AAF was conducting research on more efficient flying suits made from alpaca, and early feedback was very positive. But the military issued the considerable stockpile of bulky shearling suits, despite their proven inadequacy. [122] While investigating AAF clothing in Europe during the winter of 1943-1944, Colonel A. P. Gagge noted that the "number of bombers available for combat was determined by the amount of adequate clothing available more than by any other factor."[123]

Washburn condemned the old organization at Wright Field for its inadequacies, boldly stating his suspicions about peculiarities in the granting of AAF clothing contracts to private vendors. Suspecting high-ranking officials at Wright Field of financial benefits from "kick-backs" offered by "friendly businessmen,"[124] he argued that clothing design specifications "were drawn up so that no one but their friends could make them."[125] Washburn's diary quotes an unnamed source in October of 1943 that officials at Wright Field were using their own tailors for the production of AAF clothing rather than "qualified tailors already identified" by the Air Force.[126]

Washburn's repeated condemnation of certain AAF personnel during his first assignment at Wright Field made him a target of an apparent sting operation. While at Wright Field, a salesman offered an expensive doll as a "gift" for Washburn's newborn daughter. He accepted the doll, but suspecting a set-up by the salesman and military officials to charge him with improprieties, he deposited the present in a safe with a note explaining the nature of the transaction, and declaring the package would not be opened till after the war. These actions, he believed, would eliminate further threat of blackmail. [127] The relationship between Washburn and Wright Field officials was so strained that he believed "they were doing everything they could to trip me up and I'm sure that they ransacked my room occasionally."[128]

"Unconventional methods," was how Washburn explained the awarding of contracts at Wright Field. Inadequate processes like these were first rectified after Washburn's "banned" 1942 report and covert memorandum to Roosevelt in 1943. By early 1944, the vast majority of organizational and procedural problems had been corrected, and strict policies were enacted for the preparation, design, control, standardization, contract award, and production of all new AAF clothing.[129]

Once organizational hurdles had been surmounted, some progress was made in research, development, and eventual field testing of new AAF equipment. However, political and economic realities continued to plague Wright Field's ability to supply AAF flyers adequately with the equipment Washburn and others deemed necessary. Some of these problems were not easily corrected, since they were representative of the way in which the federal government generally carried out wartime business.

Military historian Edward Purtee points out that a critical winter flight suit, capable of protecting an airman at high altitude, was the most controversial item of equipment among developers and flyers, a significant issue in light of the increasing number of bombing missions flown at high altitude as the war continued. As early as 1935, there had been "general dissatisfaction with the shearling suits . . . but no extensive effort was made to develop any other type of suit for replacement."[130] Although the military was approached in 1940 by private industry to supply lighter and less bulky pile-woven garments to replace shearling, the AAF found "the present Air Corps sheep shearling flying clothing" to be the "best available for the purpose," and "no change in the present winter flying clothing" was contemplated.[131] The AAF continued their support for shearling up to the outbreak of World War II, despite the fact that cold-chamber tests revealed that the amount of shearling needed to keep a flyer warm in temperatures between minus 30 and minus 50 would considerably hinder the performance of an airman and "contribute toward dangerous fatigue."[132]

The increase in aerial sorties in Europe during the later years of the war increased demand for shearling, despite the negative reports on the product from Washburn and AAF flyers. Sheep farmers were encouraged to increase their supply of shearling to meet wartime demands.[133] Purtee notes that production of shearling increased from three million to over nine million pelts in response to military orders with private sheep farmers.

Flyers were ordered to adopt a "layering system" and use several types of clothing, to make up for the shortage of shearling garments. This system, affording the flyer control over body temperature and easier movement within the cockpit, soon became popular with most airmen.[134] Moreover, the War Production Board, which had oversight powers on equipment, recommended the implementation of other fabric garments that had proven effective in protecting the flyer. One such item was the "Type E" Royal Canadian Air Force suit, to which Washburn had given high marks during the 1942 McKinley expedition. This suit was found to be an improvement over shearling when used in a layered system.

Despite such positive response to a layered and less bulky system, some military officials were concerned that a drastic reduction in, or elimination of, shearling purchases from the private sector coupled with the adoption of alternative clothing items and layering schemes "would seriously upset the trade and cause great financial losses" to those "who responded patriotically to the promotional activities of the government."[135] But Washburn's report outlining the shortcomings of shearling, along with negative reports from flyers in the European Theater, did bring about additional research on alternative clothing.[136]

Although Washburn's work at Wright Field resulted in significant progress in reshaping the development and testing of new equipment, and despite the negative response to items produced from shearling and the AAF's knowledge of the inadequacies of such clothing, political and economic factors forced U.S. flyers to continue to wear such clothing. The considerable buildup of shearling stores delayed the procurement and distribution of new clothing materials and designs until all shearling stocks were exhausted.

Once the "moral obligation of the federal government" had been met, no additional orders for or requirements of shearling clothing were made after fiscal year 1944.[137] Indeed, as early as 1942-1943, the AAF had developed prototype alpaca clothing, but production to any significant degree was curtailed due to the emphasis placed on shearling. In late 1943, development and production of new clothing began for the winter of

1944, including enhancements to an electrical flying suit as well as alpaca clothing.[138]

Electric suits were effective, but problems with the circuitry were ever-present. While the design of such suits began at Wright Field in 1918, few developments were made during the interwar years. Throughout the early part of World War II, incremental advances were made, but the problem of heat regulation still persisted. By 1944, improvements in wiring and the implementation of alpaca and cotton twill undergarments significantly enhanced protection for the flyer in temperatures as low as minus 60 degrees Celsius. In the waning days of World War II, Washburn noted that the "ideal electric suit (toward which we are rapidly progressing) will be one in which . . . heat is automatically controlled by thermostats."[139] Such suits were under development at the time, but were not introduced into combat since regulatory thermostats were still unreliable.[140]

Field tests on wool-pile fabrics and alpaca were very promising as early as the winter of 1943. General Gaffney and Washburn recommended several changes to the alpaca suits being tested in cold chambers and at Ladd Field, Fairbanks.[141] Clothing made from Alpaca wool was eventually standardized and available to combat flyers in the early months of 1944.

The addition of these garments, when used in conjunction with, or in place of, electric suits, afforded AAF personnel freedom of movement with adequate protection from cold. Rayon inserts were also developed for use under larger mitten-type gloves. This allowed pilots, gunners, and navigators the dexterity needed to carry out their tasks, and provided some protection from high-altitude frostbite. The inserts were also used in conjunction with electrically heated (F-2 and F-3) gloves. Advances in footwear for stationary flyers combined an insert (still made from shearling) with a larger A-6 overboot. An electric shoe sock was also employed, in modified design, throughout the rest of the war.

The Dividends Emerge

Statistics bear out the effectiveness of Wright Field's eventual ability to design, develop, and deliver significantly better clothing and equipment after Washburn's return in the fall of 1943. For instance, injuries sustained from high altitude frostbite among members of the Eighth Air Force in Europe reached highs of 1,489 in 1943 (July-December) and over 1,700 in 1944. However, the number of injuries dramatically decreased to only 151 in 1945, when better equipment was available. Improvements were realized because the military solicited input from combat soldiers, implementation of recommendations from field test expeditions, an overall improvement in organization and administration, and standardization of processes and procurement measures.[142]

To be sure, not all the advances in clothing and equipment can be credited to Washburn. Many thousands of individuals, both civilian and military, were honest and hardworking in their efforts to supply U.S. troops with the finest clothing and fighting equipment possible. There never existed a lack of good design ideas, although production and material limitations were considerable, and the complex needs of the AAF airmen were varied and difficult to address fully. When one considers the environmental changes a pilot and crew experienced on each mission (in temperature, altitude, air pressure, and motion), it is no wonder that good clothing and equipment was not easily and quickly devised.[143] However, this very point was at the core of Washburn's frustrations and contempt. He believed the task before the United States was so grand and intricate that human ego and financial gain became unnecessary pitfalls.

Washburn's abhorrence of AAF clothing, his ceaseless accusations of improper conduct of AAF personnel, and his subsequent written reports and lobbying efforts, finally triggered a complete reorganization of winter and high-altitude clothing operations at Wright Field. One may conclude that had Washburn, Field, and Davis not taken considerable risks to inform the President and his advisors of the problems associated with equipment and clothing development, many more serious injuries would have occurred. Reflecting many years later on these events, Washburn shared with Davis his belief that his anonymous "tough memorandum to FDR" and Davis's "pictures changed the course of the whole 'Personal Equipment' program" at Wright Field.[144]

With the general disposition of cold weather equipment and clothing development on course, Washburn directed his efforts toward the development and testing of new and existing emergency clothing and equipment tailored for flyers downed in remote and harsh environments. Field tests of these items were conducted in Alaska under Washburn's direction in the winter of 1944-1945. In October of 1944, Washburn organized a four-man winter expedition to the Mount McKinley region to test "under miserable winter conditions" current emergency equipment and several new prototypes.[145]

Death and Disappearance on Mount Deception

On September 18, 1944, a month before Washburn's planned McKinley expedition, a Northwest Airlines C-47 aircraft, contracted by the U.S. Army Air Forces Air Transport Command, disappeared over the rugged Alaska Range. The plane was on a routine flight from Elmendorf Air Field in Anchorage to Ladd Airfield in Fairbanks. The men were en route to Minneapolis via Fairbanks with three crewmembers, one civilian, and fifteen U.S. servicemen on furlough to the states. The pilot, Captain Roy Proebstle, filed a flight plan before take off, anticipating a one hour and fifty-four minute flight. However, the plane never arrived in Fairbanks. Repeated attempts to contact the aircraft failed. With the fate of the airliner and its nineteen occupants unknown, officials at Ladd Air Field declared a state of emergency a half-hour after the plane was due in Fairbanks.

During the pre-flight briefing, Captain Ben Christian, who had earlier piloted the same aircraft from Fairbanks to Anchorage, had reported to Proebstle that the craft was in good working order. Christian indicated weather conditions between the two cities normal, "with winds aloft of approximately 220 degrees, 45 miles an hour at 10,000 feet; no turbulence."[146] Christian also cited overcast conditions to 8,000 feet seventy-five miles north of Anchorage, with similar conditions up to 12,000 feet, where he believed "it would be expected that an instrument operation with only light ice would be encountered from Summit to Fairbanks.[147] Before departure, Proebstle, co-pilot Peter Blivens and Flight Stewart PFC James George discussed the flight plan and weather conditions. U.S. Army Operations and Weather Service personnel reported high overcast skies with twenty miles visibility. According to the Weather Service staff, the C-47 crew "seemed satisfied that the flight should proceed."[148]

Twenty-five minutes after takeoff the plane climbed to 11,000 feet. Proebstle requested a change of altitude to just above cloud cover at 9,000 feet. Elmendorf Air Field granted permission for the change, and the captain completed this maneuver as the plane passed over Talkeetna (north of Anchorage) twelve minutes later. Proebstle reported the plane to be on course and experiencing some icing and turbulence, and estimated the plane to be over Summit in about thirty minutes. This was the pilot's final transmission, the last contact of ground crew with the aircraft.[149]

The Army Airways Communication System and the Federal Aviation Administration stations in Fairbanks, Whitehorse (Yukon Territory), and Anchorage monitored all operating frequencies for the plane's signal. The Army Air Forces contacted airfields throughout the territory, including the flight's designated alternate airport at Big Delta, approximately one hundred miles south of Fairbanks. None of the stations reported positive contact with the aircraft or knowledge of its location. However, the Army did receive two reports from stations along the Alaska Railroad of the sound of an aircraft overhead sometime that day. The military could not identify with any accuracy the location of the sounds, citing echo problems associated with the mountainous terrain.[150]

The Army immediately began an intensive air search along the route of the missing plane. A trapper reported "hearing a crash and seeing smoke near Lane Creek... about 40 miles southeast of Mount McKinley."[151] This report did not lead directly to the discovery of the plane. However, on September 21, the crew of an air reconnaissance aircraft sighted what they believed to be an SOS emanating from a signal mirror on a peak near Mount McKinley. Upon further investigation they found the "signal" to be the reflection of the sun off one of the crashed aircraft's few unbroken windows.[152] The remains of the plane lay approximately fifty miles west of its planned course, on the southeast side of an unnamed peak within Mount McKinley (now Denali) National Park, seventeen miles east-northeast of Mount McKinley proper.[153]

Rescue aircraft from Anchorage and Fairbanks searched the wreckage for signs of survivors but found none. Aerial search teams photographed the macabre scene of mangled metal strewn throughout the 9,700-foot glacial plateau where the plane finally came to rest. Approximately 1,600 feet above the main wreckage, and several hundred feet below the mountain's summit, lay one of the plane's engines, half-impaled in the icy slope.[154] Discussion of the feasibility of conducting a rescue and or recovery operation began almost immediately.

After contacting next of kin, the military issued a press release on October 4, 1944. In the release, the War Department recounted the military's search efforts and the discovery of the wreckage. It reassuringly noted that the "C-47, the Army version of the DC-3 commercial airliner, has made a remarkable safety record flying over the mountainous terrain of the Alaska Division and that the last fatal accident in which this type of aircraft was involved occurred in June, 1943."[155]

Initially, Army officials considered the cause of the accident to be some type of structural failure, resulting in the loss of a wing or engine.[156] However, photoreconnaissance of the wreckage identified all major structural components of the plane, including its engines, fuselage, and both wings. Military officials were also puzzled as to why the craft had veered nearly fifty miles off its flight plan. During a preliminary investigation into the cause of the crash, officials cited the region's turbulent and unpredictable weather as a possible factor in Captain Proebstle's decision to change course, which they believed ultimately determined the aircraft's fate.

A review of the region's weather data revealed a front in the Susitna Valley that had moved from the west toward the plane's last known location, resulting in considerable overcast conditions between Anchorage and Summit, located more than halfway between Anchorage and Fairbanks. Upper atmosphere soundings for Anchorage and Fairbanks indicated unstable air with southwest winds from forty to sixty miles an hour south of the Alaska Range, and westerly winds north of the range at comparable velocities. Given this information, the preliminary accident report stated that "severe turbulence would exist near any of the ridges of the Alaska Mountain Range."[157]

Based on the location of the downed plane and a complete review of available weather data, the preliminary report painted the following picture of the craft's final minutes aloft.

> Immediately west of the frontal zone it is expected that the top of the overcast would be materially loose, due to the strong down-slope activity on the west side of the Susitna Valley. As a result, it is expected that better on-top flying weather would be encountered west of the course, which may have contributed to his [Proebstle's] decision to remain at 9,000 feet instead of proceeding as previously planned. . . . it is expected that the top of the overcast would possibly exceed 12,000 feet, such as encountered by Captain

Christian. From the location and altitude of the wreckage it is evident that the flight did climb to near 12,000 feet as it approached Summit, however, it is likewise expected that there would be considerable leeside breaks in this overcast near the mountain range in the vicinity of Mt. McKinley that may have prompted his decision to proceed into what was apparently more favorable weather visually, without considering the possibilities of severe turbulence and down drafts.[158]

The Army's report, based on few known pieces of the puzzle, suggested that the probable cause of the accident was Captain Proebstle's decision to reroute the aircraft toward openings in the overcast skies. As a result of this action, the report noted, the plane encountered "a severe down-draft accompanied by severe turbulence that forced him [Proebstle] on instruments in a cumulus type cloud formation that resulted in his striking the mountain peak."[159]

Yet another theory soon emerged. On 21 October, Mrs. Blivens, wife of Co-Pilot Peter Blivens, received a letter from Mr. Harry Gray, a Civil Aeronautics official stationed in Anchorage. The letter stated:

> Mr. Justice, NW's {Northwest Airlines} Chief Pilot here, tells me that there was a man aboard who was en route from the islands (Aleutians} to the States and who was a camera 'bug.' This man had shown his pictures the night before and had remarked a number of times that he was extremely interested in getting more Alaskan pictures before leaving the territory. It is believed that it was at his request they proceeded to the scene of the accident for the purpose of allowing him to take pictures of Mt. McKinley. A verification of this is expected to be found on the film of the camera if it can be located. It is certain that they were in that vicinity purposely and not by error or accident because the scene of the accident is 40 degrees off course from their last reported position."[160]

In the later search of the crash site, in which Washburn would play a key role, no camera was found and no evidence uncovered to substantiate or counter Gray's statement. The absolute facts of the aircraft's loss may be buried forever in the icy snows of the Alaska Range.

Military officials from Elmendorf Air Field in Anchorage met on September 18 and 21 with Grant Pearson, Acting Superintendent of Mount McKinley National Park, to discuss a possible route to the crash site.[161] However, citing safety concerns, the Army's preliminary crash report dated 28 September, advised against such a ground expedition. The report noted "due to huge snow and ice slides that occur" along the route to the mountain, "it would be an exceedingly dangerous operation and would probably result in the loss of any person proceeding on foot."[162] Regarding recovery of the aircraft's occupants, the reports stated:

> Since there is no sign of life around the wreckage, plus the fact that to thoroughly investigate same, the entire slope would have to be inspected, it is not considered likely that any evidence of value could be found in this manner and it is therefore recommended that no further investigation be conducted.[163]

Further evidence of the military's concern with sending troops to the crash site is noted in a War Department letter to New York Congressman Ellsworth Buck dated 28 September, 1944 (the same day the military released its preliminary investigation report). The Congressman's son, Lt. O.J. Buck, was among those on board the plane when it went down. "The Commanding General, 11th Air Force, and the Commanding Officer, Ladd Army Air base," the letter began, "agrees with him that the evacuation of the bodies would require an expedition of great magnitude, including a crew capable of climbing Mt. McKinley. Therefore," the message continued, " the Commanding General, 11th Air Force states that land approach to the wrecked airplane is not considered advisable."[164]

Despite the Army's strong position on this matter, Colonial Ivan Palmer, under orders from Lt. Gen. Delos Emmons, again summoned Grant Pearson to Elmendorf Air Field on 30 September to discuss a ground expedition.[165] Pearson was a seasoned mountaineer and Park Ranger, and a member of the second successful team to climb Mount McKinley, in 1932.[166] On 3 October Pearson flew over the crash site and sketched a possible route to the plane wreck. Based on his analysis of the region, he concluded that a successful ground expedition would require a small team of four highly qualified men. However, the Army insisted on a much larger party of forty soldiers, supported by aerial supply planes, and a small mechanized contingent. Requiring a military chain of command, Emmons ordered Captain A.R. Peracca to oversee the entire operation.

According to Pearson, the Army wanted enough resources on the mountain "so that all the bodies could be brought out at once."[167] Although he agreed to the Army's terms, Pearson tempered any hopes of recovering the bodies: "by the looks of the crash from the air," he later wrote, "I could not promise to bring out any bodies as we would have to find them first, but I would take men to the wreck and return safely."[168]

When approached by military officials, Washburn agreed with Pearson's analysis of the situation as well as his doubts as to the recovery of bodies. On the day Pearson agreed to lead the recovery expedition, Washburn reviewed aerial photographs of the wreckage, in Edmonton en route to Fairbanks for his McKinley region field test expedition. Washburn's vivid description of the crash site in his diary supports Pearson's qualified statement to military officials:

> An amazing spot—just about as inaccessible as you could possibly imagine. The plane hit a nearly vertical wall of snow about 500 hundred feet below the top of an 11,000 foot peak—one of its motors stuck there and the rest of the ship slid down 1500 feet. There it lies, split open like a watermelon, with its wings broken off and scattered for a quarter mile all around it. He [the pilot] literally hit the peak of the mountain. If he'd have been a few hundred yards either way he'd have missed it completely. One could probably reach it, but oh what a climb it would be.[169]

Washburn's original expedition plan was to lead an overland journey in the vicinity of Mount McKinley with glaciologist Robert Sharp, who was serving as a civilian USAF cold weather expert. According to Washburn, the purpose of the expedition was to "field test, under miserable winter conditions, the emergency equipment normally carried in the back of all USAF aircraft flying over cold-weather terrain."[170] Two "novice" flyers would accompany Washburn and Sharp and serve as "guinea pigs" to gauge the effectiveness of prototype equipment. According to Washburn, the two "volunteers," Major Bruce Bass, a Kentucky furniture store executive, and Lieutenant Alvin Ivler, a New York City clothing design expert, "had never had any cold-weather experience at all—and thus were ideal 'typical' passengers in a USAF airplane."[171]

Washburn's expedition began at the Personal Equipment Laboratory of the U.S. Army Air Force at Wright Field in Dayton. The mission called for the testing of clothing, tents, cook stoves, and other equipage, as well as Arctic survival techniques. They planned a sixty-mile trek from Wonder Lake, thirty miles north of Mount McKinley, to Colorado Station on the Alaska Railroad via Anderson Pass. As with most of Washburn's previous expeditions, aerial supply would be at the cornerstone of his planning; this had been especially evident in 1942, when he coordinated a significant portion of the military's aerial supply efforts as a member of a joint military Mount McKinley test expedition.[172]

Pearson, who formulated the recovery plans through the first week of October, later recalled the formidable challenge:

> To get equipment for enough men needed on this trip was a tremendous task. The main factor I took into consideration was the safety of the men. Usually it takes about 3 months to organize and equip a party of four persons to climb Alaskan Mountains. I was fortunate to get Captain B. Curry to serve as supply officer who would get what supplies were needed.[173]

In less than a week, Captain Curry acquired most of the food, fuel, and equipment, and finalized logistics for delivery. However, Elmendorf Air Field did not posses adequate stores of mountaineering equipment to support the expedition. So Curry boarded a military transport plane on 9 October for Adak, Alaska, where these items lay in stockpile for the Aleutian campaign. He returned just three days later with enough equipment to outfit the entire expedition.[174] While Curry busied himself with these matters, Sgt. James Gale of the Elmendorf Air Field Rescue Squadron selected, mobilized, and briefed the entire contingent of expedition troops in a matter of days.

With the Pearson expedition taking shape, Washburn and his test party flew over the wreckage while en route from Anchorage to their base of operations at Ladd Air Field in Fairbanks. Although Washburn knew of the crash, he was not aware of the effort now being mounted to recover the bodies. As their aircraft headed north, the pilot made several passes above Mount Brooks, the peak closest to the icy mountain that claimed the C-47. By coincidence, since he planned to travel right through this very location and was a seasoned mountaineer, Washburn could not help but contemplate a feasible route to the wreckage.

> God what a wreck! If he had flown only a few hundred feet to the left or right he would have completely missed the mountain. By extraordinary chance, the mountain that he hit is only about two and a half miles from where we planned to have one of our camps—maybe we can get to the plane, but I'm afraid that it will be buried by then—we will try, at any rate. We would have to climb the north side of the peak and then descend about 1,000 feet onto the south side to get to it.[175]

On 10 October 1944, just one week after agreeing to take charge of the recovery operation, Grant Pearson met the expedition's advance party at the McKinley Park Station. The contingent consisted of twelve men, a D-6 caterpillar tractor to plow a trail through the snow-clogged Park road to the expedition's base camp at Wonder Lake, two military transport trucks, a half-ton trailer housing a mobile power plant, one radio truck, and three tons of food, fuel, and equipment.

Realizing the expedition would travel through some of the most treacherous terrain found anywhere in the world; the Army seized the opportunity to test a newly developed snow tractor, code name M-7. Equipped with a rear "half-track" propulsion system and interchangeable front wheels and skis, it could transport supplies and equipment in rugged mountain and glacier terrain. Two of these tractors would be tested and critiqued during the expedition.[176]

While the first contingent of Pearson's expedition was on its way to Wonder Lake, official word of the operation reached General Dale Gaffney and his search and rescue troops at Ladd Field. Puzzled about the change of plans, and, according to Washburn, concerned at the possibility of losing men in what he considered to be an extremely dangerous operation, Gaffney objected to the expedition[177] and convened a meeting with Washburn, Major Dick Raegle, an Arctic search and rescue expert, and

Lieutenant Paul Victor of the Alaska Transport Command. Despite his earlier private notions of reaching the crash site, Washburn publicly agreed that such an operation would be far too risky.[178]

On 12 October, under orders from General Gaffney, Washburn, Victor, and Raegle flew to Elmendorf Air Field to convince officials there to cancel the search. On the following day, the three men met with top officers of the Alaska Air Command, Colonel Ivan Palmer, General Johnson, and Lieutenant General Delos Emmons. They failed to make headway, Washburn wrote: it was a "rather futile day. Argue as we would, neither Col. Ivan Palmer nor General Johnson would agree to abandon their great expedition to haul out the frozen bodies."[179] Emmons "insisted that a determined effort should be made to reach the scene of the crash at once," Washburn noted, "regardless of the obvious possibility that further casualties might result."[180]

Yet the question why officials at Elmendorf were so determined to mount such a recovery expedition remained unanswered. Washburn believed significant pressure was being placed on high-ranking military officials by Congressman Buck, whose son was among those missing.[181] "There has been at least one well-known passenger on the plane," Washburn wrote, "and high officials in Washington were demanding a detailed explanation of what had happened."[182] Although this may have been the case, a letter soon after the crash from the Congressman to families of the victims indicated a much different position. "We can think of no better resting place," the Congressman wrote, "than in that clean Arctic snow with the great mountain above them as a monument."[183]

Congressmen Buck soon became the conduit through which most families received information about the crash. After the incident he had organized a meeting in Washington D.C. to discuss the accident and early plans to recover the bodies. Tapping his personal financial resources, Buck covered the travel expenses to Washington of those who could not afford the trip.[184] In a difficult and emotionally charged meeting, family members debated the utility and feasibility of a recovery operation. Failing to reach a consensus on the issue, they went home to await the outcome of the Army's deliberations.[185]

Washburn returned to Fairbanks from the meeting at Elmendorf where he and others had been unsuccessful in persuading the Alaskan Command to abandon their recovery plans. Turning his attention to his field expedition, he conducted numerous aerial reconnaissance flights over the proposed test site near the base of Mount McKinley, beside the Muldrow Glacier. At the same time, Pearson's recovery party cleared the ninety-mile McKinley Park road of snow, from McKinley Station (the rail link in the Park) to Wonder Lake, from which the advance team carried out several ground-based reconnaissance trips to McGonagall Pass and the Muldrow Glacier.

Pearson planned to traverse the Muldrow at the base of Mount McKinley, and then to travel up the Brooks Glacier to the base of an unnamed mountain where a route to the plane could be identified. Pearson knew the terrain quite well, having traversed the same eighteen miles in 1932 from Wonder Lake to the Muldrow Glacier as a member of the second team to summit Mount McKinley. Pearson's plan called for numerous camps along the route, creating a network of communication and supply lines complete with food, equipment, and fuel. Washburn's route to the field test site paralleled Pearson's expedition, and catching up with Pearson's party in mid October, was quite taken with the rather large-scale effort underway. "They had already forded the McKinley Fork and had 2 tractors, trailers, dozens of drums of oil . . . there's a regular road running over the hills," he wrote in his diary.[186]

Washburn encountered the Pearson expedition just as a lively debate had unfolded. Although Pearson's team had access to aerial photos of the mountain, there was considerable confusion as to which of the surrounding peaks was in fact the plane's final resting-place.[187] Having flown over the wreckage several weeks before and memorized its exact location in relation to the surrounding mountains, Washburn hand-sketched a map of the region and charted a detailed route to the crash site.[188]

In light of Washburn's knowledge of the region and extensive mountaineering experience, on November 1 Pearson invited him to join the recovery team.[189] Accepting the invitation, Washburn transferred command of his small party to co-leader Major Robert Sharp, who would now lead the three-man team on their cross-country test expedition. Washburn, Pearson, and Sergeant James Gale joined Jim Ford on his M-7 tractor and began their trek up the Brooks Glacier toward the crash site. Although the M-7 tractor could pull and carry a considerable amount of equipment, the men had great difficulty identifying negotiable routes for the vehicle on the glacial terrain and open tundra. At times, Washburn felt that these problems negated much of the M-7's value:

> Two years before [on the 1942 Mount McKinley Test Expedition], we had become very familiar with the problem of trail picking on Muldrow afoot, but trying to figure out a safe path for a 3,000-pound M-7 snow jeep to follow was an entirely different problem. Frequently, where traveling afoot was just plain arduous slogging ahead on snowshoes, the jeep would take off at twenty miles an hour for a mile or more. Then we'd overhaul it and spend an hour trying to find a practicable way to get it safely across a frozen glacial stream in a little canyon six feet deep which anyone could easily jump across, even in snowshoes.[190]

By 4 November the team moved to the 7,000-foot level and occupied the "Brooks Camp," where Washburn studied the impressive ice cascade between the camp and the upper reaches of the mountain. As he explained, the gradual elevation gain of the glacier through the mountain's upper slopes led to a

> steep ice-veneered rock mass with only one obscure passage by which a party of climbers can attain the summit ridge without great difficulty. Much of the lower part of this route lies beneath a barrier of tottering ice blocks, any one of which could wipe out several hundred yards of the trail in a matter of seconds. From the ridge camps, a steep 1,000 foot descent on the south side leads to the lonely shelf where the wreckage was discovered. A virtually impassable 3,000 foot ice fall isolates it from the head of the Eldridge Glacier below.[191]

Eight men left "Brooks Camp" a day later and began climbing toward the ridge several thousand feet above. Laboring for hours, Washburn recalled a

> long steady pull, first over patches of hard wind-packed snow and then powder occasionally knee deep. For 30 minutes we were on a pretty dangerous avalanche slope which I never relish. At 1 o'clock we hit a plateau about 1500 feet above camp . . . and at 1:30 tackled the steep (45 degree)

packed snow after putting on our crampons . . . at 4:00 we dumped our
extra food and willow wands 3550 ft. above camp (10,650) and we plowed
on to the pass 400 ft. above in ankle-to-knee deep flour snow.[192]

Reaching the pass at sunset, they witnessed a show of shadows and
colors dancing across the high peaks of the Alaska Range. This brilliant
display of nature's beauty was tempered by the scene directly below them,
as they peered down the far side of the mountain toward the plane. The
contorted remains of the C-47 lay a thousand feet below, the stark gray of
the plane standing out against the snow and ice. In the distance, a great
icefall plunged straight down to the Eldridge Glacier. From the ridge,
Washburn contemplated the arduous decent to the wreck where a "45
degree slope of hard snow with blue ice patches dropped from us to it."[193]

As the small party ended their reconnaissance and headed back, a
contingent of eleven men arrived at the "Brooks Camp" which now held
over nineteen men. The team planned to negotiate the route to the ridge
again the next day, in hopes of placing a camp directly on the ridge from
which they would descend to the plane. Convinced the mission posed
great danger for inexperienced mountaineers, Washburn became frustrated
with Pearson's insistence on placing a large party of men at the wreck site.

> Grant plans still to try to get at least one token body out of the ship, but I
> think it is more nonsensical and dangerous than ever to get a dozen or more
> inexperienced fellows up in that place . . . but the Army is very, very
> stubborn about the thoroughness of this investigation even if considerable
> danger is involved.[194]

After a review of the wreck site from the ridge above, Washburn
remained convinced that it would be next to impossible to remove anybody
from the isolated crash area. He noted that this issue took precedence over
other discussions when the men were back in camp. The "main topic of
discussion that night" Washburn later wrote, "was not how we'd get to it
[the plane]; it was how on earth we could ever get even a single body out
of the wreckage, up the shoulder, and down the icefall."[195] Also making
extraction difficult was the impending likelihood of an avalanche, as the
plane lay directly under a slope obviously prone to them.

For the next two days the Army Air Force airdropped supplies at the site of the wreckage site in preparation for the expedition's next move. Washburn, Pfc. Jake Yokel of Jackson, Wyoming, and Technician-5 Jacob Stalker of Kotzebue, Alaska, established "Ridge Camp" at approximately 11,000 feet. Yokel and Washburn descended the slope toward the aircraft on 8 November, cutting steps into the steep ice slope with their ice axes and placing a line of fixed rope along the route. They ran out of rope five hundred feet down the slope and were forced to return to camp, with what they believed to be a good plan to reach the wreck the following day.

Washburn, Yokel, and Stalker reached the plane the next day after an arduous two and a half-hour descent, during which the climbers laboriously fixed an additional nine hundred feet of rope down the ice face. By six o'clock that evening the remaining members of the advance party, in gathering darkness, joined the three men at the wreckage. As the men established their camp with the provisions dropped by the Army Air Force and settled down for another cold Alaskan winter night, Washburn felt the eerie presence of those individuals whose bodies lay buried somewhere under their isolated little camp. "By sunset twelve of us were pitching camp on that lonely shelf perched halfway up the south face" Washburn

"The fuselage was smashed and twisted in two"
Expedition leader Grant Pearson,
kneeling alongside the cockpit remains of the C-47
Negative 57-4701, courtesy Bradford Washburn Collection

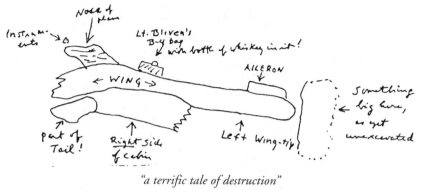

"a terrific tale of destruction"
Washburn's diary sketch of the main wreck site
Courtesy of Bradford Washburn Collction

wrote, "somewhere near us, buried deep in the wind packed snow, lay nineteen other Army men, but not a single trace of them was in sight anywhere."[196]

On 11 November, the recovery team began excavating the wreckage buried in ten feet of snow. At an altitude of 9,700 feet, the work took its toll on the men, requiring them to shovel in shifts to avoid exhaustion. "8 hours of digging yielded not a single body," Washburn later wrote, "but a terrific tale of destruction."[197] Washburn's extended diary entry for the day captures vividly the grim recovery scene, "an unbelievable wreck," he begins:

> The fuselage was smashed and twisted in two just forward of the emergency exit on the right side. . . . The doors were broken off and gone and the whole fuselage forward of the doors pinched off so that where it actually broke, it was only 3" thick with the floor and ceiling together. The wing was right side up, but was over the top of the tail assembly and the nose section. The whole wing assembly was in one piece, the left tip intact and the right end shorn off at about the mid-point. Under the wing, beside the tail and pointing backward were the twisted, snarled remnant[s] of the cockpit . . . simply a mass of wire cables, tubes and twisted aluminum.[198]

Only the control cables held the fragmented pieces of the plane together. Ten feet behind the plane's cockpit and next to its excavated left wing, the team uncovered a B-4 bag belonging to Co-pilot Blivens, "In it a bottle of whisky unpadded and intact," Washburn noted, "it must have fallen out

*"the motor still was stuck at an angle 220 vertical feet below the ridge
and 1540 above where the plane lies"*

Jim Gale inspects the port engine of the C-47
below the summit of Mount Deception

Negative 57-4716, courtesy Bradford Washburn Collection

of the pilot's luggage and mail compartment." The contents of the bottle
disappeared in a very few minutes.[199] "We found a box of chocolates,
Washburn continued, "and some perfect Doublemint chewing gum in
Bliven's bag too."[200]

The team also uncovered the shattered plywood backrest of the pilot's
seat next to Bliven's bag and "half of a safety belt . . . not broken . . . just
undone" Washburn noted.[201] In fact, not one safety belt was found
fastened, and playing cards lay strewn about the wreckage, evidence perhaps
of the men's final activity before the plunge into the mountain. A soldier's
cap and toilet kit belonging to Congressman Buck's son, Lt. O.J. Buck,
lay in deep snow, and scattered furlough orders littered the area.[202] After a

full day of digging, the plane lay uncovered and in three sections, with its port engine imbedded in ice some 1,500 feet above the aircraft. A trail sliced into the ice by the plane's left wing before impact had directed the men's eyes to the engine above.[203]

Next morning the men tunneled ten feet beneath the plane and all around a fifteen-foot section of the fuselage. A frustrated Pearson confessed, "we have dug out the main parts of the airplane . . . but failed to find any bodies. There was nothing in it except a few blood stains."[204] The team uncovered a trail of debris and personal items, but the mountain covered all signs of the dead, and all evidence of the cause of the crash that would either contradict or support the military's official position of the events leading to the disaster.

After two days of exhaustive searching, Pearson conceded that the bodies could not be found and decided to end the expedition. "I took a census of opinions of the men and all believed the finding of the bodies was hopeless," he reported.[205] On 13 November, the main party broke camp and Pearson directed Washburn and Gale to begin the difficult task of climbing up to the plane's port engine in hopes of finding some helpful information on its condition and possible connection to the crash.[206]

The two men climbed to a point about seven hundred and fifty vertical feet above the engine. Here a large cornice of ice above a fifteen-foot overhang blocked the way. Cutting a hole through the ice, they tied one end of the rope to an ice-axe several feet in back of the ridge, tying the remaining end around Gale's waist. He rappelled through the cornice and down to the motor, with Washburn close behind. Washburn's report described the scene as follows:

Perched on a 53 degree slope and driven 24"into solid ice, the motor still was stuck at an angle 220 vertical feet below the ridge and 1540 above where the plane lies. Beyond it for a hundred yards was a mass of small articles of wreckage, still splattered and stuck all over the hillside . . . a hillside of solid blue ice except above the motor, where the hard snow (about one foot deep) still was stuck on the surface. The motor was clearly the left one. The plane's left wing first hit, then it twisted around, the motor crashing, then the nose, the right wing escaping injury. It must have then slid backward, then over and all the way down. An oxygen bottle, wire, cable and a mass of smaller objects were scattered all over the slope beyond the motor.[207]

After a short yet thorough investigation and photographic reconnaissance of the site, the two men fought their way back across the slope in a fierce wind and plummeting temperatures. Sgt. Richard Manuel and Pvt. Elmo Fenn awaited the pair's return in hopes of continuing on to the mountain's summit. Nearly overcome by the elements, Washburn recalled how he and Gale finally reached the safety of the ridge:

> Our hands were numb from pulling ourselves up the hand line and we both finally had to hauled up the overhang and through the cornice like sacks of meal. When we reached our friends on the ridge they were congealed from waiting for us—a frigid northwest wind was sweeping the ridge . . . We beat the snow out of our gloves and sleeves, wiped the icicles from our eyebrows, re-adjusted our rope and started quickly up the ridge toward top . . . No ascent had ever been made of its summit, so we figured that the Army would not mind our taking a 45-minute leave of absence for this little side trip, now that our jobs were done.[208]

A short climb led them to the summit where the entire Kantishna region, Mt. Hayes (of which Washburn had made the first ascent with his wife Barbara in 1941), and the entire McKinley massif stretched out before the men. From this vantage point, Washburn calculated the mountain's height to be lower than that of adjacent Mount Brooks. As a last matter of business, Manuel and Fenn erected a makeshift summit-flag fashioned from yellow parachute cloth fastened to a piece of wood. Their flag whipped in the cold mountain wind, a testament to the men buried below as well as the mark of the climbers' accomplishment.[209]

Making a quick descent to "Ridge Camp" the team continued down the ice cascade to the Brooks Glacier. After a well-deserved dinner, they welcomed the bright lights of Jim Ford's M-7 tractor as it pulled into camp in a fierce snowstorm. The four summiteers accepted Ford's invitation for a ride back to the lower part of the glacier, where Washburn hoped to rejoin Bob Sharp and the rest of his test expedition. "At Nine O'clock at night, in the pitch dark and in the midst of a wild blizzard, we chugged steadily along at fifteen miles an hour, our headlights clearly picking up one willow trail marker after another in their brilliant beam," Washburn recalled. "What a ridiculous way to be traveling along an Alaskan glacier and what an incongruous end to a thoroughly fantastic experience," he added.[210] The tractor and its passengers reached Washburn's team at the "Brooks Moraine Camp" in less than an hour; the M-7 proving its utility after all.

The remaining members of Pearson's recovery party descended the glacier the following morning and continued the long walk to base camp at Wonder Lake. From here the men made their way to Anchorage. On 24 November, when the last members of the team reached Elmendorf Air Field, the expedition came to an official close, almost two months after it began.

While the Pearson expedition was winding down, Washburn rejoined his test team, who set course on 14 November for their final push to Colorado Station—their last destination. Supported by air supply and ferrying loads over steep and rugged terrain, the party, predominantly led by Sharp while Washburn had been assisting the Pearson expedition, reached their final destination on 6 December.[211] In temperatures ranging from twenty degrees above zero to forty-six below zero, Sharp and his two "guinea pigs" traversed more than one hundred miles almost entirely on snowshoes. After leading the initial field test expedition to the Muldrow Glacier, leading the recovery team to the crash site, making the first ascent of the mountain, and then rejoining his expedition as they concluded their tests, Washburn had accomplished a great deal in this Alaskan winter. The test expedition ended on 9 December, when the small team of four boarded an AT-11 aircraft at McKinley Park Headquarters and left for Ladd Air Field in Fairbanks.[212]

Bradford Washburn left Fairbanks two days before Christmas. While flying south, his plane circled the 11,826 foot mountain in hopes of catching one last glimpse of the C-47, but he was disappointed: "the whole camp, crash and all is so completely buried under new snow that not a trace of either is to be seen."[213]

After the recovery team arrived in Anchorage, an Army Air Force transport from Ladd Field flew over the C-47 site and dropped three floral wreaths onto the plateau where the nineteen bodies lay hidden beneath the snow. As a lasting monument, members of the expedition suggested naming the mountain in honor of the men buried there, but from the very outset of his involvement Washburn had unofficially dubbed the peak "Mount Deception" for the mysterious circumstances surrounding the accident. Supporting his unofficial name for the peak was the total absence of the plane's occupants at the wreckage site.[214]

Despite Washburn's suggestion, Pearson argued that the mountain's name should more closely relate to the men and their connection to the peak.[215]

> As this mountain is not on the map nor has it been named, I believe a name should be placed on it as a memorial to those who lost their lives in the crash. Washburn suggested the name Mt. Deception. I believe a more fitting name could be found. All of the men, except for one civilian and the plane's crew of three, were on their way to the states on furlough. How about the name FURLOUGH MOUNTAIN.[216]

The U.S. Board on Geographic Names found Washburn's suggestion more appropriate and officially named the peak Mount Deception. On 8 January 1945, Congressman Ellsworth Buck penned a moving and final letter to the families of the men who died on Mount Deception. In it, the grieving father offered words of comfort, strength, and perseverance:

> Non melting mountain snows gradually solidify into ice, which in turn forms glaciers. Glaciers move but a few feet a year. The men are thus perpetually and cleanly buried for thousands of years beyond possibility of their resting places being disturbed.
>
> Unanticipated and instantaneous death! A sublime, uncontaminable resting place! Despite our losses, we have much for which to be thankful.[217]

New Horizons

Washburn's final field expedition to test emergency and survival equipment came in the waning months of the war, from March through May of 1945. The test site was a familiar location; from the McKinley River to the Brooks Glacier and slopes of Mt. Silverthrone (13,800 feet), eleven miles northeast of McKinley. Washburn's team found dramatic improvements in the equipment now available to the fighting man (sleeping bags, gloves, goggles, tents, and boots), with the majority of items tested rating either good or superior in both quality and effectiveness.[218] These findings underscored the significant progress made in the development, production, and deployment of crucial clothing and equipment in support of Army Air Force flyers. Writing in 1946, Washburn summarized his thoughts about his efforts at Wright Field and about the men who worked so diligently on U.S Army Air Force clothing and equipment problems:

> Although there is scarcely a man in any branch of our services who does not feel that some of his equipment was far from perfect, you will not find one in ten thousand who would prefer to renounce all of his American food and equipment in exchange for that issued by any other of the warring powers. The United States equipped its fighting men better than any other country in the world.[219]

In a letter to his parents immediately after the war, Washburn lamented that his work at Wright Field was "an awful struggle," yet boasted of his "smashing victory over the old guard." Washburn savored the "victory" and remained steadfast in his conviction that "it is worth fighting for ideals even if they seem absurdly high to most people." Washburn, like the majority of citizens emerging from the dark cloud of war, confessed to his parents, "I feel as if a chapter in my life had finished and a new one was about to begin."[220]

Curiously, Washburn's life had already begun to change before war's end. His last Alaska field test for the military was to the Mount Silverthrone region next to Mount McKinley and the expedition would provide the catalyst for Washburn's further exploration of Mount McKinley. While camped on Mount Silverthrone Washburn instructed engineers at Ladd Field in Fairbanks to air lift to him field survey equipment, so he could "lessen the inevitable boredom" of the field test by conducting a systematic survey of as much as the area as possible. He noted that each of his military expeditions to the McKinley region had been seriously "handicapped from start to finish by [the] lack of a good map."[221] He began a preliminary survey of Mount McKinley and the surrounding region, determining the position and height of McKinley's taller south peak (20,320 feet) and establishing a more accurate height for the mountain's north peak—just

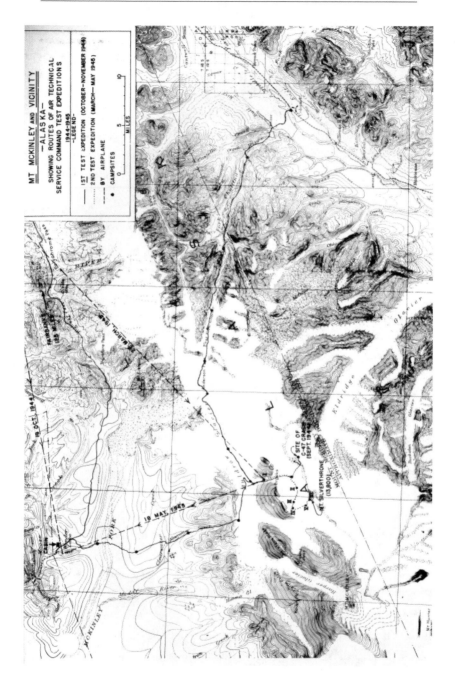

"His last Alaska field test for the military was to the Mount Silverthrone region"

Route map of Washburn's 1944-45 AAF winter test expeditions

Courtesy of Bradford Washburn Collction

853 feet shorter than its companion. This information represented the first truly accurate survey data obtained of the mountain.

Washburn's brief yet fruitful survey work was soon followed by an Air Force aerial photographic flight over McKinley's Muldrow and Traleika glaciers in June of 1945. The United States Coast and Geodetic Survey later incorporated these single-lens vertical photographs and Washburn's McKinley control data in the first detailed large-scale map of the region between Mt. Brooks and McKinley. Although the map was never published, Washburn later confessed that the project "strengthened [his] interest in making a thorough attack on this whole area."[222] Over the next fifteen years Washburn returned often to McKinley, incrementally expanding his initial survey and photographic work to encompass the entire McKinley massif. In 1960, in association with the Swiss Institute for Alpine Research, he produced the most visually aesthetic and strikingly accurate topographic map of Mount McKinley published to date.[223]

Washburn's wartime expeditions to and survey work throughout the McKinley region crystallized his relationship with the mountain, and provided a foundation for his lifelong interest in studying McKinley's unique landscape, environment, and history. In the post-war era, Washburn would climb the peak twice more, becoming the first person to climb the mountain multiple times, and would use his personal connections in the military to further geologic, topographic, and scientific research on the mountain. Washburn's use of the mountain as a research platform resulted in the authoritative map of the mountain, and enabled him to become the foremost authority on the region's history and topography. Today, Washburn's photographs, maps, books, journal articles, and popular magazine stories continue to entice McKinley mountaineers to attempt new and exceedingly difficult ascents. By 1960, Washburn's personal and professional involvement with Mount McKinley was so intimate and interwoven that he would, from then on share with the mountain a significant portion of his own identity. The names Mount McKinley and Bradford Washburn will forever be linked.

4

Mount McKinley: Maps, Hollywood, and Cold War Science

"I was totally overcome with emotion when at 5:30 we reached the summit and the whole amazing panorama burst upon us." Bradford Washburn

Discovering the Landscape

After World War II, thirty-five year old Bradford Washburn returned to Boston and resumed his duties as director of the New England Museum of Natural History. He had left a young yet competent assistant, Miss Peggy Baker in charge of the still-struggling museum. Washburn later recalled, "I dreaded finding a revolt on my hands when I returned. But I had great confidence in Peggy Baker. And she did a superb job."[1]

Washburn wasted little time in exploring new ideas to invigorate the old institution. His plan called for a tour of the new Rochester Museum of Arts and Science, personally conducted by the soon-to-retire director Dr. Arthur C. Parker. Parker was so taken with Washburn that he soon offered the young explorer the director's position once he officially stepped down. As author Mary Desmond Rock notes, "The temptations were great, as Brad assessed his situation in 1945."[2] Washburn was faced with resurrecting an institution in dire financial straits with no long-term plan for future development. Additionally, Washburn believed that the museum Trustees had long neglected the museum and needed to take a more active role in its future. In a memorandum dated 13 December, and read before the Board on 14 December 1945, Washburn outlined the steps needed to retain his position and to move the institution forward. Among them, he noted "The Board must visit the Museum frequently and learn of its problems at first hand, or its members cannot work intelligently toward a common goal. In Rochester," he continued, "I was deeply impressed by the confidence of the Board in their staff and their director and its detailed knowledge of the Museum and its problems."

*"Obtaining seismic
profiles of both
Crillon Lake and
Crillon Glacier"*

Richard Goldthwait
conducting the first
seismic soundings
in Alaska on the South
Crillon Glacier

"And focus all of our efforts on the first ascent of the west buttress"

Bill Hackett approaching the edge of Kahiltna Pass at 10,000 feet. The Peters
Glacier can be seen below

"Evenings were spent repairing equipment and enjoying the spoils of Washburn's use of air transport to supply such a remote camp"

Expedition members in Crillon Lake

"Bradford, sixteen years old . . . achieved an impressive list of successful ascents including the Matterhorn (14,690 feet)"

The Matterhorn and shadow

Negative 4226, copyright Bradford Washburn, courtesy of Panopticon Gallery, Waltham, MA

"A veritable textbook of glacial features"

Woodworth Glacier, Tasnuna Valley

Negative 1825, copyright Bradford Washburn, courtesy of Panopticon Gallery, Waltham, MA

"It's like looking out the windows of heaven"

The Alaska Range from 40,000 feet.
The photo is taken just above the West Fork of the Yetna River

Negative 8277, copyright Bradford Washburn, courtesy of Panopticon Gallery, Waltham, MA

"This abyss would measure nearly 9,000 feet deep from rim to floor"

Climbers in the Great Gorge, Ruth Glacier

Negative 57-6358, copyright Bradford Washburn, courtesy of Panopticon Gallery, Waltham, MA

"The U.S. equipped its fighting men better than any other country in the world"

Ice blocks and climber, Mount Silverthrone, 1945

"distant, stupendous mountains covered with snow and apparently detached from one another"

Mount Foraker (17,400') and Mount McKinley (20,320) from Cook Inlet, where Captain George Vancouver described the peaks in April 1794. Half of McKinley's height is hidden by the earth's curvature.

"A detailed and literal description of the mountain terrain"

The chain of the Aiguille Verte from the Aiguille du Midi

Washburn continued with additional conditions.[3] These included the Trustee's immediate commitment to secure appropriate storage and office space. In addition, Washburn sought approval for a tour of the country's prominent museums to "gather material from which to start plans for a new building as soon as possible." He also proposed to infuse the Board with what he called "prominent Bostonians" committed to a new institution and "who are willing to work hard toward its realization." Washburn finally proposed a name change, at an appropriate time, to the New England Museum of Science. (The name change, when it came, was to the Museum of Science.).[4] Although Washburn confessed that the Rochester position had a significant attraction to him, "the job lacks one feature in which I, as an individual, place a great deal of importance—Dr. Parker's seventeen-year fight for city support and a new museum has been won." He continued, "Rochester no longer presents as great a creative challenge as is still ours here in Boston."

On the issue of compensation, Washburn's salary had been addressed earlier in the month, with the Board, fearing Washburn's interest in the Rochester position, approving an increase from $3,000 to $4,200 a year; still far below the $5,800 salary that would have come with the Rochester offer.[5] The day following Washburn's declaration to the Trustees, 14 December, Trustee Harold Coolidge notified Washburn that the Board had accepted almost all of his "recommendations." On 15 December 1945, Bradford Washburn enjoyed the full support of the Trustees and busied himself in preparing for the future.[6]

Although Washburn focused his efforts on a comprehensive makeover of the museum, his passion for exploration and interest in the McKinley region consumed his free time. For the next fifteen years Washburn dedicated most of his research and fieldwork toward the development and production of the most accurate and artistic map of Mount McKinley. Washburn had conducted a preliminary ground survey of McKinley, and had led an aerial photographic reconnaissance of the peak and its surrounding environs for the National Geographic Society nearly a decade earlier.[7] His mountaineering accomplishments and growing fame enabled him to orchestrate diverse and even disparate entities toward a common goal. These entities included the U.S. military, the National Geographic Society, and Hollywood juggernaut RKO Radio Pictures.[8]

The end of the Second World War saw the start of the Cold War, when significant federal monies were directed into military research and development programs. Historian Stuart W. Leslie has argued that the Cold War redefined American science, and notes that in the decade following World War II, the Department of Defense "became the biggest single patron of American science, predominantly in the physical sciences and engineering but important in many of the natural and social sciences as well."[9] On this subject, historian of science Harvey Sapolsky noted, "Collectively, military agencies were the main federal sponsors of university-based research in the initial years after World War II."[10] In short, when military funding eclipsed all other potential patrons, Washburn positioned himself to reap the benefits of a mutually beneficial relationship with U.S. military agencies. Much of this work took place on Mount McKinley.

The early history of geographic exploration throughout the McKinley region is well documented.[11] Using the mountain as a platform for field science, Washburn created a bridge from late nineteenth century McKinley explorers to those of the mid-twentieth century. In many ways, Washburn is to late-twentieth century McKinley explorers what Alfred H. Brooks and William Field were to turn-of-the-twentieth-century field geologists and glaciologists in Alaska.[12]

Mount McKinley, the tallest mountain in North America, rises over 20,320 feet above sea level as monarch of the Alaska Range.[13] The range constitutes a great arc of glaciated peaks stretching from the Canadian border in the east to the Aleutian Range in southwestern Alaska. The mountains are comprised of Cretaceous and Paleozoic rock as well as granite batholiths intruded into volcanic and sedimentary rock.[14] The mountains block and capture the relatively warm, moisture-laden air of the Pacific Ocean, drawing nearly all precipitation from the air before it reaches Alaska's vast interior. As a result, glaciers along the southern slopes are much larger than those situated on its northern flanks.[15] The landscape immediately surrounding Mount McKinley has been shaped by two distinct glacial episodes. The first event, the Healy Glaciation during the Wisconsin Glaciation, seventy thousand years ago, resulted in a significant buildup and advance of the Alaska Range's southern glaciers, and forming a massive ice field that covered a considerable portion of southern Alaska. The Riley Creek Glaciation during the late Wisconsin period between twenty-five thousand and ninety-five hundred years ago, although less dramatic than its predecessor, also played a considerable role in carving this landscape.[16]

The region surrounding Mount McKinley, with its glacial-carved valleys, mosquito-infested taiga, and ice-clad peaks, posed a considerable challenge to European explorers.[17] After Vitus Bering's discovery of the mainland of Alaska in 1741, Russian fur traders began slowly to venture inland, uncovering an increasingly mysterious landscape. Before white contact, Native Alaskans migrated and hunted throughout the region, and revered the great peak that was often incorporated into their creation stories.[18] During the late eighteenth century, the vast interior of then Russian America was largely unknown, and its spectacular inland mountains were yet to be explored. In 1794, British navigator and explorer George Vancouver, anchored in what is now known as Knik Arm, noted "distant stupendous mountains covered with snow and apparently detached from one another; though possibly they might be connected by land of insufficient height to interrupt our horizon."[19] Most McKinley historians regard this as the first recorded reference to Mount McKinley and its companion peak, Mount Foraker.[20]

Russian expansion through Alaska during the late eighteenth and early nineteenth century continued inland from the resource-rich marine coastline. By the 1830s, significantly more information on Alaska's geography had been collected by fur traders of the Russian American Company. These efforts were coordinated and directed by the Russian governor of Alaska, Baron Ferdinand P. von Wrangell, who relayed information from his many traders back to St. Petersburg. In 1834, one such trader, Andrei Glazunov, documented a great mountain "called Tenada," which is clearly depicted on Wrangell's 1839 map of Russian America.[21]

As the lucrative fur trade began to fade in the mid-nineteenth century, so did Russian interest in Alaska. Following the transfer of Alaska from Russia to the United States in 1867, there was little impetus for the U.S. government to explore their newly acquired territory. It was left to hardy prospectors, driven by the promise of the North's rich gold fields, to uncover the topographic mysteries of Alaska, including the McKinley region. It is to this group of pioneers, says Alaska geologist Alfred Brooks, "that we owe our extension of geographic knowledge."[22] In 1878, a small group of prospectors camped on the shores of the Tanana River at the future site of Fairbanks discovered alluvial gold, and noted to the south the large snow-capped peaks of the Alaska Range and Mount McKinley.[23]

Miners tried their luck throughout the territory in the latter part of the nineteenth century, requiring the U.S. government not only to exert its sovereignty over the region, but also to gather geographic data, provide security, and maintain order in the frontier. Several of the Army reconnaissance expeditions ordered to various locations throughout Alaska were responsible for pioneering explorations in the McKinley region. Lieutenant Henry Allen, leading an expedition to the McKinley area in 1885, noted that the Alaska Range comprised some "very high snow clad peaks."[24] Prospector Frank Densmore praised McKinley's grandeur so often that in 1889 fellow miners christened the peak Densmore's Mountain.[25] In 1894 in the Cook Inlet area south of the Alaska Range, gold was discovered that brought a swarm of miners to the region. Eventually, they traveled north in great numbers toward the Alaska Range, undoubtedly gaining on the way rich geographic knowledge of the area. However, by the very nature of their trade, miners were (and perhaps still are) less than forthcoming regarding an area's geologic (and topographic) composition. Perhaps this is why word of Densmore's great peak did not make it to the outside world.

The lure of Alaska gold also attracted William Dickey, a Princeton-educated prospector, who worked his way from Cook Inlet to McKinley's lowlands. Dickey's account of the 1896 field season, published in the *New York Sun,* first brought public attention to the peak, which he proclaimed the "highest in North America," estimating its height at "over 20,000 feet high."[26] Dickey also gave the name to the mountain by which it is now known: "We named our great peak Mount McKinley, after William McKinley of Ohio, who had first been nominated for the Presidency, and that fact was the first news we received on our way out of that wonderful wilderness."[27]

Although Dickey's report drew some public and government attention to McKinley and Alaska's interior, it was the discovery of gold in the Klondike that placed the territory and its considerable mineral resources in the forefront of political and economic discourse. Financial appropriations were made to the United States Geological Survey (USGS) that began a series of systematic explorations and surveys throughout Alaska, including the McKinley region.[28] Six USGS parties were dispatched to Alaska in the summer of 1898, four of which traversed the environs surrounding the mountain.[29] George Eldridge led one such expedition, on which topographer Robert Muldrow made the first "scientific" calculation of the mountain's height, finding it to be 20,464 feet tall, supporting Dickey's assertion that the peak was indeed the continent's tallest.[30] Additional reconnaissance expeditions were dispatched by the USGS and the War Department during the summers of 1898 and 1899, each adding significantly to the geographic understanding of the McKinley landscape.[31]

In 1902, Alfred Brooks of the USGS explored from Cook Inlet to the Yukon River. Brooks's reconnaissance, which lasted two months and covered eight hundred miles, continued previous surveys in the region, completing the first survey and exploration of the foothills surrounding McKinley. In August of that year, Brooks became the first documented white man to set foot on the mountain's slopes.[32]

In addition to the vast amount of geographic, geologic, and topographic information the expedition collected, news of Brooks's "ascent" in the McKinley foothills drew considerable public attention that "caused popular interest in the results of the expedition out of proportion to their importance." Brooks tells how "an intense curiosity sprang up" among mountaineers regarding a feasible route to the mountain's summit. To satisfy this demand, "an article was published outlining briefly what appeared to be the most feasible routes to the base of the mountain".[33] He recommended a northern approach, claiming that a southern route from Cook Inlet would be far too long. Within months of Brooks's publication, two mountaineering parties descended upon the peak, each determined to make the first ascent of North America's tallest mountain.[34]

The Mountaineers Arrive

The first expedition to attempt Mount McKinley started in Fairbanks (by way of Nenana), in May 1903, under the leadership of Alaska District Judge James Wickersham. Although Wickersham's expedition failed to reach the summit, he did reach an elevation of about four thousand feet, to the bottom of mountain's avalanche-strewn north wall.[35] Just two months after Wickersham's expedition left the mountain, Dr. Frederick Cook, a New York physician and veteran of several polar expeditions, brought an expedition sponsored by *Harper's Magazine*. Although Cook's party also failed to summit, they did reach the head of the Peters Glacier, climbing as high as ten thousand feet on the mountain. Despite such impressive accomplishments, Cook's expedition was fraught with personal conflicts.[36]

Returning to Mt. McKinley in 1906, Dr. Cook claimed to have made the first ascent of the peak with companion Ed Barrill. Cook's claim almost immediately came under suspicion, first from expedition members who were not with Cook during his "ascent," and later from the broader mountaineering and exploration community. The debate was, and continues to be, significant in the history of Mount McKinley exploration.[37] Despite Cook's claim, several teams also tried their luck on McKinley's ice-encrusted slopes. None reached the mountain's 20,320-foot South Peak until June 7, 1913 (Washburn's third birthday), when the Reverend Hudson Stuck, Harry Karstens, Walter Harper, and Robert Tatum stood atop North America's tallest peak. The Stuck expedition is widely credited with making the first successful summit of Mount McKinley.[38]

From Harvard to Hollywood

After Hudson Stuck's expedition, the mountain remained unchallenged for nearly two decades. In the summer of 1932, premier American mountaineer and Bell Laboratories engineer Allen Carpè led a scientific expedition to Mount McKinley under the auspices of Chicago University physicist Dr. Arthur H. Compton. The expedition's cosmic ray investigations, explained Carpè to his friend and colleague Francis Farquhar, were to be added to other data collected by Compton's global research teams "for a wide program of investigations of cosmic rays at high elevations in different parts of the earth."[39]

Through the 1920s and 1930s, physicists began aggressive investigations into the nature of cosmic rays, discovered in 1912 by Austrian physicist Victor F. Hess. The origin of cosmic rays was a matter of controversy during the inter-war years.[40] Hess's discovery of a strange form of subatomic radiation, whose energy far exceeded that of any known form of terrestrial radiation, was subsequently confirmed between 1913 and 1919 by German physicist W. Kohlhorster. Kohlhorster, like Hess, employed hot-air balloons to reach an altitude of 28,000 feet where he noticed a correlation between intensity of cosmic ray radiation and altitude.

However, some physicists, like Robert Millikan of the California Institute of Technology, were hesitant to accept the results. He carried out a comprehensive research program from 1923 to 1926 on the origin of cosmic rays. This work was undertaken in a variety of environments and mediums, including high alpine lakes, at various depths in the ocean, and through unmanned sounding balloons in the upper atmosphere. As physicist Bruno Rossi noted, "Millikan's experiments convinced himself and nearly everyone else in the scientific community that the radiation discovered by Hess did come from beyond the earth's atmosphere. And it was Millikan who gave the name Cosmic Rays to their radiation."[41] The nature of cosmic rays intrigued scientists because the very existence and characteristics of this celestial radiation challenged conventional wisdom and the accepted scientific models. However, questions still lingered about whether the intensity of cosmic rays increased or decreased with a change in latitude. Millikan contended that latitude had no effect on the strength of radiation, while Chicago University physicist Arthur Compton believed otherwise.

In 1932, Compton set out to confirm his theory by organizing a global research program to test his theory. Sixty-nine research stations were established throughout the globe in geographically diverse regions. Allen Carpe's 1932 Mount McKinley Cosmic Ray expedition was one component of this global effort. Carpe's expedition ended tragically when he and companion Theodore Koven fell to their deaths into a crevasse on the Muldrow Glacier. Although their research was not complete, field data obtained before their death was retrieved by members of the Lindley-Leak expedition. This team, descending after making the second successful ascent of the peak, had investigated the vacant campsite of the two men. Members of the expedition forwarded the data to Compton,[42] who wrote that it indicated a "rapid increase with altitude noted by previous observers . . . but also the fact that at each altitude the intensity is greater for higher latitudes than near the equator."[43] The findings also indicated that cosmic rays were charged particles, a notion held by Compton but contested by Millikan, who believed that cosmic rays were photons. If Millikan were to accept Compton's findings, then such charged particles would be distributed unevenly around the earth by the planet's magnetic field, and as historian Daniel Kevles pointed out, "the intensity of cosmic rays would vary with latitude," a notion dismissed by Millikan.[44]

Physicists continuing to study the atom through the 1930s found that cosmic rays were an excellent means by which matter could be probed. As historian David Devorkin noted, "everyone knew, however, that what they were catching in their detectors were not the original cosmic rays, called 'primaries'; but the secondary byproducts of the collisions of primaries with particles in the earth's atmosphere." So the study of primaries drew significant attention as the subject of numerous research programs until such efforts were curtailed by the outbreak of World War II. With the end of the war and the emergence of the Cold War, however, research into cosmic ray radiation resumed.[45]

After World War II Bradford Washburn understood the significance of obtaining a portion of the considerable amount of military funding and logistical support available for expeditionary science. In October of 1946, four months after the Washburns' third child, Betsy, was born, RKO Pictures executive Paul Hollister contacted Washburn to organize and lead a large-scale mountaineering expedition. Washburn agreed and solicited support from the military and the American scientific community for financial, scientific, and logistical support. Hollister encouraged Washburn to develop a critical link to the scientific community, taking advantage of his experience in carrying out large-scale expeditions and his ability to generate both public and institutional support for high-publicized explorations in remote regions. Hollister looked to the academic community in particular to lend an air of "scientific legitimacy" to the expedition.

Since RKO Pictures had purchased the movie rights to a very successful and popular book, Hollister pitched to Washburn the idea of an expedition to obtain authentic mountaineering footage for the movie. Although the actual location was scheduled for the Alps, dramatic high-altitude footage was needed for a short public-relations film, and to provide training for RKO cameramen who would film the full-length movie on location.[46] Hollister first considered Mount Everest, but Washburn persuaded

Hollister that Mount McKinley would be a more feasible option, because it was situated between two military air fields, Anchorage and Fairbanks.[47] With McKinley agreed upon, Hollister and Washburn set out to create an attractive program of theatrical and scientific significance. "The New England Museum agreed to undertake this project," Washburn later wrote, "provided that RKO made it financially possible for the museum to carry out a number of purely scientific objectives."[48]

In a confidential letter to Roy Larsen of *Life Magazine*, in which he explored possible media coverage for and joint collaboration in the expedition, Hollister explained that

> Our own self-interest in offering the essential out-of-pocket costs is simply this: We own a book called The White Tower by James Ramsey Ullman, which has now sold upwards of 700,000 copies, which we are going to make into a distinguished picture—and I mean distinguished. Its story concerns alpine climbing. The more often people can read about high mountain climbing, the more receptive the audience will be to our picture when it comes out. It's just that simple.[49]

Indeed, as Washburn later wrote, Hollister was keenly aware of the public-relations benefit of having a short documentary made of the expedition. This could serve as the perfect marketing tool for a large-scale Hollywood film.

> It was not Mr. Hollister's idea to have a small party which would merely study the use of heavy electrically operated camera equipment on a large mountain. He wanted to have Operation White Tower, as the expedition came to be known, a self-supporting enterprise which would photograph a half-hour short subject, while its personnel were learning the limitations of studio equipment on a big peak and while the public was becoming even further imbued with the two magic words "White Tower," an important factor in the advance publicity strategy for any feature film.[50]

James Ramsey Ullman's novel was set in the throes of World War II: a woven story of love, war, and the personal challenges that motivate individuals to face and perhaps conquer their inner fears and conflicts. The book's inside flap, capturing the gist of Ullman's story, provides insight into Hollister's enthusiasm for the entire project.

The White Tower raises its savage and sublime immensity of rock and snow and ice high above Europe torn by war and hate. In bygone years of peace this great mountain challenged the most experienced climbers of every nation—and none who tried the ascent from the Alpine valley of Kandermatt had ever succeeded.

The tides of war have left a strange human flotsam in neutral Switzerland. And in remote Kandermatt there are six oddly assorted people who desire above all else to climb the White Tower despite (or because of?) its dangers—each for a private reason of his own. Andreas Benner, the Swiss guide who has lived all his life in its shadow, has dreamed from earliest boyhood of making the terrible ascent which cost his father's life. His is the least complicated reason. Nicholas Radcliffe, the English geologist, was in his younger days a great climber. High on Everest he had watched Mallory and Irvine disappear forever in that dark cloud just below the summit cone. To him the White Tower symbolizes the high adventure of his lost youth. To Paul Delambre, the Frenchman, the mountain is an escape from dilettantism into the reality of action, a chance to live for once outside the mirror of himself. For Siegfried Hein, Wehrmacht officer and expert Alpinist, the conquest of the great snow peak represents another triumph for the Third Reich and racial superiority.

But what of Martin Ordway, the American bomber pilot whose presence in Kandermatt is baffling even to himself? Why is it that he can not return to the war he has left involuntarily without first pitting his hard-tried courage against the White Tower? And what is it out of her haunted past that impels Carla, the Viennese girl, to join Martin in his assault upon that lofty citadel? Of these and many other things, including love and death, the reader learns as he lives through this superb account of an epic adventure.[51]

A key character in Ullman's story was that of the Viennese beauty Carla. So Hollister supported the idea of including a woman on the expedition. However, he believed that the expedition needed several "angles" on which it could be sold not only to the general public, but also to the military and scientists whose support and expertise were vital to the plan's success.[52] In an effort to draw public attention to the expedition and create pre-release interest in the movie, Washburn suggested a woman be added to the expedition. "You made a brilliant suggestion in wanting to get the first gal up there," Hollister wrote, "it seems to me that this would be publicity of the first magnitude." Hollister also suggested to Washburn that since the movie called for two actors to scale the mountain, "how would you like to take the leading male and or leading woman to the top of the goddamn mountain." He suggested that "the man can do anything athletic that would be required. As to the girl, just assume that she has the usual equipment—whatever that is." Yet he reassured Washburn that he was not "going publicity crazy," as this was a "serious venture" that must include all the "scientific or pseudo-scientific angles that will justify the venture in a wide variety of directions." [53]

Although Hollister tried to present the expedition as a "serious venture," his overriding motive clearly was public relations. Nevertheless, he contacted Harvard astrophysicist, director of the Harvard College Observatory, Dr. Harlow Shapley, to explore the possibility of developing scientific components for the expedition. Hollister encouraged Washburn to "get into a closed room with him and ask him to suggest how many ways [the] expedition might make a real scientific contribution."[54] Preliminary discussions with Shapley were productive: "He (Shapley) has some extremely practical ideas with regard to McKinley and is going to discuss them with a group of cosmic ray physicists" Washburn reported.[55] "He believes that a considerable sum of money could be secured, either from a private foundation or from the Government for this enterprise."[56] Indeed, the Naval Research Laboratory (NRL) viewed research into the origin, characteristics, and behavior of cosmic rays to be a "practical application because cosmic radiation represents a potential hazard to operations of high-flying manned vehicles and to instrumentation, particularly transistors, to be used in earth satellites."[57]

Eventual support for the expedition's cosmic ray work was secured through the U.S. Navy's Office of Naval Research (ONR), founded in 1946, which supplied significant financial resources for basic research.[58] In fact, from 1946 through 1950, which historian Harvey Sapolsky called the golden age of academic science, ONR was the primary federal agency supporting academic research. A relatively remote and energetic expedition such as Washburn proposed fit well into ONR's research and funding mandates. "ONR was able to use public funds to support promising opportunities in science," Sapolsky noted, "free from the considerations of geography."[59] A previously classified document covering the activities of the Geophysics Branch of ONR from 1947 to 1948 contained specific directives encouraging sponsorship of field research expeditions to "relatively inaccessible areas of the Earth." ONR believed that such expeditions were an "outgrowth of Man's native curiosity" and a way to "discover new principles which control our environment." The understanding and possible control of the environment was a high military priority, since officials at ONR believed that "the society which knows the most about its environment . . . is going to be more likely to win the next war." The final justification for continued ONR support of remote expeditions was based less on military interests and more on sheer emotion: "In addition to these reasons for expeditions but not the least in importance, expeditions are fun."[60]

While Shapley developed scientific options for the program, Washburn unveiled to Hollister a bold and multidisciplinary plan that included a myriad of objectives. He envisioned the McKinley program as an ideal way to continue the survey work on McKinley initiated during the waning days of the war. The goals of this expedition, he wrote to Hollister, "in addition to the purely adventurous objectives of climbing the mountain, would be to obtain valuable survey data on its yet unmapped upper portion . . . and other scientific projects that might be proposed by Shapley."[61] He also suggested a series of reconnaissance and aerial photographic flights "to make photographs to use in place of a map during the actual climb."[62]

Aerial resupply of the expedition was to be supported by military C-47 aircraft at 18,000 feet, where a "comfortable camp could be parachuted so that the high altitude survey work and other projects . . . could be carried out from a reasonably warm and comfortable base." Moreover, large quantities of "scientific supplies could be chuted to the 18,000 ft. camp," Washburn noted, where the "highest observatory ever established anywhere in the world" would be occupied.[63] Washburn reassured Hollister that he and Shapley could create a project that would be "interesting, dramatic, practical and distinguished." "If you don't get $15,000 worth of mountain publicity out of it," he declared, "I'd eat my flying suit."[64] RKO quickly approved Washburn's plan. Although details of the scientific components were still in discussion, the expedition was scheduled to begin in the spring of 1947.[65]

"God forbid that I should ever become a 'hard-boiled' scientist"
Washburn surveying from the summit of 20,320 foot Mount McKinley,
in the thin, twenty-below-zero air temperature
Negative 57-5392, copyright Bradford Washburn, courtesy Panopticon Gallery, Waltham, MA

On October 31 1946, Washburn met at the Harvard College Observatory, with some of the nation's leading scientists, Harlow Shapley and Donald H. Menzel of Harvard, and Bruno Rossi of the Massachusetts Institute of Technology, to discuss the viability of high-altitude research programs for the expedition.[66] Shapley reported "neither the Harvard nor MIT cosmic ray men have a particular interest in the problems that could be tackled on Mount McKinley." However, several alternative suggestions were made, including the recruitment of Professor Ira A. Bowen and Dr. Harold Babcock of the Mount Wilson Observatories, who were "working with Millikan on studies related to the magnetic field of the sun and high altitude in high latitudes." Shapley also indicated "Professor Marcel Schein of Chicago University would have an interest in this direction."[67]

Schein indeed found the opportunity appealing, as he notified Shapley:

I have in mind an experiment on the production of mesotrons which has to be carried out with a system of counter telescopes. There is a chance that in addition we might be able to fix up some ionization chambers for investigation of giant atmospheric showers. We also could send along some photographic plates for measuring the frequency of nuclear disintegration (stars) caused by cosmic particles.[68]

Before World War II, Schein had made the first observations of highly accelerated protons, believed to be the elusive cosmic ray primaries.[69] After the war, the US military began an energetic program to develop long-range rockets capable of delivering various military and scientific payloads into and through the upper atmosphere. Although rockets could reach altitudes higher than either balloons or aircraft, their flying time was limited, and as David DeVorkin points out, rockets were "far from a pristine environment for cosmic-ray research." Schein preferred the use of balloons "because they had longer flights, and maintained known altitudes in space." He also saw the benefits of establishing a stationary high-altitude research hut on McKinley that was capable of obtaining data over a prolonged period of time.[70] Plans for the cosmic ray work, under the direction of Schein and with the advice of Shapley, were solidified by mid January of 1947. The scientific program required a large research hut to be erected at eighteen thousand feet (as Washburn had envisioned) to house a system of telescopes (weighing three hundred pounds), high-voltage batteries, photographic recorders, heaters, an ionization chamber, and spare parts. "Because the major scientific goal of the expedition was Cosmic Ray research in Denali Pass," Washburn later wrote, "the Army Air Forces agreed to furnish air support, in order to effect the establishment of this special camp."[71]

Washburn soon secured several additional scientific components for the expedition, including the collection of geological samples from the "tops of both peaks of McKinley in order to tie into work already done in the adjacent lowlands by the U.S. Geological Survey." He also developed plans for the collection of climatological data with instruments furnished by the U.S. Weather Service and cold-climate field tests to be carried out by representatives of the Army Air and Ground Forces "of various articles of new equipment and food throughout the expedition."[72] Not only would this new program enable Washburn to continue further research on winter clothing for the Air Force, it solidified his relationship with the military and reinforced their support for the expedition.

Meanwhile, Paul Hollister was busy greasing the political wheels far in advance of the party's arrival in Alaska. He sought the support of his long-time friend and Alaska territorial governor Ernest Gruening. In a letter to Gruening, Hollister contended that the publicity will "not be aimed at a few thousand, but as many as millions of readers and listeners" who will be interested in the "much sensational scientific material to be collected." Such a program, Hollister believed, would "also help your territory" and this is why "I know darn well you . . . will probably want to aid and abet it." Although he emphasized the expedition's "scientific objectives," the Hollywood slant he planned was to "include in the party 'for the first time on any stage' a photogenic woman—who is Mrs. Washburn herself."[73]

"As an old and expert publicist yourself," Hollister wrote, "you will see that this has powerful and favorable publicity possibilities for the territory." He prodded Gruening to "put the scheme in the top of your head along with 4 or 5 Martinis, let it slosh around and ferment there a while."[74] Although we will never know if Gruening followed Hollister's suggestion, we do know that he supported the expedition and asked to be "informed just when the expedition is going to start so that I can make sure that it is properly welcomed."[75] To gain maximum publicity for the climb, the joint expedition between RKO Pictures and Washburn's New England Museum of Natural History was named "Operation White Tower," after Ullman's *The White Tower*.[76]

Operation White Tower

Through the winter and spring of 1947 Washburn assembled a group of seasoned mountaineers and explorers to support the team's less experienced scientists and cameraman. Expedition members included Bradford and Barbara Washburn, Grant Pearson (Chief Ranger, McKinley Park and leader of the 1944 Mount Deception expedition), Sergeant James Gale (10th Rescue Squadron, also a member of the Mount Deception expedition), George Browne (son of pioneer Alaskan mountaineer and artist Belmore Browne), Lieutenant William Hackett (Army observer), Robert Lange, Hugo Victoreen (directing the expedition's cosmic ray research program), Earl Norris (dog driver), William Deeke and George Wellstead (RKO movie photographers), Hakon Christenson (ski-plane pilot), Harvey "Red" Solberg (radio operator at Camp Eielson), Len

Shannon (the RKO public relations representative who later quit the expedition on April 28), and William Sterling (Shannon's replacement).

George Browne and Bob Lange arrived in Anchorage on March 15 to organize the expedition's supplies. Two days later James Gale and pilot Hakon Christensen conducted an aerial survey of the Muldrow Glacier and marked with twigs a potential site to serve as a landing strip. [77] Brad and Barbara Washburn reached Anchorage, Alaska, on March 27, and continued the task of sorting and organizing the mountain of equipment as well as finalizing the expedition's plans. [78] A few days later, Washburn made the first of several photographic reconnaissance flights to an elevation of 23,500 feet, to evaluate his proposed climbing route. [79] On March 30 Browne and Lange flew to 5,700-foot McGonagall Pass, where they established the expedition's base camp. At the same time, the Wonder Lake radio station, which would serve as a critical survey station marker and radio link to the outside world, was established. As Washburn noted, "our efficient Signal Corp operator (Sergeant Harvey Solberg), assisted by Mr. Moore, a Signal Corps engineer, had this station (WXE-2) operating perfectly by April 3." [80]

Expedition members and supplies were ferried to the mountain over several days by Christensen, with the final flight made on April 9. Through April and May, the team methodically moved up the mountain, the survey work occupying a significant portion of Washburn's time. His expedition account captures the process as follows:

> The method which we used for making our long survey shots between the hills just north of Muldrow Glacier and the main control station at Wonder Lake 20 miles away was simple but very successful. On our 8 a.m. radio schedule with Wonder Lake we made another schedule 3 hours later. By then we had packed our light Forest Service SPF radio telephone set to the top of McGonagall Peak 800 feet above camp and set it up beside our theodolite. The theodolite was focused on the Wonder Lake Ranger Cabin where Sgt. Solberg ran our radio relay station, about 100 yards from the key survey station in the Wonder Lake region. At 11 a.m. we contacted Solberg on our radio and told him we were ready to observe. He took a large mirror over to the survey station and kept flashing us with it till we told him on the radio that we had made the necessary number of repetitions of our angle

and that they checked properly. This system required flawless visibility between these points as well as good radio and survey teamwork. The survey work was bitterly cold, as the lowlands around Wonder Lake were rarely clear except with the light cutting northerly or northeasterly breeze. Later on this same system was used successfully from both Gunsight Pass and Browne Tower.[81]

By mid April the majority of the team had arrived on the Muldrow Glacier and advance base camp was well established. Earl Norris's dog-team hauled the expedition's food and fuel up the glacier, but McKinley's miserable weather often delayed Washburn's plans, playing havoc with the movie-making and his overall scientific efforts. "While dog teaming went ahead very nicely despite wretched conditions under foot," Washburn later wrote, "the movie program and surveying were held almost at a standstill."[82] Nevertheless, through snowstorms, fog, and cold, the team continued to advance up the glacier, establishing Camp II or the Great Serac Camp at 8,500 feet, on May 8. Washburn mixed exhausting days of hauling with interludes of detailed survey work:

> Survey work, geological collecting and photography were made even longer
> by heavy back-packing relaying of virtually our entire outfit through the
> steep parts of both icefalls where dogteaming was quite out of the question.
> We had no air-drops between McGonagall and 11,000 ft. hence our
> packing program of 600 pounds of movie gear and about 500 pounds of
> dog feed in addition to our own food, clothing and camping equipment was
> very heavy. Dog teaming was so miserably hard and required so many relays
> that we might easily have done better to do without dogs and depend
> entirely on air support. But conditions of this sort are most unusual on
> Muldrow and must occur very rarely.[83]

Day after day, though their advance was slow and laborious, progress up the mountain was made. "On May 12 after a wicked siege of back-packing movie equipment, batteries, food and a dozen sacks of evil-smelling dried fish (dog-food), up the Great Serac," Washburn declared, "our last contingent arrived at 11,000 feet where Jim Gale and Victoreen had already established a splendid 3-igloo village."[84] Washburn used igloos throughout the expedition, and they quickly became popular with team members. "I believe our use of igloos on Operation White Tower," Washburn wrote, "is the first time that they have been steadily relied upon as a shelter on a major mountain expedition. They were wonderful." His analysis continues:

> Although they were somewhat humid and never could be kept really warm inside, they were never at all cold. They did not flap in gusty wind. They didn't have to be dug out after a heavy snowfall. Almost best of all, once built, they were up for weeks, as long as the weather stayed cold. On a cold night, the temperature dropped to 15 or 20 below zero inside a tent almost the moment the stove was turned off, even though it had been 60 or 70 above with the heat on. . . . When we broke camp, we simply rolled up our sleeping bags and crawled out, just as if we were leaving a house. If we had to reoccupy a camp that we had evacuated a week or two before, all we had to do was shovel a drift of snow out of the doorway, open the vent in the roof and set up housekeeping.[85]

Washburn, Jim Gale, and Robert Craig set out on May 13 to reconnoiter the route to Browne Tower (named after mountaineer and artist Belmore Browne) via Karstens Ridge, named after Harry Karstens, a member of Reverend Hudson Stuck's team that made the first ascent of the mountain in 1913. The Ridge allows safe, although exposed, access from the lower

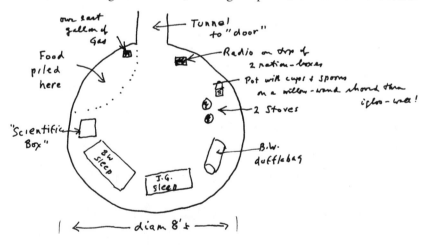

"The men sought refuge here, with a terrific storm raging all about them"
Washburn's diary sketch of a typical igloo campsite
Courtesy of Bradford Washburn Collection

elevations of the Muldrow Glacier at about 11,000 feet, to the mountain's upper reaches of the Harper Glacier. It provides an alternative route around the treacherous icefall resulting from the Harper's plunge down to the Muldrow Glacier. Like Karstens Ridge, the Harper was named for a member of Stuck's party, Walter Harper, the first person to reach McKinley's summit.

Through the remaining days of May, the team established additional camps at Browne Tower and at 16,400 feet. Gale and Washburn moved into the latter camp on May 20 while the rest of the expedition continued to haul equipment and food in anticipation of establishing the team's high camp above 18,000 feet. "We put up our tent in a gusty 40-mile wind," Washburn wrote, "which rapidly increased to sixty or more. The thermometer which had dropped to better than 20 below zero during the last two nights at Browne Tower rose to −10 minimum and a wild blizzard raged about us for 18 hours."[86] The weather that evening was a harbinger of things to come.

For nine straight days the Great Storm, as it was named by the expedition, punished the team. After setting up their camp on the 20th, Washburn and Gale decided to construct an igloo at 16,500 feet. "There we spent as unpleasant an afternoon as I have ever experienced," Washburn later recalled, "building an igloo in dense fog, gusty wind and drifting snow with the mercury barely above zero."[87] The men sought refuge here, with a terrific storm raging all about them. With winds exceeding ninety miles an hour, the two did not venture outside of their icy home for an entire forty-eight hour period. According to Washburn, the wind was "screaming" and "one of my crampons actually *blew off my ice axe* and fetched up on *top* of the igloo."[88] The weather played havoc with Washburn's plans. He privately admitted "our progress in the last month has been pretty sad in many ways."

Reports from other team members lower down on the mountain were no better. Washburn noted "the radio from 11,000 cheerily reported 100 miles of wind, 2 tents blown flat (one of them a new Army pentagonal tent) and all hands holding down the cooktent for dear life. Barbara reported savage gusts, dense fog and heavy snow at Browne Tower. McKinley Park Headquarters, 14,000 feet below us, reported heavy warm rain and the buds coming out on the trees!"[89]

Much to Paul Hollister's liking, news stories dispatched by the expedition kept the public informed of the team's battle with the Great Storm. Although reports of the expedition's challenges were for the most part complimentary, not all reports were positive. The climb was portrayed in the Anchorage press as melodramatic, with a less than sporting atmosphere, noting that military air support "prepares the way and tenderly watches over each rod of the distance traveled." The expedition was described as a "pampered holiday of the self publicized Bradford Washburn party."[90] Although the work of RKO cameraman Bill Deeke was applauded on the release of a short documentary account of the climb the following year (1948), one Fairbanks newsman found the narrative to be "written with a pen dipped alternately in syrup and scented ice by a frail young man {Washburn} who had just rolled in crushed rose petals."[91]

On May 25, assessing the slow progress of the expedition, Washburn questioned the feasibility of conducting Schein's cosmic ray work. He confessed "today for the first time we are beginning to wonder whether we can actually succeed in pulling off Vic's [Hugo Victoreen's] scheduled cosmic ray program at 18,000."[92] The blizzard that besieged the party not only delayed the expedition's climbing and survey schedule, it jeopardized Schein's and Victoreen's entire research program. "Vic's Geiger counters are all destroyed [by the last storm]," Washburn wrote, "and we have wired Schein . . . for replacements."[93] But Victoreen indicated to Washburn "that it would be virtually impossible to replace the lost counters in less than a month" and Washburn canceled the program on May 27.[94] He explained his reasons for doing so in a telegram to Paul Hollister at RKO's New York office:

> We have appraised the cosmic ray program thoroughly and have decided it cannot be continued. . . . Please explain unfortunate but unavoidable situation to Schein.[95]

On June 4, just one week after Washburn canceled the program, he received a telegram from Schein, via radio from Anchorage, indicating the importance Schein placed on the McKinley work:

> Counters replaced. Counters have already been sent to Anchorage via N.W. Airlines, carrying instructions that they be dropped with other cosmic ray

18,000 equipment . . . . It would be highly profitable to undertake even part if not all of cosmic ray program without endangering life or health of personnel.[96]

"Vic is pleased as punch," Washburn noted, adding, "so am I. I hate to admit I'm licked and somehow or other we'll do this."[97]

The Great Storm ended on May 30. On June 5 the entire team joined Washburn and Gale within a couple of hundred yards of Denali Pass, above 18,000 feet. Barbara, RKO cameraman Bill Deeke, and Washburn reconnoitered a route up McKinley's South Peak to 19,200 feet while Bill Hackett and Robert Lange "chopped a route out of the pass up the steep 800 ft. buttress of the North Peak. When June 6th dawned clear, cool (-27) and windless," Washburn wrote, "we were ready to move in either direction."[98]

As Washburn prepared for the summit, an entertaining yet impractical request came in via radio from Hollister's marketing office:

RKO radioed us an impassioned plea to have us receive, by parachute, a full-scale, colored, plastic model of Rita Hayworth (whom Hollister had apparently selected to star in the film) dressed in a very scanty bathing suit. We were to carry her to the top and photograph her there with Barbara and

"RKO radioed us an impassioned plea to have us receive, by parachute, a full-scale, colored, plastic model of Rita Hayworth"

1947 Operation White Tower Expedition members on the North Peak. The photo was taken on Washburn's 37th Birthday (June 7, 1947)

Negative 57-5414, copyright Bradford Washburn, courtesy of Panopticon Gallery, Waltham, MA

our team. My answer—to our regret as well as theirs, was a firm no! A month later, at the end of the expedition we discovered Rita, leaning sadly in a corner of the 10th Air Force Rescue Squadron's supply room in Anchorage![99]

With backpacks loaded down with an average of forty pounds of movie and survey equipment, the team began their two thousand-foot climb up McKinley's South Peak at 10:30 A.M. on June 6. "We had a beautiful climb through almost cloudless and windless skies," Washburn reported. However, as the team broke 19,000 feet, the weather turned less friendly. "The temperature was about 20 below zero now and an icy SE breeze hit us as we tackled the steep summit drifts. The skies to the S and SW were rapidly clouding in and a high milky overcast sped above us to take the place of the clear blue of the forenoon."[100]

Despite the deteriorating weather, the team continued its march toward the summit. At 4 P.M., Hackett, Lange, and Barbara Washburn, the first woman to do so, reached the summit of Mount McKinley. "We were moving steadily upward, the summit inching ever closer. And then, all of a sudden, we were there," Barbara later wrote, "standing on the roof of North America at 20,320 feet above sea level, with a thrilling panorama of Alaska stretched out before us—almost 100,000 square miles in a single sweep."[101] The remaining team members joined the summit group twenty minutes later; Washburn and Deeke took the opportunity to film the dramatic scene along the summit ridge.[102] Once on the summit, Hackett

"all of a sudden, we were there"

The Washburns on the summit of Mount McKinley. Barbara became the first woman to reach the summit, June 6, 1947

Negative 57-5394, copyright Bradford Washburn, courtesy of Panopticon Gallery, Waltham, MA

and Lange erected the survey equipment, which the two men had carried the entire day. Washburn started his survey work almost immediately after reaching the summit, securing with a heavy Swiss theodolite, "key angles desired by the Coast and Geodetic Survey," with particular attention to "accurate readings on the North Peak and Mt. Silverthrone." This direct extension of his 1945 Silverthrone survey work, providing data critical to ground control for future survey efforts, was the first survey conducted on the slopes and summit of Mount McKinley.[103] As Washburn struggled in frigid winds to work the delicate theodolite, Deeke filmed the entire effort for RKO. With the survey and photographic work done, the team began their descent, making a detour for rock samples "80 ft. down a very steep crusty slope on the south side in order to collect geological specimens of the McKinley granite."[104]

Later that evening, a melancholy Washburn noted: "At 5:30 after a good handshake all around we left the top . . . I guess for the last time in my life—it was for me at least a dramatic moment as we left: one of sadness, happiness and triumph mixed together." At day's close, the team celebrated with a "nightcap of the tiny bottle of whiskey given us by the Baptists the night we left [Anchorage]".[105]

June 7 dawned clear and still, a perfect day to celebrate Washburn's thirty-seventh birthday. "I should have known he would want to do something special," Barbara Washburn declared, "Just as I was settling down for a restful day of reading and letter writing, Brad opened the tent flap and shouted, 'Let's climb the North Peak! We'll never get a perfect day again!'"[106]

After a breakfast of grapefruit, cereal, bacon, and coffee (the clear benefit of military air support) the team set out for the 19,470-foot North Peak at 11:00 A.M. In the meantime, Victoreen, Pearson, Browne, and Deeke remained in camp to put the finishing touches on the cosmic ray hut. After a few hours of climbing the team reached their goal and quickly set up the survey equipment in calm conditions and a temperature of minus ten degrees.[107] "Surveying from the North Peak, although not recommended as a sport at 10 below zero, was still a picnic compared with the job the day before on South Peak. We were lucky to have perfect conditions," Washburn wrote. "The weather was so perfect that we surveyed, photographed and drank in the magnificent view for three full hours atop the North Peak." At 5:20 the team left the summit. Washburn later wrote, "A more perfect day on the heights would be hard to imagine."[108] During a brief lunch break at noon, Washburn placed his angle-book down and rested his pencil atop the open pages. At 19,470 feet, the pages didn't even flutter.

Resting in the confines of the high camp, Washburn later rejoiced in the expedition's success: they had carried out an impressive survey program, Barbara had become the first woman to climb the mountain, Washburn the first person to climb the south peak twice, and the party the first to climb both summits. RKO cameraman Bill Deeke assured Washburn that he had secured enough quality footage to make Hollister pleased with the expedition's results, and at last preparations for the pending cosmic ray research were progressing well.[109]

The cosmic ray hut, composed of eleven separate parts, and weighing about eight hundred pounds, was air-dropped on a windless day by parachute to the high camp at eighteen thousand feet. Victoreen erected the research hut and was ready to begin the work by June 10. However, delays in shipping and poor flying conditions delayed the delivery of the critical Geiger counters until June 16. Victoreen, Gale, and Lange stayed at high camp to carry out the cosmic ray program while the others began their descent. Washburn's team reached McGonagall Pass just as the scientific equipment was delivered to the high camp. Victoreen began his program on June 17 and continued his efforts for ten days.[110] As Victoreen worked high on the mountain, Washburn reached the lowlands with the rest of the team members and began a survey of the mountain's lower regions from four survey points between the Eielson area and Wonder Lake.[111] This data would not only be used to develop Washburn's map of the McKinley massif, but also would provide a "basis for contouring the new map of this area now being prepared in Washington."[112] On July 10, after completing the cosmic ray program, Victoreen, Gale, and Lange joined Washburn at Wonder Lake, bringing Operation White Tower to an end after ninety-two days on the mountain.

The expedition was a total success. The team had completed each facet of its scientific and photographic objects. Victoreen's cosmic ray data was hailed by physicists Thomas Carr, Schein, and Ian Barbour (co-authors of the scientific analysis of the McKinley cosmic ray work), who later wrote that such work had previously been "attainable only in short-duration plane flights." The information was incorporated into Schein's considerable database of cosmic ray data and compared with similar work performed on Mt. Evans (14,250 feet) in Colorado. Although the McKinley data indicated a negligible latitude effect, it "strongly indicates," the researchers found, "that an additional production of mesotrons" of rather low energy "takes place in the atmosphere between these two altitudes" [on Mount Evans at 14,250 feet and at 18,000 feet on Mount McKinley].[113]

Mapping the Mountain Landscape

Washburn's passion for mapping McKinley can be traced to events that occurred over a decade before the White Tower expedition was conceived. In 1936, he had led a National Geographic Society—Harvard's Institute for Geographic Exploration-sponsored aerial photographic reconnaissance of the mountain. On July 12 and then again on July 16, expedition members had boarded a Lockheed Electra monoplane in Fairbanks piloted by S. E. Robbins, circling around and just below McKinley's summit at an altitude of twenty thousand feet. Wearing oxygen masks, mittens, and cold-weather flying suits, Washburn, radioman Robert Gleason, and data recorder Albert Linc Washburn (no relation) flew over the ice-encrusted upper slopes of the mountain.[114] Washburn choreographed the photographic work by directing Robbins through McKinley's maze of rock and ice. "Gleason had prepared for me a telephone mouthpiece connected to a set of headphones on Robbins," Washburn explained. It enabled him to "co-ordinate perfectly in getting the ship into the correct position for each photograph."[115]

The plane's cabin door was removed so Washburn could take oblique photographs of the peak. An old gas-can placed in the open doorway served as his seat. Washburn knotted a hemp rope around his waist and tied the other end to the opposite side of the aircraft, which, as he later noted, allowed him to "lean just far enough out the opening to take pictures—and no further."[116] From this precarious vantage point, Washburn photographed the peak from numerous angles and confirmed the location of Mount Hunter, whose existence was yet to be verified. Washburn used a fifty-pound Fairchild K-6 Aerial Camera, given to Harvard's Institute for Geographic Exploration by his mentor Captain

Albert Stevens. He later described the K-6 as an "archaic . . . hideous, obsolete, bulky, heavy old thing which is absolutely perfect for the use to which I put it."[117] For the twenty-six year old explorer, this McKinley experience reinforced a long-standing love for exploration and discovery; he became "more and more fascinated by the magnificent wilderness of the McKinley massif." As he later admitted, his "interest in its peaks and glaciers was so whetted that I returned in both 1937 and 1938," to make additional photographic investigations.[118] During his aerial reconnaissance of the mountain in the summer of 1937, Washburn reported to the National Geographic Society that he obtained a "good many photographs" of the mountain's southern flanks and several taken "from an altitude almost 2,000 feet above the summit . . . which also were notably lacking from our last summer's series."[119] In 1938, Washburn photographed McKinley once again, as well as other areas throughout the Alaska Range and the mountains of the St. Elias Range.

This wealth of photographic information, the foundation on which Washburn built his exploration of the McKinley region, provided critical data to direct his subsequent ground and aerial surveys of the mountain a decade later. During his 1942 U.S. Army expedition to Mount McKinley, Washburn complained that the entire program was "handicapped from start to finish by lack of a good map." On a later military field test in 1945 to Mt. Silverthrone in the McKinley region, the need for a reliable map was even more apparent, and as a result he initiated a preliminary survey of the mountain and its surrounding landscape. Washburn later explained that the Silverthrone experience "got me gently started on the project."[120] The opportunity to create the first detailed and comprehensive map of McKinley resulted from Washburn's uncanny ability to link large-scale expeditionary science with private, corporate, and government patrons. Operation White Tower was the large-scale expansion of those now-modest efforts first initiated by Washburn in the 1930s and during the war, only realized because of his unique ability to marshal the right patrons, financing, and partners.

And what became of Hollister's plan to transform Ullman's book into a "distinguished picture"? *The White Tower* was released in 1950, starring Glenn Ford as Martine Ordway, Alida Valli as Carla Alton, Claude Rains as Paul DeLambre, Cedric Hardwicke as Dr. Nicholas Radcliffe, and Lloyd

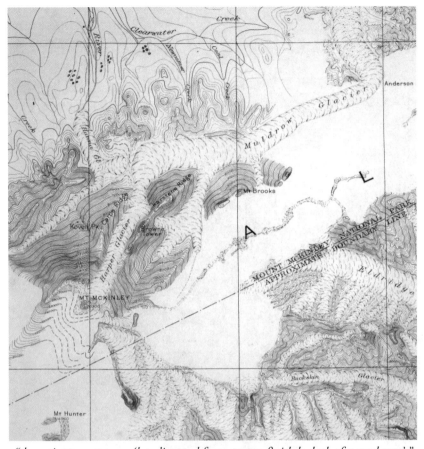

"the entire program was 'handicapped from start to finish by lack of a good map' "

This pre-World War II USGS map of the Mount McKinley region was used by the 1942 U.S. Army Test Expedition. It was the most accurate map available until Washburn published his 1960 edition

Courtesy of Bradford Washburn Collection

Bridges as Mr. Hein. Hollister's movie can occasionally be seen today on cable television.

When Operation White Tower came to an end in the summer of 1947, Washburn had accumulated a plethora of survey data of the McKinley massif and surrounding lowlands. The data were later enhanced and complemented by a series of vertical mapping photographs taken from an altitude of forty thousand feet from a military B-47 aircraft. From 1949 through 1952, the USGS incorporated these photographs and Washburn's 1947 survey data into their expanded McKinley mapping program, from

"If you make a map topographically almost perfect in its detail, all of a sudden the whole map looks like reality"

Washburn's 1960 Mount McKinley map provided detail previously unavailable and has become the authoritative resource for McKinley climbers and researchers.

Courtesy of University of Alaska Press

which they produced the map of *Mount McKinley National Park* and related topographic data sheets. This information constituted the first comprehensive view of the peak.

According to Washburn, the USGS "did not expect to push survey work into the high mountains for some time."[121] As a result, the opportunity to realize his long-standing goal of developing and producing a truly comprehensive map now presented itself. Over the next dozen years, Washburn choreographed five additional survey expeditions to the McKinley region, in which he would obtain all the survey data he would need for the project. In the process, he accumulated an additional string of firsts: the first helicopter landing on the Muldrow Glacier in 1949; the first ascent of McKinley's West Buttress in 1951; becoming the first person to reach the summit three times, and the first to set the now universally accepted elevation of the mountain at 20,320 feet.[122]

Washburn later described the process of mapping the mountain in this fashion: "I wish I could say that this map is the result of an orderly, long-range plan, slowly and carefully brought to fruition. Unfortunately it is not."[123] Although his survey lacked a year-by-year action plan, he took advantage of several opportunities to continue his work. In addition to establishing survey stations throughout the McKinley area, Washburn choreographed a number of B-29 and B-47 high-altitude photographic flights in 1951 and 1955, and used helicopters to transport numerous survey teams into the heart of the McKinley massif.[124] As part of this unique program, Washburn led a 1951 expedition to climb McKinley's West Buttress, a route he had discovered and proposed to mountaineers several years earlier.[125] The expedition had a number of scientific objectives that included an extension of his survey work and the acquisition of geological samples for the University of Denver.[126] Washburn believed his new route would provide a safer and more practical path up the mountain. Marcel Schein, who crafted the 1947 cosmic ray research program, had earlier proposed the creation of a more permanent cosmic ray observatory on McKinley. However, according to Washburn, Schein eventually changed his mind because of advances in particle accelerators that afforded a controlled and more economic way of investigating cosmic rays.[127]

Although Washburn's accomplishments were generally celebrated, they did draw some outspoken criticism from those who perceived his work to be self-serving. In fact, one of the nation's leading environmentalists considered continued Cold War research on McKinley inappropriate. Naturalist, outdoorsman, scientist, and ardent conservationist Adolph Murie, writing to University of Alaska archeologist Otto Geist, showed his disdain for Washburn's work: "We all feel that Washburn, with his commercialization of the Mountain, has already desecrated it enough, enough for one little man." In the fall of 1949, following Washburn's pioneering use of helicopters on McKinley, which demonstrated their feasibility in supporting large-scale research, Murie's brother, Olaus, spoke out against Washburn's effort to secure additional funding from the Office of Naval Research. The pair was convinced that Washburn was "trying to make it appear that the Navy wants these projects he is promoting; actually he is pulling all possible strings to get the projects approved so that he can get lecture material." Adolph admitted to Geist that he did not know the importance of establishing a high altitude Cosmic Ray research presence on McKinley, but confessed, "even if the mountain is convenient in such studies, I still think that it should not be so used."[128]

Despite Schein's withdrawal from the project and the Muries' objections, Washburn pressed forward in the belief that a safe route to McKinley's upper slopes was feasible. Preparations for the 1951 expedition progressed quickly, and Washburn was consumed with the extensive planning required for yet another large-scale expedition. While in Fairbanks, which served as expedition headquarters, Washburn was the celebrated commencement speaker at the University of Alaska's graduation ceremony, and received the first of his many honorary doctorates. His long-time friend, climbing companion, and President of the University Dr. Terris Moore presided over the ceremony.

The newly honored Dr. Washburn left Fairbanks for McKinley Park soon after the ceremony, to begin his survey work on May 27. In addition to serving as the President of the University of Alaska, Terris Moore was an extremely competent pilot. The two men developed a plan to use Moore's ski-wheel -equipped Super Cub aircraft to transfer expedition members and equipment to the mountain. A landing along Washburn's proposed West Buttress route had not yet been tried, and the possibility intrigued both men.

On June 2, Moore piloted his plane to McKinley Park where he picked up Washburn for a test flight. The men flew over the Ruth Glacier, the Ruth Amphitheater, and pierced the low-hanging fog to see the summit of Mount McKinley ten thousand feet above the aircraft.[129] "The fantastic ice and rock of the Rooster Comb, Mount Huntington, and McKinley were savage and impressive beyond description," Washburn wrote. His account of the first attempt on June 2 to find a safe and practical glacial airstrip captures the drama of this path-breaking effort.

> Terry's little plane is so slow that we could easily circle at 60 mph within the confines of this amazing valley. We climbed slowly to 12,000 feet, then crossed the 11,000-foot pass between Mount Hunter and McKinley's South Buttress, and emerged at last over the broad valley of the Kahiltna Glacier. But, alas, the spot where we had hoped to land was deeply shrouded in fog. So we proceeded over Kahiltna Pass to try a landing in the upper basin of Peters Glacier.
>
> The weather was all clear over the Peters, and we landed on perfect, dry snow with scarcely a bump: altitude 7,750 feet. No human being had ever landed where we now stood. There was a slight southwest breeze. We were thrilled at the tremendous face of Wickersham Wall that now towered nearly 12,000 feet above us to the top of McKinley's North Peak.
>
> I hope that we can use this little ship to get in to the Kahiltna Glacier later this month. In certain ways it is better than a helicopter, as it is OK in soft snow and can land on quite a grade safely. It is incredible what a feeling of safety we get in Terry's little plane—a Super Cub 150 with ski-wheels, able to land safely on either its wheels or skis. The plane has a propeller that's slightly longer than usual for better performance at high altitude. When we took off from the Peters Glacier, despite an uphill run, we were in the air in slightly over a hundred yards.[130]

Ten days later Washburn returned to the mountain using pioneer aviator Don Sheldon's Super Cub aircraft. Although a landing was not tried, Washburn did identify the perfect landing strip for Moore's ski-equipped plane. "We flew clear up the glacier to the upper end of the great 6,200-

foot plateau about abreast with Mount Hunter," Washburn recalled, "There are at least five miles of absolutely smooth, level snow with no crevasses or even bumps." Washburn found the key to his West Buttress route: a landing strip one-third the way up the mountain and capable of supporting large teams of climbers and their associated supplies."[131]

On June 18, Bradford Washburn and expedition member Henry Buchtel rendezvoused with Terris Moore at Chelatna Lake. The weather was cloudy with rainsqualls in the area, but the men were so eager to set out that little could dash Washburn's determination. "Terry and I decided that we'd take a try for a Kahiltna Glacier landing," Washburn wrote, "So we changed into our winter underwear right on the spot, there being no girls within forty miles in any direction."[132] The men packed the plane with essential equipment to establish a base camp, and at five P.M. Moore and Washburn took of for the Kahiltna Glacier.

As they approached the peak, the plane was engulfed in thick clouds and Moore struggled to find his way through to a Kahiltna landing. The flat light conditions made landing on the glacier problematic, but an hour after takeoff a thread of sunlight pierced the clouds and gave Moore the

"We pounced on the opportunity, landing immediately and perfectly, not even a bounce"

Terris Moore, who made the first-ever landing on the Kahiltna Glacier, poses with members of the 1951 West Buttress Expedition at the 10,000 foot Advanced Based Camp. Left to right: Terris Moore, Henry Buchtel, Washburn, Bill Hackett, and Jim Gale

Negative 57-5732, copyright Bradford Washburn, courtesy of Panopticon Gallery, Waltham, MA

landing conditions he needed. "We pounced on the opportunity, landing immediately and perfectly, not even a bounce," Washburn declared.[133] They unloaded the equipment and Moore quickly left to retrieve Buchtel. As the empty plane sped off and the surrounding mountains echoed with the sound of Moore's engine, Washburn went to work setting up the team's base camp. Buchtel and Moore arrived on a second flight at 8:50 with the clouds slowly encircling the tiny camp. As Washburn explained, "Foraker was gone for good and the Kahiltna Peaks were rapidly vanishing as Terry, Henry, and I emptied the plane of its load and turned it around. Terry speeded on his way again at 9:04 p.m. Now there were two of us on the vast Kahiltna Glacier."[134] Little could Washburn have known that his tiny camp site would someday evolve into a virtual city of hundreds of climbers and tourists who each summer visit Kahiltna base camp to either climb the mountain or just experience the beauty of the landscape.

Over the next few days Washburn and Buchtel carried loads of equipment to an elevation just short of Kahiltna Pass (10,300 feet), where Washburn planned to establish the expedition's Advance Base Camp at 10,000 feet. On June 20 Moore unexpectedly arrived with team members Jim Gale and Bill Hackett, making two trips through awful weather. The following day the men packed heavy loads up the glacier in the sweltering ninety-degree sun, relying on their snowshoes to keep them afloat atop the slush of the Kahiltna's summer snow cover. The day was long and the four men finally climbed into their single tent at 12:30 A.M.

The men awoke late the next morning to the sound of a C-47 airplane dropping supplies, a ton in all. Before long the clouds began to roll in and the men worked quickly to erect a recently delivered wall tent. The eight-by-ten tent with a ceiling reaching eight feet high was quite a luxury for a team in such a remote and inhospitable environment. The Birds Eye Company supplied the expedition with an abundance of frozen foods; the men crafted a "freezer" in the glacial ice to keep the goods from spoiling.[135]

With the camp now settled and well supplied, Washburn turned his full attention to the survey work. On the afternoon of June 25 the team set out for Pass Peak (later named Mount Capps) on which Washburn made a number of sightings. Photographs were also taken of the terrain to identify unnamed landmarks for future reference. Dr. Land, a pioneer in photographic techniques and creator of the Land Camera, supplied Washburn with the groundbreaking instant-developing film that has enjoyed widespread popularity throughout the world. Washburn kept the team on an aggressive work schedule, starting the day of the 26th at 5:30 in the morning. The team's survey point for the day was Peak Z (later named Kahiltna Dome), that afforded Washburn a perfect vantage point, at 12,535 feet, from which to survey. "This is the key survey station for the entire area southwest of McKinley." Washburn's diary entry best describes the day's events:

> We reached the top of Peak Z at 10:20 after a long, hard haul with heavy loads of survey gear, an eight-foot marker pole, food, and cameras. While Bill [Hackett] and I surveyed, Henry [Buchtel] and Jim [Gale] made an igloo to use as shelter in case of storm, or rest and eat in while chilly survey work was being done. To describe the view is impossible, it is that stupendous. Ten jet fighters flew over us during the day, as well as a C-47 cargo plane. Two of the jets played around us, zooming and diving at 600 mph—once screaming past us only fifty feet above our igloo, with McKinley in the backdrop.[136]

Equipment was continuously ferried up the mountain, and by June 30 a well-stocked cache was in place at 13,000 feet. Washburn moved the team one thousand feet further, to reconnoiter the route to the base of the West Buttress at 14,000 feet. From this vantage point the team would climb a steep 40-60 degree ice-encrusted slope to a campsite at 16,000 feet. Washburn was pleased with the progress, and equally thrilled that the rest of his team (John Ambler, Thomas Melvin "Mel" Griffiths, Jerry Moore, and renowned American mountaineer Barry Bishop) had now joined the team at their Advance Base Camp. This latter group had made their way from Wonder Lake by pack train and then picked their way through the crevasse-strewn Peters Glacier to join Washburn. By the close of the evening, Washburn proclaimed "terrific progress" and confessed he could see "no major problems ahead of us—exactly like it appeared in my aerial photographs."[137]

Aerial support of Washburn's party continued throughout the expedition. For the most part, these aerial freight deliveries were successful. However, some tested Washburn's patience. The delivery of July 2 was a good example. A B-18 bomber was dispatched to deliver food, equipment, a radio, and Washburn's coveted film supply. "In the first drop," Washburn explained, "the parachute became detached from the load and Jerry Moore's new radio was smashed completely and a dozen film-packs sent to me were wrecked." Washburn was not impressed with the pilot's skills either, declaring him "stupid beyond words," because he was "apparently using one of the tents as a marker for his drops and almost destroying it with one of his boxes.[138]

Putting the aerial bombardment behind him, Washburn departed for Peak Z (Kahiltna Dome) and completed his survey work from this point by ten o'clock that evening. After a brief snack of beans and tea in the expedition's igloo, Hackett, Gale, and Washburn erected a survey marker on top of the igloo, hoping they could later use the site as a key point during the post-climb survey program. At one thirty in the morning on July 4 the men descended to 11,000 feet and climbed Pass Peak where they "sleepily surveyed another hour to correct a few errors in last week's work." At four o'clock in the morning they returned to camp, "tired but happy," in Washburn's words, "the survey work on the Kahiltna all completed. We couldn't have had a more perfect night for the job. We can now stow our trusty theodolite away and focus all of our efforts on the first ascent of the West Buttress."[139]

Later that morning, as the team awoke to sunny skies, Washburn decided to move camp up to 13,000 feet, at a spot he named Windy Corner. After five hours of heavy hauling, the team (Jim Gale, John Ambler, Henry Buchtel, Bill Hackett, and Washburn) arrived at the new camp, to be welcomed by a fast-brewing storm. As the wind began to build and the snow began to fall, the men worked quickly to erect their tent and fashion yet another igloo, complete with a tunnel joining the two structures. "There's nothing like an igloo for comfort in bad weather," Washburn declared, and as the storm intensified the following day, with winds gusting to 60 mph, he noted, "We are certainly wise to have named this spot Windy Corner."[140]

When the weather cleared on July 6, Washburn, Gale, and Hackett set out to tackle the steep wall that allows access to the West Buttress and McKinley's upper slopes. The loose, deep snow slowed the team's progress, forcing the men to use their shovels to dig steps into the slope. At 15,500 feet the exhausted men sought refuge inside a large crevasse where they rested sipping tea, while the rest of the expedition ferried equipment and supplies to the same elevation. The rest seemed to reenergize Washburn and Gale, and they decided to continue climbing.

Taking up to thirty chops to carve each solid-ice step, the work was hard and exhausting at such an altitude. But steady progress prevailed, and at 7:15 P.M. Washburn and Gale crested the ridge at slightly over 16,000 feet. To make the route safer, the men installed a fixed line anchored into the ice by wooden pickets. As Washburn explained, "From now on, that miserable slope would be no less steep, but ready for safe climbing."[141] Meanwhile Hackett built an igloo in the bergschrund (the spot where a portion of a moving glacier separates from the ice frozen to the rock) and Washburn and Gale retreated to the sanctuary of the little "icehouse."

Hackett, Gale, and Washburn set out the next day and slowly scaled the fixed rope, taking a break at 16,000 feet for a hot lunch and to survey the landscape. "My but this is a magnificently spectacular route," Washburn commented. "The views of the Kahiltna Glacier, of Mount Foraker and Mount Hunter, are stunning in every conceivable combination of light and shadow."[142] Negotiating the route between 16,000 and the high camp at over 17,000 feet was relatively straightforward for the team. Here the men cached their packs and headed back to the camp below, stopping only to collect geologic samples for future investigation.

On July 9 they moved the entire camp to 17,200 feet, from which they would make their summit attempt. After building an igloo and preparing the campsite, they settled in for a warm and well-deserved dinner of Lipton soup, frozen hamburger, peas (frozen), minute potatoes, bread, butter, and strawberries (frozen). The well-rounded meal was the courtesy of the many aerial supply drops by Army aircraft throughout the expedition. A meal such as this would be the envy of any modern-day McKinley climber who must endure weeks of freeze-dried food. A relatively warm home, good food, and an easy evening prepared the men well for the final push to the summit the following day.[143] On July 10, 1951, Washburn, Gale, and Hackett began their climb into the history books. Washburn's diary entry late that evening captures each step of the now-standard climbing route on North America's highest mountain:

It was wonderfully clear and calm and we decided to take a crack at both Denali Pass and the summit of McKinley if the weather held. Jim [Gale], Bill [Hackett], and I left camp at 10:20 a.m. equipped for anything. It was 20 degrees and no wind as we tackled the steep western slope of Denali Pass. This was the last unknown section of our new route up McKinley. In 1947 we had looked down this slope from Denali Pass, and we've always been sure it would be a steep but speedy climb.

The sastrugi—the wavelike ridges of rock-hard, wind-blown snow often encountered on slopes like this—were enormous. The westerly winds must have howled across that bleak slope. The going was never really steep (the maximum was about a 40-degree angle) and the hard, icy snow alternated with breakable wind-crust over ice—essentially just what we expected. We took lots of pictures, moved slowly, and enjoyed ourselves a lot. And we reached Denali pass at 12:15—in just two hours!

Reaching Denali Pass was the climax of this expedition: exactly what we had wanted to do. This route was now established as the shortest, safest, and easiest way to the top of Mount McKinley. We all shook hands joyously. Anything more that we did was pure frosting on the cake, as we now stood on ground well known to all three of us. Jim and Bill and I were all on the successful 1947 ascent of Mount McKinley, members of the summit party that also included my wife, Barbara—first woman to the top!

We stopped at the pass to examine the big cache of food and equipment that we'd left there four years ago. We found a ghastly mess. The yellow parachute that we'd left to cover our cache was in tatters and flapping in the wind, and a shovel was lying on the snow, a hundred yards east of the pass. There was horrible confusion at the cache. A subsequent climbing partly, wanting supplies, had apparently cut the parachute off the cache, taken what they needed, and then just left it open to the elements.

Wind-driven snow fill every nook and cranny of that carefully protected cache. Two sleeping bags were filled with snow, and one of our stoves was out in the open. The whole cache was a solid, immovable mass of material cemented together with ice and snow. What criminal negligence. We were lucky that we weren't in serious need of the gear.

We dug deep enough into the cache to see that some sugar and oatmeal were dry inside a five-gallon can. Then we walked to the thermometer cache and opened it to check the minimum-temperature thermometer, which would indicate the coldest reading for Denali Pass in the past four years. It read minus 59 degrees Fahrenheit – a frigid spot.

At one o'clock the weather was steadily getting better, we decided that we would make a try for the top. We had plenty of willow wands in hand, and at the very least we would get the trail well-marked for a good distance. There were big plumes of ice fog over both the North and South peaks, but I figured that as the afternoon went on and it began to get colder, those clouds would slowly disappear. It helps to be an intimate friend of this dear old mountain.

As we climbed slowly up the ridge, to our amazement we ran into lots of our 1947 willow wands. They had all been broken off, though, flush with the icy surface of the snow. My guess is that they had become loaded with frost and that the added wind resistance had snapped them. We found these little relics at intervals all the way.

At 19,000 feet we went into the fog and the breeze got brisker. I climbed a little to the left of our old route, heading for the hollow between the 19,000-foot shoulder and the formation known as Archdeacon's Tower. We made this first thousand feet in exactly an hour. Jim and Bill were having a bit of hard going with the altitude, so I took all the trail markers and my cameras and put them together in my pack. This was the only time I've ever seen Jim Gale really tired. Curiously enough, I've never felt better, and the forty-pound load including the cameras (a tiny C-3 Leica, a Bell & Howell 141-B 16mm movie camera, and a 4x5 Speed Graphic) seemed not to bother me a bit. I was having one of those really good days.

Our approach to the summit was made blind, using a detailed knowledge of the mountain and using willow wands that we stuck in the snow to literally survey us in a straight line across the huge, level snowfield between the Archdeacon's Tower and the final summit slope. I set the basic course, marking the way with the wands, then Jim and Bill would yell when I swung either way of a straight line.

We stopped for a forty-five minute lunch in the dense fog and warm sun before going up that final hillside. We then wallowed through knee-deep powder snow for fifteen minutes because we had left our snowshoes behind. The skies were clear everywhere but on the very top of McKinley. This made me sure if we continued moving slowly ahead that it would all clear as soon as the air began to cool off around 4:30 or 5:00 P.M.

That was a good theory. At 4:30 we were toiling up the summit cone among huge sastrugi when it suddenly started to clear. As we reached the crest of the shoulder, it cleared completely and we could see the big bamboo pole that we'd left on the summit four years ago.

From here it was only a short climb to the top, so I unroped and Jim and Bill went ahead while I photographed them against a cloudless blue sky. As I worked my way up after them, the view to the south was staggering. A 10,000-foot wall dropped off to the Kahiltna Glacier where we had landed three weeks ago. The green of the Tokositna Valley was wonderful to see, creeping far up among the ice peaks. Mount Hunter, which had long dominated our view, now looked utterly insignificant.

I caught up with the others atop the last big hump on the ridge, a hundred yards short of the top. I was totally overcome with emotion when at 5:30 we reached the summit and the whole amazing panorama burst upon us.

Our stay on top was geared to the weather and photography. When we arrived, there was only a light breeze. The temperature was at about zero and there were only a few scattered clouds to the northwest. We set to work to make a good series of movies and stills of both the top and the view. It was very cold work for the hands.

Forty-five minutes went by all too fast, and then all three of us were ready to leave. The wind was coming up again, and there was no longer any warmth from the lowering sun. We were all beginning to shiver.

We hated to leave. The view was so marvelous in every direction: our old friend Mount Hayes, far to the east; the Coast Range behind Anchorage, at least 150 miles to the south; and scores of mountains, lakes, and rivers stretching to the western horizon. I remembered for a moment the wonderful remark by Robert Tatum, who stood on this spot with the first-ascent party on June 7, 1913: "It's like looking out the windows of Heaven."

At 6:15 we tied our old bit of orange bunting back to the top of the bamboo pole and bade farewell to the summit. This was surely my last visit to this place. Then we headed off down the ridge, Jim Gale and I both admitted later that tears had trickled down our cheeks as we left.[144]

*"Jim Gale and I both admitted later that
tears had trickled down our cheeks
as we left"*

Bradford Washburn stands atop Mount
McKinley in 1951, the first person to
reach the summit
of Mount McKinley three times

Negative 57-5932, copyright Bradford
Washburn, courtesy of Panopticon Gallery,
Waltham, MA

Washburn's route, aided by ski-equipped airplanes, opened up the mountain to "casual" explorers and established McKinley as a feasible climbing destination for professional and amateur mountaineers.

The first ascent of the West Buttress completed, the men crawled into their small igloo at 9:00 P.M., ten hours after setting out. The small party spent the next two days descending to Kahiltna Pass at 10,000 feet, where Washburn radioed Terris Moore in Fairbanks and asked that the team be picked up. On July 13 at 9:15 P.M. Moore descended upon the camp to retrieve Washburn along with ninety pounds of equipment. The two men landed at the small community of Kantishna, in the shadow of McKinley, where they grabbed a short nap in a tiny cabin near the landing strip.

Moore flew back to the mountain early the next morning, returned at almost 4:00 A.M. with Bill Hackett, then made a further flight to the Kahiltna to get Jim Gale, the last of the three-man party. During the day, without Washburn's knowledge, Barry Bishop, Henry Buchtel, and John Ambler reached the summit, following Washburn's well-marked trail. Mel (Thomas Melvin) Griffiths and Jerry More reached the summit on July 15. On the same day, Washburn and Hackett traveled to Wonder Lake, where they completed a key component of the overall survey program. "The telescope of my beloved Swiss T-3 theodolite instantly picked up our target on Peak Z after locating our huge igloo target," Washburn wrote. "This successfully ties our new survey on the western side of McKinley to the major network that we want to establish here on the northern side."[145] During the next seven days Moore battled bad weather and deteriorating landing conditions on the Kahiltna to pick up the remaining expedition members. "All's well that ends well," Washburn declared on July 23. "We are all safely off the mountain, and Mount McKinley's West Buttress has been climbed with total success."[146] Washburn's West Buttress route is now the standard route by which the majority of climbers attempt the mountain each year. Ski-plane transport from Talkeetna, just south of the mountain, to the Kahiltna Glacier has spurred an industry of pioneer bush pilots who fly over a thousand climbers and tourists to the Kahiltna from this quaint Alaskan community.

"Washburn's West Buttress route is now the standard"

Washburn's West Buttress route superimposed
over one of his most popular McKinley photographs.

"Mount McKinley's West Buttress has been climbed with total success"
The 1951 West Buttress route superimposed over Washburn's now-classic 1960 map.
Courtesy of Bradford Washburn Collection.
Artwork courtesy of Greg Glade, Top of the World Books

Following the expedition, the survey data was added to that of
Washburn's previous expeditions, as well as the information obtained from
the USGS and the U.S. Coast and Geodetic Survey. By 1958 Washburn
had accumulated enough data to begin preliminary work on the McKinley
map. He returned to the mountain in the summer of 1959 to carry out
final observations and conduct a vegetation study of the region, to ensure
both the accuracy and aesthetic value of the final product. Compilation
of the McKinley survey data began in Switzerland in the summer of 1958.
The Swiss, Washburn knew, were masterful cartographers; he believed his
vision of the map could be realized only through such craftsmanship. The
Swiss Institute for Alpine Research supplied financial and logistical support

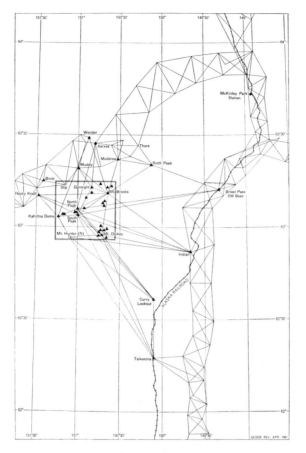

"the survey data was added to ... the information obtained from the USGS and the U.S. Coast and Geodetic Survey"

Triangulation diagram showing the integration of Washburn's survey data with that of the U.S. Coast and Geodetic Survey

Courtesy of Bradford Washburn Collection

for the project, and cartographic artwork and production was sponsored by the Swiss Federal Institute of Topography.[147] Published in 1960, the map is a brilliant mixture of artistic topographic relief and cartographic accuracy. Washburn's ability to organize and lead such an undertaking was tested by the sheer magnitude of the project. Over the course of fifteen years, from 1945 to 1960, support for Washburn's project was secured from a number of seemingly disparate individuals, organizations, and institutions including the U.S. military, Boston's Museum of Science, the US Coast and Geodetic Survey, the USGS, the National Geographic Society, Harvard's Institute for Geographical Exploration, the United States Office of Naval Research, the Swiss Institute for Alpine Research, and the American Academy of Arts and Sciences, the latter providing significant financial resources for the map's actual publication. Individual funding for the project came from many of Washburn's public lectures as well as the generous financial support of his long-time mentors, Dr. Hamilton Rice and Captain Albert Stevens.[148]

The map's scale is an impressive 1:10,000, with five-meter contour-lines that detail the massif as no other before or since.[149] Brian M. Ambroziak and Jeffrey R. Ambroziak, authors of *Infinite Perspectives: Two Thousand Years of Three-Dimensional Mapmaking*, note that Washburn's McKinley map "combines shaded relief with a soft range of blues that give the effect of an atmospheric haze over its entirety." They further note that "by using the same palette for the contours, they do not overpower the map nor do they become the primary graphic element, as is often the case" with other maps. Finally, the authors declare, "This map of Mount McKinley, with its high degree of artistic and scientific achievement, represents a renaissance in mapmaking."[150]

Washburn's map advanced understanding of the peak in two dramatic and practical ways. The artistic detail allows both mountaineer and scientist to evaluate and execute climbing and future research efforts on the mountain. At the same time, it allows armchair explorers to experience the mountain world without setting foot in Alaska. The map is appealing not just to the McKinley mountaineer but also to those who enjoy the lure and sheer magnitude of the mountain landscape

Mr. McKinley

For nearly seven decades, from 1936 to the present, Washburn, now in his nineties, has studied, photographed, climbed, and surveyed Mount McKinley, forming a bridge between generations of early McKinley pioneers and modern-day climbers and scientists. Washburn's survey expeditions and the resulting map that constitutes his long-term work in the McKinley region was a natural extension of the remarkably accurate (for the time) work of turn-of-the-century explorer-cartographers such as William Dickey, Robert Muldrow, and George Eldridge. In 1955, the accepted altitude of McKinley's taller southern peak, calculated by the USGS and U.S. Coast and Geodetic Survey with the help of Washburn's field work, was established at 20,320 feet.[151] This figure, obtained with the most modern equipment of the time, aerial photography, and modern logistical support, is strikingly close to the 1896 estimate made by William

Dickey of 20,000 feet, Robert Muldrow's 1898 observation of 20,464 feet, and D.L. Reaburn's 1902 determination of 20,155 feet. Although Washburn's 1960 McKinley map provides detail and clarity not previously available, one should recognize the significant contributions of those early pioneer explorers.

Washburn's fascination with measuring Mount McKinley did not end with the public release of the map in August 1960. In September of that year, Washburn incorporated a new Cold War technology into his continued study of the mountain. The U-2 photo-reconnaissance aircraft was developed to obtain accurate, and thus strategic, high-altitude photographs of land-based images (primarily military infrastructure of the former Soviet Union) over broad geographic areas. On September 6 1960, just four months after a U-2 aircraft piloted by Gary Powers was shot down over the Soviet Union, the Air Force took U-2 photographs of Mount McKinley from an altitude of 68,000 feet.[152] Washburn eagerly assimilated the information into his continued study of the peak.

Washburn's encyclopedic knowledge of McKinley's unique landscape has, for decades, made him the ultimate McKinley resource for mountaineers, scientists, explorers, and photographers the world over. Starting in the late 1940s, he has tempted would-be McKinley mountaineers by proposing new and more challenging climbing routes, and an eager audience throughout the world responded to these challenges. He methodically published detailed route-lines on a myriad of vivid black-and-white oblique photographs of McKinley, providing blueprints for increasingly difficult and more interesting ascents of the peak.

In 1957, he proposed a summit route up McKinley's steep and exposed South Face.[153] In 1961, guided by Washburn's photos and extended correspondence, Riccardo Cassin, one of Italy's most distinguished mountaineers, led a successful ascent of this route, now known to mountaineers as "The Cassin Ridge."[154] Two years later, Washburn recruited a group of young yet able Harvard College mountaineers to attempt a direct route up McKinley's northern avalanche-strewn slopes. As David Roberts, a member of that group, later wrote, Washburn "urged on us a 'line' he had scouted from the air that went straight up the east-central section of McKinley's 14,000-foot Wickersham Wall."[155] Later that summer, the Harvard team took the route Washburn had encouraged them to consider, climbing their way into McKinley history with the first ascent of the avalanche-strewn wall named for the Fairbanks judge who six decades before had been the first to challenge North America's tallest peak.

Washburn also encouraged young scientists to build upon the work of McKinley's early pioneers as well as his own research base. For instance, in 1979 Washburn secured the resources for a series of seismic profiles of the Muldrow Glacier, conducted by the University of British Columbia. The results revealed that the thickness of the Muldrow Glacier's ice fluctuated between 1558 feet to 1617 feet, far deeper than Washburn had expected. He surmised that if the glacier were this thick, other glaciers on the mountain would be even thicker.[156] While flying over McKinley's Great Gorge in the summer of 1937 for the National Geographic Society, Washburn was overtaken with the immense flow of the Ruth Glacier through its vertical rock walls. Almost ten years after the Muldrow seismic findings, Washburn convinced University of Alaska glaciologist Keith Echelmeyer to conduct an extensive seismic profile of the Gorge. Echelmeyer's findings supported Washburn suspicions. The Gorge was one of the deepest in the world, the glacier 3,770 feet thick. For perspective, if totally void of ice, this abyss would measure nearly 9,000 feet from rim to floor. The Grand Canyon is 5,300 feet deep.

Washburn's relationship with Mount McKinley has spanned more than six decades, linking his name forever with the peak. His pioneering aerial photographs of the mountain in 1935, subsequent climbs in 1942, 1947, and 1951, his embrace of Cold War funding and scientific partnerships, and use of the most advanced technologies and transportation to carry out remote expeditionary field science, have afforded him a unique perspective and intimate knowledge of North America's highest mountain. Washburn's rich photographic archives of black-and-white pictures of McKinley are continually in demand by thousands of mountaineers, scientists, and photographers worldwide. Washburn is truly the grand old man of the mountain: Mr. McKinley.

5

From Sledge to Shuttle

"For many of us the only tie between us and science is this interest in geography." Bradford Washburn, speaking before the American Geographical Society

The Washburn Legacy

Washburn's career as expeditionary scientist, mapmaker, and photographer did not end with the 1960 publication of the McKinley map. Later he would direct several cartographic projects, from the rugged southwestern United States to the massive Himalayan Plateau of Nepal and China. In 1971, at the age of seventy-one, he began a seven-year surveying project of the Grand Canyon for his long-time patron, the National Geographic Society. Spanning five field-seasons between 1971 and 1975, the project required Washburn and his wife Barbara to be transported by helicopter to over three hundred remote survey sites. Washburn once again took advantage of the latest technology, using lasers to obtain the most accurate readings possible. The finished map of the Grand Canyon was published in the July 1978 issue of the *National Geographic Magazine.*[1]

Having perfected the use of laser technology during the Grand Canyon survey, Washburn returned to Mount McKinley in 1977 to make the first laser readings of the mountain, in an effort to fix its true geographic position. Washburn's work, aided by a climbing team from the National Outdoor Leadership School (who placed a series of laser prisms on the mountain's taller South Peak) found the mountain to be 18.37 feet southwest of its previously calculated position.[2] Washburn's interest in using technology to investigate McKinley's unique environment did not stop there; he would also employee the latest GPS technology to further his research agenda in the decades that followed.[3]

In 1980 Washburn retired as director of Boston's Museum of Science, after a long and rich administrative career. Under his forty-plus years of

"In 1971, at the age of seventy-one, he initiated a seven-year surveying project of the Grand Canyon"

The Washburns surveying from Dana Butte in the Grand Canyon

Courtesy of Charles O'Rear

leadership, the museum had evolved significantly from its modest beginnings. Established in 1830 by physician Dr. Walter Channing and twelve other prominent Bostonians, the Boston Society for Natural History began with an interest in "collecting and discussing specimens from the field of natural history."[4] The Society's initiatives included a public lecture series, the development of a modest library and collections, and a scientific survey of the Commonwealth of Massachusetts. In 1861 the Society secured land, through an act of the state legislature, to build a permanent museum. The following year work began, and the New England Museum of Natural History was dedicated two years later in 1864. Although the museum grew modestly through the rest of the century, by the time Washburn accepted the directorship, the museum was well worn and in need of immediate attention.[5]

When in February 1939 Washburn assumed the directorship, the museum was the most visible component of the organization. Washburn inherited a budget of approximately thirty-two thousand dollars. At his retirement in 1980 the budget exceeded three and a half million dollars. Total salaries in 1940 were just less than twenty five thousand dollars; in 1980 that number had grown to over $1.3 million dollars. The museum had physically grown from a modest three-story brownstone on Berkeley Street, erected near the first building of the Massachusetts Institute of Technology, to a physical plant exceeding five million cubic feet along Boston's Charles River. In 1980, approximately one million people visited the museum, a far cry from the roughly thirty-five thousand who toured the original museum in 1940. During his forty-one year career, Washburn raised nearly forty-five million dollars for the museum's expansion, programs, displays, outreach efforts, and administration.[6]

Washburn's expeditions certainly helped to raise the profile of the museum, but his embrace of education and outreach were the keys to public awareness and eventual fund-raising. In 1947 the museum launched a path-breaking nature tour on which live animals, collections, film, and educational kits were loaded into a station wagon and shared with dozens of children's camps throughout New England. In October of the following year the museum broadcast "Living Wonders," the first live educational television show to use animals. The museum also unveiled its traveling planetarium, the first of its kind. The planetarium toured New England, to the enjoyment of school children everywhere, with programs conducted by such individuals as Charles A. Federer, Jr, of the Harvard Observatory and formerly with the Hayden Planetarium. [7]

Washburn's museum also capitalized on the public's interest in atomic energy, technology, and space travel. The museum sponsored "Eclipse Parties," where the public could view, though the institution's telescopes, the two lunar eclipses occurring in 1949. When querying staff about the phenomenon the guest of course became more aware of the museum's value to the community. And when it came time to lay the cornerstone for the first phase of the new Museum of Science building in December of 1949, Washburn made sure that a congratulatory message from the Governor of Connecticut arrived via a Sikorsky helicopter, to the delight of onlookers. Edwin A. Land photographed the ceremony using his path-breaking, instant-developing Polaroid camera. The images were given to Washburn and interned in the building's structure. [8]

Throughout the 1950s the museum highlighted prominent discoveries in science with displays and ceremonies that generated interest in the institution's activities. A model of the atom U-235 was developed in association with MIT and Harvard scientists, and hung prominently in the museum's new East Wing. Washburn was joined in 1951 by Board president Carlton Fuller and MIT President Karl Compton in a celebratory lighting of the model. Later in the decade, in 1958, the museum unveiled the new Charles Hayden Planetarium, an immediate favorite with the public.[9]

In the 1960s the museum welcomed many new exhibits and dignitaries, including astronaut Alan Shepard. Taking advantage of the heightened interest in space travel, the museum unveiled a simulated Apollo 8 command module for children to experience. Interactive displays, lunar rovers, and giant dinosaurs all added to the interest in and public support of the museum well into the 1970s. By 1980, Washburn's dream of a grand science museum had been realized.[10]

Never one to allow time to pass idly, in 1981 Washburn found himself engaged in high-level negotiations with the Chinese and Nepalese governments to re-survey Mount Everest, the mountain that had first

"The mountain that had first captured his attention as a teenager"
Scale model of Mount Everest based on Washburn's survey
that included the Space Shuttle Columbia
Courtesy of Boston's Museum of Science

captured his attention as a teenager, when he attended a lecture by Everest veteran Captain John Noel. This effort, involving scientists, cartographers and mathematicians from ten nations, was funded, in part, by his long-time patron the National Geographic Society.

In addition to ground-based surveys of Everest, Washburn added the technology and scientific capacity of the U.S. Space Shuttle *Columbia* to his ever-growing arsenal of scientific instrumentation—a resource authors Ron Graham and Roger Read have described as the ultimate survey platform.[11] In December 1983, *Columbia* astronauts took a series of overlapping infrared photographs of Mount Everest from an altitude of 156 miles above the earth, covering an area of more than thirteen thousand square miles. To these photographs Washburn added a series of high-altitude images taken from a Learjet at an altitude of forty-one thousand feet. Washburn's integration of technology, international scientific teams, aerial photography, willing patrons, survey expertise, and unending energy, resulted in the production of the most accurate map of Mount Everest available to date.[12]

Through the 1990s, he continued to refine his Everest survey data, employing several scientific and mountaineering teams to measure the mountain's ever-increasing altitude by GPS, laser, and theodolite.[13] Now in his nineties, Washburn no longer scales the great peaks of the world; rather, he continues to organize remote, large-scale scientific expeditions from his home and office in Massachusetts. In a 1996 letter to David Rawle, a fellow Groton School classmate, Washburn explained his motivation for continued geographic exploration:

> As we get older and do more thinking about what we DID instead of what we're going to do, I find that it's been wonderful to try to identify what I would like to do today IF I was still 35 or 40, but with all the exciting machinery of today in hand—Satellites, laser, radio and new geologic techniques. Then I try to find some fellows who are 35-40 who'd like to do what I WISH I COULD DO—and help them get the money to do it and give them the battle-plan . . . . If they succeed, I get almost as much of a thrill out of their success as I would if I had done it with them.[14]

Washburn's recent practice of choreographing scientific expeditions from a distance has roots in nineteenth-century American expeditionary science.

For instance, the exploration of North America by Lewis and Clark (1803-1806) was made possible by the vision, ambition, and patronage of President Jefferson, who might have attempted such a journey had not his age and demands of the presidency precluded it.[15] And just as Dr. Hamilton Rice and Captain Albert Stevens made possible several of Washburn's expeditions, Washburn now has become the patron and scientific leader for a new generation of field scientists and explorers, enabling expeditions through an extensive network of personal contacts. This style of exploration worked especially well before World War II. In the post-war era, Washburn continued to rely on personal networks to carry out his scientific agenda, a style becoming increasingly more difficult with the vast expansion of scale and stratification of the natural and social sciences. Washburn's continued work on both Everest and McKinley might not have been possible without the characteristic "Washburn style" of integrating seemingly disparate organizations and interests toward a scientific and geographic objective.

The thread throughout Washburn's work is the quest for geographic knowledge and the belief that geography serves as a unifying discipline.[16] The field of geography has long been challenged as a separate, viable, and even practical academic discipline. Yet Washburn has used geography's multiple utilities, and even its perceived lack of clearly defined parameters, to explore, analyze, describe, and spatially represent the landscape. Washburn argues, and his career demonstrates, that geography transcends a multitude of academic and applied areas, and provides a vehicle for broad field investigations.

It is unlikely that Washburn's career would have been as successful as it has been, if he had more clearly followed a particular discipline. Perhaps the physicist would have seized the opportunity to carry out cosmic ray research on McKinley in the summer of 1947. But would the physicist have had personal connections with the U.S. military to support such an expedition, or an interest in conducting research on cold weather clothing, in path-breaking surveys on the summit of North America's tallest peak, capturing both moving and still photography, or in securing high altitude geologic data? Would the physicist have had the ability to mass-market a grand expedition to scientific, corporate, or private patrons? And would the physicist have taken on the enormous burden of conducting all of these efforts during a single mountaineering expedition, in one of the most inhospitable environments in the world? Geography and geographic exploration, argues Washburn, has provided the perfect framework in which to carryout his lifelong pursuits. In 1997, when the National Research Council published an assessment of geography in the United States, their findings reported a propensity for geographers to study both "vertical" integration of characteristics that define place as well as the "horizontal" connections between places. The study of these relationships has enabled geographers to pay attention to complexities of places and processes that are frequently treated in the abstract by other disciplines."[17] Speaking before a meeting of the American Geographical Society, Washburn declared, "For many of us the only tie between us and science is this interest in geography."[18]

More than a century ago, James Bryce, the British ambassador, described geography as a "meeting point between the sciences of Nature and the sciences of man."[19] Washburn's explorations are a vivid example of Bryce's declaration. Geography, Washburn noted, provides a means to explore and understand the "complex relationships between man and materials and science."[20] To illustrate this point, Washburn wrote:

> We realize that geography, the study of our earth, was, for almost all of us, the logical avenue into most of our other intellectual interests, whatever they may be. One rarely finds anthropologists or astronomers at the annual meeting of the chemical society—or physicists and mathematicians at a paleontological discussion—Yet tonight this room is filled with top experts from all of these fields and many others besides.[21]

Indeed, Washburn shares the sentiment of both James Bryce and nineteenth-century British geographer Halford Mackinder, in 1887 an outspoken champion of the integrating nature of geography. Mackinder argued that an "abyss" existed between the "natural sciences and the study of humanity." Mackinder, David Livingstone noted, "allocate[d] geography the task of reintegrating society and environment."[22] Washburn's work demonstrates his unique ability to integrate the natural and social sciences through geographic exploration; spanning at least a portion of Mackinder's "abyss" that today still remains.

Although the interdisciplinary nature of geography has made it a target for academic purists, it still provides Washburn with a flexible and productive forum in which to explore and study.[23] Although Washburn's vast collection of photographs and vivid maps are the most celebrated results of his fieldwork, Washburn's expeditions made possible the collection of significant scientific and geographical information. Scientific fields have increasing become more stratified and specialized in recent decades, but Washburn was able to bring together experts from many different fields to explore a remote and harsh environment.[24] His investigation of Mount Everest is just one recent example in a long career.

Washburn has been described in many ways: photographer, mountaineer, explorer, administrator, scientist, and cartographer. Washburn's insistence on accuracy goes beyond a broad concern for the product he delivered to patrons. In a 1993 interview, Washburn shared this philosophy:

> If you make a map topographically almost perfect in its detail, all of a sudden the whole map looks like reality. And the more beautiful and realistic a map is, the better it conveys its information. If you believe that one's appreciation of the natural world as a whole is greatly enhanced by intimate knowledge of detail, then beautiful, accurate maps make perfect sense. . . . This sort of map is much more than a representation of geography or a tool to make hikers navigate . . . it is a rendering of the fascinating undulations of the earth's surface.[25]

Washburn's expeditions of geographic discovery have been, in part, the product of a cunning entrepreneur, explorer, mountaineer, visionary, and enabler. "My mother often worried that I would become a mountain guide," Washburn recalled, "so she was relieved when I started working at the museum."[26] Yet, in an interesting way, Washburn has become a guide for millions of people who have read his articles, absorbed his photographs, or admired and used his maps. He has provided a means by which many non-mountaineers may appreciate the mountain world, and for non-explorers to explore.

Washburn joins an impressive community of geographic explorers and expeditionary scientists who, over the centuries, have pieced together the planet's mosaic of flora, fauna, and landscape. He has his own vision of and appreciation for his role in facilitating understanding of the natural world, often ending his public lectures with this quote from Aristotle:

> The Search for the Truth
> Is in one way hard—and in another easy
> For it is evident that no one of us can ever
> Master it fully . . . or miss it wholly
> Each one of us adds a little
> To our understanding of Nature
> And, from all the facts assembled,
> Arises a certain grandeur.

Washburn's love of the mountains and prowess as a mountaineer, developed as a young boy in New England, were the perfect precursor for his use of the mountain landscape as a natural laboratory. Washburn's first Alaskan expedition to Mount Fairweather in 1930, developed after a successful string of ascents in the Alps, served as a frustrating lesson in large-scale geographic exploration. The expedition could not achieve any significant altitude, and he later failed to reach the summit of Mount Crillon in the summers of 1932 and 1933. Yet during the latter expeditions he employed aerial photography and reconnaissance, utilized camp-to-camp radio communications, and carried out path-breaking geophysical work on Crillon Glacier. Almost at the same time, Admiral Byrd was using similar technologies and scientific methodology during his Antarctic fieldwork. Washburn's early expeditions to Fairweather and Crillon built upon turn-of-the century survey and glaciological investigations carried out by pioneering scientists, such as Israel Russell, Tarr and Martin, and William Field. Washburn, ever persistent, finally reached the summit of Crillon on his third attempt in 1934 after executing additional glacial and cartographic investigations.

In 1935 Washburn spent over three months traversing the uncharted mountain wilderness of the Wrangell—St. Elias region for the National Geographic Society. Again he utilized the airplane, radio communications, and aerial photography to map nearly five thousand square miles of previously unknown terrain. During the expedition he discovered and named a number of mountains and glaciers and updated the conventional

"his long-standing relationship with the National Geographic Society has by far been the most productive and interesting"

Recipients of the National Geographic Centennial Award. Standing, l to r: Senator John Glenn, Dr. Robert Ballard, Dr. Kenan Terim, Dr. Bradford Washburn, Dr. Jane Goodhall, Gilbert M. Grosvenor, Dr. Richard Leaky, Thayer Soule, Sir Edmund Hillary. Seated, l to r: Dr. George Bass, Dr. Harold Edgerton, Jacques Cousteau, Dr. Barbara Washburn, Dr. Mary Leakey, Dr. Frank Craighead, Jr., Dr. John Craighead

Courtesy of Bradford Washburn Collection

understanding of the region. The mountain landscape again served as a bridge between field science and mountaineering in 1936 when he conducted a series of aerial photographic surveys of Mount McKinley.

Washburn's consistent partner throughout most of his career has been the National Geographic Society. The Society made possible many of Washburn's expeditions and supported each of the three broad themes: Washburn's role as an innovative explorer and independent geographer; the role of geography as a disciplinary bridge; and the dynamic relationship between American field science and mountaineering. By the time Washburn established himself in the early 1920s as a competent mountaineer and photographer, the Society was well on its way toward making photography an integral part of its overall philosophy. "This vision for the magazine – appealing to the reader's sense of curiosity," observed historian Susan Schulten, "rested upon the extensive use of photography."[27] Washburn's large-format photographs of remote and newly discovered mountains and glaciers fit well into Grosvenor's vision. "The Geographic had by 1921 come to symbolize something that endures to this day. In fact the Geographic took on its modern form and style in these years, coming to rely primarily on photography for its success," Schulten argues.[28]

By examining Washburn's geographic and scientific expeditions one can better understand the scope and importance of his discoveries in Alaska and the Yukon. Although Washburn's work has been welcomed and appreciated by geographers, geologists, and glaciologists, for example, many expeditionary scientists and field geographers have not fared as well.[29] On this subject, historians of science Henrika Kuklick and Robert Kohler wrote, "Scholars derive their own status from that of their subjects. . . . Defining scientific rigor by the standards of the laboratory, scholars have judged the field to be a site of compromised work."[30]

Certainly Washburn's body of work offers a powerful answer to those who believe fieldwork to be of less value than laboratory research. Most field scientists accept the controversies that sometimes accompany their work. Washburn showed his awareness of these realities in this simple declaration to Gilbert Grosvenor: "God forbid that I should ever become a 'hard-boiled scientist.'"[31] It is also true that Washburn's ability to bring together many disparate agencies, patrons, and institutions on a large scale certainly opened him to criticism beyond those of field science in general.

The Muries' stinging attack on Washburn's "desecration" of Mount McKinley is one such example. However, in retrospect, their concerns were unfounded. Today, air and ground research on McKinley are restricted by the National Park Service to assure minimal impact on the mountain. Moreover, Washburn's demonstration of the relative safety and ease of the West Buttress has resulted in the concentration along this route of nearly three-quarters of the mountaineering activity on McKinley, and his photographs, publications, and map of McKinley have brought international awareness, understanding, and appreciation of a region that most people will never experience. However, it is important not to overstate Washburn's contribution to the modern environmental movement. To be sure, environmental organizations know the power a photograph can have on public perception, and Washburn's work has done more to inform the general public about McKinley's unique environment than it has negatively affected either the mountain or the region.

Through his life's work, Washburn has generated a more complete understanding of McKinley and the mountain world in general, and from this understanding has come a greater appreciation. The best description of Washburn's mountain photography is that of Clifford S. Ackley, Ruth and Carl Shapiro Curator of Prints, Drawings, and Photographs at Boston's Museum of Fine Arts:

> Perhaps the central visual message of Washburn's aerial photographs is the revelation of how the earth works. This is at once good science and expressive art. All the earth's secrets, its geological movements, its upheavals and erosions, the slow march and retreat of glaciers, the essential interconnectedness of the earth's bones, veins, and muscles, are laid out before us with exemplary clarity.[32]

Reflecting upon Washburn's career it is natural to contemplate his legacy, a rather curious and challenging exercise. I have posed this question to many individuals and have had the same question asked of me on other occasions. To the mountaineer, Washburn's pioneering ascents, vivid mountain photography and maps on which climbing routes can be planned, are widely admired. The expert in photography points to the aesthetic quality of Washburn's work and his ability to overcome the significant challenges of operating in remote areas. Glaciologists and geologists, almost without hesitation, celebrate the scientific and educational value of Washburn's aerial photographs with their detailed records of the position and conditions of glaciers, resulting in the deep understanding described by Ackley. Cartographers see in Washburn's maps a striking accuracy and attention to detail. Appreciating the skill with which his many surveys were conducted, they celebrate Washburn's ability to embrace emerging technologies over the course of nearly seven decades of work. And in the circle of explorers, Washburn's pioneering use of air transport, camp radios, the use of aerial photographs to chart exploration into remote regions, and his ability to marshal significant scientific and financial support are always mentioned. To the educator, Washburn's Museum of Science stands as his true, physical legacy, and has provided a model for educational innovations in other museums.

Washburn's interdisciplinary approach to his multiple careers makes a single study of his life quite a challenge. A separate volume could be written on each area of Washburn's expertise: mountaineer, photographer, scientist, explorer, cartographer, educator. However, by weaving together the different components of his career one can appreciate Washburn's accomplishments and gauge their importance to multiple academic disciplines as well as their value to the general public. His legacy reaches far beyond Boston or any particular academic community. His influence is wide-ranging, and his achievements will be long remembered.

Notes

Abbreviations

BW—Bradford Washburn

BWC—Bradford Washburn Collection, University of Alaska Fairbanks, Rasmuson Library, Alaska and Polar Regions Archives, Fairbanks, Alaska.

BWPP—Bradford Washburn Personal Papers (to be added to the Bradford Washburn Collection at the University of Alaska Fairbanks), Fairbanks, Alaska.

ETO—European Theater of Operations

GSA—Geological Society of America

NGS—National Geographic Society

NRC—National Research Council

ONR—Office of Naval Research

OSRD—Office of Scientific Research and Development

QMC—Quartermaster Corps

USGS—United States Geological Survey

Preface

1. Moore, *McKinley*.
2. BW and Cherici, *The Dishonorable Dr. Cook,* 97.
3. For a tribute to Moore's life see Katrina Moore, *Borestone to Bering Strait*.
4. Over the course of several years, I have conducted numerous oral history interviews with BW, Terris Moore, and other prominent American mountaineers. These interviews will be deposited in the Rasmusen Library of the University of Alaska Fairbanks.
5. The NGS, *Mount Everest*. See also BW, "Mount Everest," 653-59.
6. For issues related to biography as "history," see Schweber, "Writing the Biography of a Living Scientist," and Soderquist, "After the 200th Hour."

Introduction

1. Saulkeld, "Skinning One Skunk," 36.
2. BW and Roberts, *Mount McKinley,* 17.
3. BW, taped interview with Mike Sfraga, 15 July, 1992, Boston.
4. For a broad overview, see Kirwin, *A History of Polar Exploration,* Livingstone, *The Geographical Tradition,* and Lever, "Vilhjamur Stefansson," 233-47, especially 233-36.
5. Amundsen, *The North West Passage;* see also Amundsen, "To the North Magnetic Pole," 485-518. For his conquest of the South Pole, see Amundsen, *The South Pole*. For Amundsen's "race" with Scott to the South Pole, see Huntford, *The Last Place on Earth*. For Scott's expedition, see *Scott's Last Expedition* and *Scott's Last Expedition: The Journals*. For a new perspective see Solomon, *The Coldest March*. See also Amundsen, *My Life as an*

Explorer and Boddington, *Antarctic Photographs.*

6. See Huntford, *The Last Place on Earth.*

7. See Peary, *The North Pole.* For the Cook-Peary controversy, see Hunt, *To Stand at the Pole,* Eames, *Winner Lose All,* Freeman, *The Case for Dr. Cook,* Herbert, *The Noose of Laurels,* Rawlins: *Peary at the North Pole,* Henson, *A Negro Explorer,* and Roberts, *Great Exploration Hoaxes.* The best one-volume study is Bryce, *Cook and Peary: The Polar Controversy Resolved.* See also BW and Cherici, *The Dishonorable Dr. Cook.*

8. See Cook, *My Attainment of the Pole* and *Return From the Pole.*

9. Riffenburgh, *The Myth of the Explorer,* 165-90.

10. Goetzmann, *New Lands, New Men,* 433.

11. Goetzmann, *Ibid.,* 5, Cronon, Miles, and Gitlin, "Becoming West," and Nash, *Creating the West.*

12. Turner, *The Frontier in American History,* 1.

13. More detailed survey of geographic regions followed these broad discoveries, and exploration took on a more "scientific" focus. See Bowler, *The Norton History of The Environmental Sciences,* 390. For the U.S. Geological Society, see Rabbitt, *Minerals, Lands, and Geology.* See also Bartlett, *Great Surveys,* Powell, *The Exploration of the Colorado River,* Worster, *A River Running West,* and Dolnick, *Down the Great Unknown.*

14. Goetzmann, *New Lands, New Men,* 4. See also Goetzmann, *Exploration and Empire.*

15. John K. Wright, "The Field of the Geographical Society," 548-52.

16. Riffenburgh, *The Myth of the Explorer,* 119-37.

17. Taylor, ed., *Geography in the Twentieth Century,* 1-3. See also Bowler, *Norton History,* 196. On professionalism, see Ross, *The Origins of American Social Sciences.*

18. Goetzmann, *New Lands, New Men,* 1-2.

19. Jules Verne popularized this notion of exploration.

20. Pyne, "A Third Great Age of Discovery," 38.

21. *Ibid.,* 25, 34. The International Geophysical Year signaled a unique and significant event in global scientific cooperation. Although Pyne is correct on the significance of the IGY, it could be argued that the scientific initiatives during the Second World War more accurately define a Third Great Age of Discovery. See DeVorkin, *Science With A Vengeance.*

22. See Sorrenson, "The Ship as Scientific Instrument in the Eighteenth Century," 221-36.

23. Kuklick and Kohler, "Science in the Field," 2-3.

24. Goetzmann, "Paradigm Lost," 25.

25. Pyne, "From the Grand Canyon to the Marianas Trench," 189. See also Thrower, *Maps and Civilization,* 160, 163,173-74, 177, 186, 194, 199, 210, 229.

26. Bowler, *The Norton History,* 391. For a broader perspective, see Oleson and Voss, eds., *The Organization of Knowledge.*

27. Pyne, "From the Grand Canyon to the Marianas Trench," 189. Recent studies in history of science, for instance Kohler, *Partners in Science,* have addressed the role of patronage, but have not highlighted the role of individual entrepreneurs. For one exception, see Lucier, "Commercial Interests and Scientific Disinterestedness," 245-67.

28. See Hevly, "The Heroic Science," 76.

29. The role and significance of the field scientist/geographer is discussed in

Kuklick and Kohler, "Science in the Field," 1-14. See also Kohler, "Place and Practice," 189-210.

30. The significance of aerial photography in the study of landscape was well appreciated in Canada from the early 1920s. Canadian geophysicist Tuzo Wilson championed the use of such technology, stating that "many features of glacial origin can be recognized and mapped" from the air. See Wilson, "Structural Features," 493, and John Tuzo Wilson, interview with Ronald Doel, transcribed tape recording, Toronto, 16 February 1993, 44-45, Niels Bohr Library, American Institute of Physics, College Park, Maryland. See also Wilson, "Glacial Geology ," 49, and Zaslow, *Reading the Rocks,* 372.

31. For a history of the Office of Naval Research, see Sapolsky, "Academic Science and the Military," 379-99. For the "golden age of academic science," see p. 385.

Chapter 1

1. Peary, *The Snow Baby.* BW, interview with Mike Sfraga, unrecorded, Anchorage, September 16, 1994.

2. BW, "Response by Bradford Washburn" (Speech delivered at the King Albert Memorial Foundation Award Ceremony, St. Moritz, Switzerland, 3 December 1994), 2. Similar speeches, correspondence, and documents have been received by Mike Sfraga from BW. Hereafter they will be cited as BWPP (Bradford Washburn Personal Papers). This material has been added to the Bradford Washburn Collection (BWC) at the University of Alaska Fairbanks.

3. Botsford, "Catching up with Brad Washburn," 13.

4. BW, interview with Mike Sfraga, tape recording, not transcribed,
Boston, Massachusetts, July 18, 1992.

5. "*Life* Visits the Mayflower Descendants," *Life Magazine,* November 29, 1948, 132. BW, interview with Mike Sfraga, Boston, Massachusetts, July 1992.

6. Fagen, "Philip Washburn."

7. "Western Union Gets Anglo-American," *New York Times,* December 17, 1910, 1; "E. J. Hall, Developer of Telephone, Dies," *New York Sun,* September 18, 1914; "Edward J. Hall: Vice-president of the American Telephone and Telegraph Co., Died at Watkins, N.Y., September 17, 1914," *The Telephone Review,* October 1914, 279.

8. BW, "Biographical Summary," unpublished biographical notes, BWC, "Biographical Information," Box 1, File 90-072, Alaska and Polar Regions Archives, Elmer E. Rasmuson Library, University of Alaska Fairbanks, 2. Unless otherwise indicated, correspondence, diaries and other related material are included in the BWC.

9. *Ibid.*

10. BW to Dr. Jan Fontein, BWPP, June 22, 1983.

11. Dr. G. A. Reisner to BW, BWPP, April 22, 1920.

12. BW to Mike Sfraga, November 3, 1995.

13. BW, "Biographical Summary," 4.

14. BW, "Fishing: What A Boy Thinks," 12.

15. *Ibid.*

16. *Ibid.*

17. *Ibid.*

18. BW to Mike Sfraga, BWPP, September 15, 1994. Charles Washburn was a Harvard graduate and engineer who served as a member of the Massachusetts General Court and later in the United States Congress 1906-1912.

19. Henry Washburn to Edith Washburn, BWPP, June 22, 1922.
20. *Ibid.*
21. BW, taped interview with Mike Sfraga, Boston, November 19, 1989.
22. BW, *Bradford on Mt. Washington,* 80.
23. *Ibid.,* 77.
24. BW, taped interview with Mike Sfraga, Boston, July 18, 1992.
25. BW to Mabel Colgate, BWPP, n.d., December 1924. Mabel was Washburn's half-sister.
26. BW to Mabel Colgate, BWPP, October 26, 1924.
27. BW to Mabel Colgate, BWPP, n.d., March 1925.
28. BW to Mabel Colgate, BWPP, February 15, 1925.
29. Washburn's passion for recording weather data can be compared with similar practices in the colonial period. James Fleming divides the history of U.S. meteorology into four periods, the first of which was the "era of individual, isolated diarists before 1800" who recorded weather data without the benefit of reliable instrumentation or institutional support. Nevertheless, they "contributed to meteorological science by keeping records of the local weather and climate." See Fleming, *Meteorology in America: 1800-1896,* xvii-xviii.
30. BW to Mabel Colgate, BWPP, n.d., 1925.
31. BW to Mabel Colgate, BWPP, n.d., 1970.
32. Groton School, "The Athletic Association," BWPP, 36.
33. BW, "Groton Memories," speech delivered at Washburn's sixty-fifth Groton School class reunion, Groton, Massachusetts, May 1994, 1. BWPP.
34. *Ibid.,* 2.
35. BW, "Groton Memories," 2. BW, interview with Mike Sfraga, Anchorage, September 16, 1994.
36. Henry Bradford Washburn Jr., *The Trails and Peaks of the Presidential Range of the White Mountains.*
37. BW, "Biographical Summary," 5.
38. Tissot, *Mont Blanc,* 60. BW, taped interview with Mike Sfraga, Boston, July 18, 1992.
39. Clark, *The Alps,* 50.
40. *Ibid.*
41. *Ibid.,* 51, 274.
42. BW, "Response by Bradford Washburn," 3.
43. BW, "Bradford Washburn's remarks at the Groupe de Haute Montagne," (Speech delivered to the French Alpine Club, Chamonix, France, February 1995), 2. BWPP.
44. Holzel and Saulkeld, *First on Everest.* See also Breashears and Saulkeld, *Last Climb.*
45. BW, "Captain Noel's Lecture," *Third Form Weekly,* BWPP, October 9, 1926.
46. BW, interview with Mike Sfraga, Anchorage, September 16, 1994.
47. BW, "Europe and the Alps," Diary, June 24 to September 4, 1926. Box 1, 92-147. Diary entries will be noted with a "D" throughout text.
48. BW, "A Boy on the Matterhorn," 190; BW, "I Climb Mont Blanc."
49. Edith Washburn to Mabel Colgate, BWPP, May 29, 1927.
50. *Ibid.*
51. BW, *Among the Alps with Bradford. Bradford on Mt. Washington* was published in 1928, and the final book in the series, *Bradford on Mt. Fairweather,* was published in 1931.
52. BW, taped interview with Mike Sfraga, Boston, July 18, 1992.
53. BW, "The First Ascent," 102. For a brief, contemporary review of Washburn's European ascents, including the Aiguille Verte, see *High Magazine Sports,* "Alpine Special," February 1995, 53.
54. BW, taped interview with Mike Sfraga, Boston, July 18, 1992.

55. BW, "Aerial Photography: Alaska and the Alps," 19.
56. *Ibid.*
57. *Ibid.*
58. BW to Mike Sfraga, BWPP, February 21, 1995.
59. *Ibid.*
60. *Ibid.*
61. BW, taped interview with Mike Sfraga, Cambridge, Massachusetts, July 23, 1992.
62. BW, "Biographical Summary," 7.
63. NGS Memorandum, BWPP, undated, 1930.
64. BW, taped interview with Mike Sfraga, Boston, July 18, 1992; Gilbert M. Grosvenor, transcribed speech given in honor of The Alexander Graham Bell Medal of the NGS, BWPP, November 6, 1980.
65. BW and his wife Barbara were named the 2002 National Geographic Society's "Explorers in Residence."

Chapter 2

1. Sharp, *Living Ice: Understanding Glaciers and Glaciation,* 49; William Field, *Mountain Glaciers,* 4.
2. Glaciation in Alaska has been primarily alpine in nature. See Hamilton, Reed, and Thorson, eds., *Glaciation in Alaska,* 2; Field, *Mountain Glaciers of the Northern Hemisphere,* 4.
3. Molnia, *Alaska's Glaciers,* 89.
4. Field, *Geographic Study of Mountain Glaciation,* 2.a.1.3.
5. Molnia, *Alaska's Glaciers,* 64.
6. *Ibid.,* 76.
7. *Ibid.,* 77.
8. Krashieninnikov, *Explorations of Kamchatka: 1735-41,* 121. There is some confusion as to whether Bering intended to name the mountain or the cape nearest his anchorage—Cape Elila. See Sven Waxell, *The American Expedition,* 105. Bill Hunt believes cartographers transposed

Bering's intended Cape Elila to St. Elias, the largest peak on the expedition's exploratory maps: "It remains customary to credit Bering with naming the mountain even though the evidence does not confirm it." See Hunt, *Mountain Wilderness,* 13. A few days before Bering's discovery, Chirikof had sighted Prince of Wales Island in the Alexander Archipelago. See Hunt, *Mountain Wilderness,* 7.
9. Steller, *Journal of a Voyage with Bering 1741-1742,* 65.
10. La Perouse, *A Voyage Around the World, vol. 1,* 364-416.
11. Israel Russell, "An Expedition to Mount St. Elias," 63-64.
12. *Ibid.,* 63.
13. *Ibid.*
14. *Ibid.*
15. George Vancouver, *A Voyage of Discovery,* 1552.
16. Berton, *The Arctic Grail,* 16-17.
17. Dall, "Report on Mount Saint Elias," 159.
18. Sherwood, *Exploration of Alaska: 1865-1900,* 81; see also "Note on Mount Logan," *American Geologist* 13 (1894): 292.
19. Sherwood, *Exploration of Alaska: 1865-1900,* 75.
20. Buwalda, in John Muir, *Studies,* ix.
21. *Ibid.,* xxv.
22. *Ibid.,* 17-74.
23. For an account of Muir's observations in Alaska, see *Muir: Travels in Alaska.*
24 Sherwood, *Exploration of Alaska: 1865-1900,* 76.
25 *Ibid.,* 36.
26 Blake, "The Glaciers of Alaska," 96-102; Russell, *Glaciers of North America,* 75. For the emergence of glacial studies in Europe, see Seligman, "Research on Glacier Flow," 228-238. In Europe during the late 1860s, glaciers began a dramatic recession after decades of

advances that threatened water supplies and led to systematic widespread surveys. See Mathis, "Glaciers," 149-219. For a popular account, see Bolles, *The Ice Finders*.

27. Wright, "The Muir Glacier," 1-18.

28. Read, "Studies of Muir Glacier," 19-84. See also Field, "Glaciological Research in Alaska," 124. Field contends that glaciology "attained the status of an independent earth science" before the Second World War. Field, *Some Aspects of Glaciers*, 3; see also Ahlmann, "Forward," 3-4, and Hevly, "The Heroic Science," 66-86.

29. Russell, "An Expedition to Mount St. Elias," 192. This was the first field expedition sponsored by the NGS. See Bryan, *The National Geographic Society*, 31.

30. *Ibid.*, 194.

31. de Filippi, *The Ascent of Mount St. Elias,* 79.

32. Merriam, *Harriman Alaska Expedition*. For a review of the expedition's glacial surveys, see Gilbert *Glaciers and Glaciation*. For the significance of the expedition's results, see Field, "Glaciological Research in Alaska," 125. See also Goetzmann and Sloan, *Looking Far North*.

33. Tarr and Martin, *Alaskan Glacier Studies,* ix-x. The duo also conducted field research in 1905 and 1906.

34. Field, "The Fairweather Range," 460-72.

35. BW, taped interview with Mike Sfraga, Cambridge, Massachusetts, June 23, 1992. Also attending Field's 1926 presentation was fellow Harvard student Terris Moore, later to become the second president (1947-1951) of the University of Alaska. Moore credits Field with enticing him to climb in the then-virgin peaks of southeast Alaska. Moore, taped interview with Mike

Sfraga, Boston, January 25, 1993.

36. Mount St. Elias, 18,008 feet was climbed in 1897; see de Filippi, *The Ascent of Mount St. Elias*. Mount McKinley was scaled in 1913; see Stuck, *The Ascent of Denali*.

37. BW, *Bradford on Mt. Fairweather,* 7.

38. *Ibid.*

39. *Ibid.*

40. BW, *Bradford on Mt. Fairweather*, 9.

41. *Ibid.*, 12.

42. Charles Houston, speech delivered to the American Alpine Club meeting, Denver, Colorado, December 5, 1993.

43. BW, "Back-Packing to Fairweather," 61.

44. BW, *Bradford on Mt. Fairweather*, 15.

45. *Ibid.*, 16.

46. *Ibid.*, 26.

47. Klotz, "Notes on the Glaciers of Southeastern Alaska," 524-26.

48. Brooks, *Preliminary Report on the Ketchikan Mining District,* 31.

49. BW, *Bradford on Mt. Fairweather*, 78.

50. BW, "Back-Packing to Fairweather," 61.

51. *Ibid.*, 81; BW, "A Preliminary Report," 219. This report was written to encompass all work done through the 1930s.

52. Geologic and fossil samples were added to a rather small yet significant collection taken by a number of expeditions to the region, including that of Mertie in 1917. See Mertie, "Geography and Geology of Lituya Bay," 117.

53. BW, *Bradford on Mt. Fairweather*, 82, 35; BW, "Back-Packing to Fairweather," 61.

54. "Will Try to Climb Mt. Fairweather," *New York Times*, June 13, 1932, 8.

55. The important role of various types of vehicles in support of field science is discussed at great length in David DeVorkin, *Science With a Vengeance*.

56. Sargent, 1929.
57. BW, "A Preliminary Report," 222.
58. BW, "The Conquest of Mount Crillon," 363.
59. William Field surveyed and photographed this region in 1926, yet BW did not reoccupy Field's stations. See Field and Brown, *With a Camera*, 60-62. I would like to thank Suzanne Brown, Professor William Schneider, and the University of Alaska Fairbanks Oral History Project for making available to me a preliminary copy of this very important oral history of William Field. Washburn's calculated height of Mount Crillon exceeded that of early Boundary Commission estimates at the turn of the century by a mere one foot, placing it at 12,728 feet.
60. BW, interview with Mike Sfraga, November 19, 1989.
61. "Snowstorm Balks Mt. Crillon Climb," *New York Times*, August 27, 1933, sec. 2, p. 4.
62. *Ibid.*, p. 1
63. A detailed map was produced under the auspices of the Institute for Geographic Exploration at Harvard University from data attained by Washburn's Crillon expeditions of 1933 and 1934. This survey material was added to that of the U.S. Coast and Geodetic Survey of 1926 and coastal aerial photographs of the U.S. Forest Service of 1929. See BW and Goldthwait, "Lituya Bay and Mount Crillon District." Topographic data of Crillon's upper slopes were compiled in 1933 and 1934. Measurements were made by aneroid "spot-heights," the data from which supplemented previous fixed ground-based triangulation. A subsequent series of oblique aerial photographs taken by BW in 1934 completed the data collection.

64. BW and Richard Goldthwait, "Movement of South Crillon Glacier," 1654.
65. BW, "The Conquest of Mount Crillon," 365.
66. Richard Goldthwait, "Seismic Sounding on South Crillon and Klooch Glaciers," 496.
67. Harvard University's Committee on Geophysics supported a number of field initiatives throughout the 1930s, the majority of which were under the auspices of Harvard faculty. This highlights the degree to which Washburn's work was considered important. Few published studies discuss Harvard's role in support of such work.
68. BW, "The Harvard-Dartmouth Mount Crillon Expedition," D, May 30-August 17, 1934, 20, 24, 27. Box 2. file 3.
69. BW and Goldthwait, "Movement of South Crillon Glacier," 1655.
70. BW, "The Conquest of Mount Crillon," 365.
71. *Ibid.*, 1658; BW and Goldthwait, "Movement of South Crillon Glacier," 1660-63.
72. Chamberland, "Instrumental Work on the Nature of Glacier Motion," 1-30.
73. See for instance, Mothes, "Dickenmessungen," 121-44; Brockamp and Mothes, "Seismische Untersuchungen," 482-500.
74. BW, "The Harvard-Dartmouth Alaskan Expeditions," 484.
75. *Ibid.*, 498.
76. Funding for the committee's research came from a number of external patrons. In particular, the Rockefeller Foundation contributed funds in excess of one hundred thousand dollars through the 1930s. See Committee on Experimental Geology, "Thirty-seventh meeting of the Committee on Geophysical Research," January 18, 1940, box

UA V 420.125, Division of Geological Sciences files, Harvard University Archives.

77. Such an interdisciplinary framework was quite common at this time. Historian of Science Ronald Doel has argued that the committee resembled that of a "transient institution," addressing academic questions outside the more traditional academic disciplines. Doel, "Defining Cooperative Research."

78. Mather was one of Washburn's advisors at Harvard. In 1938 they co-published "The Telescopic Alidade and Plane Table." See also Bork, *Cracking Rocks and Defending Democracy.*

79. See Committee on Experimental Geology, "Memo to Committee on Geophysical Research," n.d., Division of Geological Science files, box UA V 420.125. Seismic exploration became a fundamental component of many geophysical departments and institutes of major universities in the 1930s. See for instance, Doel, "The Earth Sciences and Geophysics," 10. Seismic exploration was quite common in oil prospecting. Harvard faculty used seismic exploration to better understand Earth's structure, publishing extensively throughout the 1930s and 1940s on this subject. See for instance, Munro, *Geophysics at Harvard,* 30-32. For an excellent synthesis of major patronage for exploration geophysics, in particular that of the Rockefeller Foundation, the significant source of funding for Harvard's foray into geophysics, see Kohler, *Partners in Science,* 256. After 1945, geophysical investigation at Harvard expanded, forcing the school to solicit additional patrons. A very pointed text entitled "Geophysics at Harvard," complete

with an opening aerial photograph of Alaska's Bernard Glacier by BW, was distributed in an effort to lure additional funding. See Monro, *Geophysics at Harvard.*

80. R. A. Daly to C. G. Morgan, September 30, 1933.

81. Goldthwait, "Seismic Sounding," 496.

82. *Ibid.,* 496. Goldthwait returned to Crillon Glacier in the 1960s, documenting its cycle of recession and advances as well as the prehistoric and historic changes that had occurred in the surrounding area. See Goldthwait, McKeller, and Cronk, "The Fluctuations of Crillon Glacier System," 62-74, and Field, *Mountain Glaciers of the Northern Hemisphere,* 188-189. For related work in Glacier Bay, Alaska, see for instance, Goldthwait, "Dating the Little Ice Age," 37-46. Eventually, Goldthwait would follow in his father's footsteps, rising to become one of the most distinguished American glaciologists of the twentieth century. For a synopsis of Goldthwait's career and abbreviated bibliography of his publications, see Albert Lincoln Washburn, "Memorial to Richard Parker Goldthwait: 1911-1992," 167-70.

83. For an early history of aerial photography and photogrammetry, see McKinley, *Applied Aerial Photography.* McKinley was an instructor in aerial photography during the First World War for the U.S. Army Air Corps and served as aerial surveyor for Admiral Byrd's Antarctic expedition.

84. BW, "Harvard-Dartmouth Mount Crillon Expedition," 10.

85. *Ibid.,* 11.

86. *Ibid.,* 12.

87. *Ibid.,* 13-14.

88. *Ibid.,* 1. The aerial exploration was supported by a five hundred-dollar

grant from the Penrose Fund. Penrose would underwrite the follow-up glacial investigations in 1936. In addition, three thousand feet of photographic film as well as an additional five hundred dollars from Grantland Rice.

89. *Ibid.*, 30.

90. Gilbert, *Harriman Alaska Expedition*, 58-63; Tarr, "The Yakutat Bay Region," 54-59; Tarr and Martin, *Alaska Glacier Studies*, 131-45.

91. *Ibid.*, 139-41. Tarr died in 1913.

92. BW, "Morainic Banding of Malaspina Glacier," 1885.

93. Maynard Miller found Nunatak Glacier to have receded about six and one half miles during the same period. Miller, "Observations on the Regimen of Glaciers," 40.

94. BW," The Harvard-Dartmouth Mount Crillon Expedition," 30-31.

95. Field, *Mountain Glaciers*, 225.

96. BW, "The Harvard-Dartmouth Mount Crillon Expedition," 30. The Hubbard Glacier was advancing at the time of Washburn's expedition. This advance continues to this day, with a total advance of approximately three kilometers, or 20-30 meters per year. Bruce Molnia, interview with Mike Sfraga, October 24, 2003.

97. Field, "Glaciological Research in Alaska," 127.

98. *Ibid.*

99. BW, "The Harvard-Dartmouth Mount Crillon Expedition," 30.

100. BW, "Morainic Banding," 1981.

101. *Ibid.*, 31.

102. Russell, "An Expedition to Mount St. Elias, Alaska," 57, 122. Field, *Geographic Study of Mountain Glaciation,* 21; Field, *Mountain Glaciers*, 233-34; BW, "Morainic Banding," 1881; Tarr and Martin, *Alaskan Glacier Studies*, 44.

103. Dall, *Coast Pilot,* 212.

104. *Ibid.*, 176.

105. Russell, *Glaciers of North America,* 3.

106. Russell, "Mt. St. Elias and Its Glaciers," 170; Russell, "An Expedition to Mount St. Elias," 185-86. The Malaspina is the largest Piedmont glacier in North America spanning 850 square miles. See Henning, Olds, and Rennick, *Alaska's Glaciers*, 87.

107. Tarr and Martin, *Alaskan Glacier Studies*, 44.

108. *Ibid.*

109. BW, "Morainic Banding," 1882.

110. Tarr and Martin, *Alaskan Glacier Studies*, 168. See also Tarr, "Recent Advance of Glaciers," 277-86.

111. Tarr and Martin, *Alaskan Glacier Studies*, 175.

112. BW, "Morainic Banding," 1882.

113. Post, "Effects of the March 1964 Alaskan Earthquake," 38-41; Miller, "The Role of Diastrophism," 296.

114. BW, "Morainic Banding," 1882.

115. Current research is still being conducted on many of Alaska's glaciers in an effort to identify the mechanism or mechanisms responsible for glacial flow and surges. Recent data indicate mechanisms responsible for glacial surge are more a function of faulty "plumbing" within the glacier rather than a result of climactic change. See Kamb et al., "Glacier Surge Mechanism," 478-79. Professor Will Harrison, Geophysical Institute, University of Alaska Fairbanks, credits Austin Post with first advancing such a theory.

116. Robert Sharp, *Glaciers* (Eugene: University of Oregon, 1990), 68; Michael Hambrey and Jurg Alean, *Glaciers* (Cambridge: University of Cambridge Press, 1992), 64.

117. For the evolution of Forbes' theory see J. D. Forbes, *Travels Through the Alps of Savoy* (Edinburgh: Simpkin, 1843). See also J. E. Fisher, "The Formation of Forbes Bands," *Journal*

of Glaciology 1, (1951): 580-81, J. E. Fisher, "Forbes and Alaskan 'Dirt' Bands on Glaciers and Their Origins," *American Journal of Science* 245 (1947): 137-45.

118. Sharp, *Glaciers*, 63.

119. Hambrey and Alean, *Glaciers*, 64; Waddington, "Wave Ogives," 325.

120. King and Lewis, "A Tentative Theory," 913-39; see also Sharp, *Living Ice*, 36.

121. Forbes, *The Theory of Glaciers,* 25.

122. BW, "Morainic Banding," 1887.

123. *Ibid.*, 1888-1889.

124. Waddington, "Wave Ogives," 326.

125. *Ibid.*

126. *Ibid.* In 1948, The Arctic Institute of North America initiated "Project Snow Cornice," which built significantly upon the work of BW and others within the Seward-Malaspina system. See Field, "Glaciological Research in Alaska," 127-28.

127. On Muir's contributions, see Fox, *John Muir.*

128. BW, "Harvard-Dartmouth Mount Crillon Expedition," 31.

129. BW, "Harvard-Dartmouth Mount Crillon Expedition," 37-42.

130. *Ibid.*, 44.

131. *Ibid.*, 44.

132. *Ibid.*, 44.

133. *Ibid.*, 45.

134. *Ibid.*, 45, 46.

135. Byrd, "The Conquest of Antarctica by Air," 127-238.

136. Needell, *Cold War and the American State,* 18-19. I would like to thank Allan Needell for his permission to read an earlier draft manuscript. See also Needell, "Lloyd Berkner and Science-Statesmanship," 294.

137. Berkner to Dellinger, May 11, 1929, Dellinger files, RG 167, Box 19; quoted in Needell, *Horizons of Lloyd Berkner,* 29.

138. BW, "The Harvard-Dartmouth Mount Crillon Expedition," 17-18.

139. *Ibid.*, 18.

140. *Ibid.*, 17; BW, "The Conquest of Mount Crillon," 367.

141. BW, "The Harvard-Dartmouth Mount Crillon Expedition," 43.

142. Aerial photography was used to map the frontier of India during this time. See Crone, "Mapping From the Air," 149-53. See Salt, "Photographs From the Mount Everest Flight," 54. See also Thrower, *Maps and Civilization,* 163-229.

143. Flemer, "Photographic Methods and Instruments," 619-735.

144. Bagley, "The Use of the Panoramic Camera," 7.

145. *Ibid.*, 14.

146. Sargent and Moffit, "Aerial Photographic Surveys," 144.

147. Byrd, *Little America.*

148. Graham and Read, *Manual of Aerial Photography,* 4; Thrower, *Maps and Civilization,* 163.

149. Robinson, "Geographic Cartography," 558.

150. Graham and Read, *Manual of Aerial Photography,* 9-10.

151. Doel, "Expeditions and the CIW," 79-87.

152. BW, interview with Mike Sfraga, Boston, June 23, 1992.

153. Roberts, "Bradford Washburn," 46. See also BW and Decaneas, *Bradford Washburn: Mountain Photography.*

154. For the career of Sella, see Clark, *The Splendid Hills: The Life and Photographs of Vittorio Sella*; see also Lunn, "Vittorio Sella," in *A Century of Mountaineering,* 126-29, and Sella et al, *Summit.*

155. Miller, "Observations on the Regimen of the Glaciers," 20.

156. Gilbert Grosvenor to BW, October 12, 1934, Gilbert Grosvenor files 510-1-2117 Washburn, Bradford, NGS Archives, Washington, D.C. The author thanks the NGS for allowing access to the Society's rich

archival resources and for unique access to Mr. Grosvenor's papers.

157. BW to Gilbert Grosvenor, 23 November, 1934, Gilbert Grosvenor files 510-1-2117 Washburn, Bradford.

158. *Ibid.*

159. *Champaigne-Urbana News,* November 27, 1934, 3. Gilbert Grosvenor file 510-1-2117 Washburn, Bradford.

160. BW to Gilbert Grosvenor, December 11, 1934. Gilbert Grosvenor File 510-1-2117.

161. *National Geographic Magazine,* "Father Hubbard's Alaskan Explorations," 625-26.

162. *Champaign-Urbana News,* 3.

163. BW, "The Harvard-Dartmouth Mount Crillon Expedition," 54-55.

164. BW to Gilbert Grosvenor, 11 December 1934. Gilbert Grosvenor files 510-1-2117 Washburn, Bradford.

165. *Ibid.*

166. Lutz and Collins, *Reading National Geographic,* 24. See also Schulten, *The Geographical Imagination in America.*

167. *Ibid.*

168. Pauly, "The World and All That's in It," 518.

169. Abramson, *National Geographic,* 131; see also Grosvenor, *The National Geographic Society and Its Magazine.*

170. *Ibid.,* 132.

171. *Ibid.,* 135; also quoted in DeVorkin, *Race to the Stratosphere.*

172. *Ibid.,* 136-42. The *Geographic* supported numerous expeditions that incorporated aerial photography and surveys; see for instance Simpich, "Skypaths Through Latin America," 1-79; Goddard, "The Unexplored Philippines," 311-43; Albert Stevens, "Photographing the Eclipse of 1932," 581-96.

173. Lutz and Collins, *Reading the National Geographic,* 29.

174. Gilbert Grosvenor to BW, November 6, 1934. Gilbert Grosvenor files, Yukon Expedition, NGS Archives, Washington, D.C.

175. BW to Gilbert Grosvenor, 6 November 1934. Gilbert Grosvenor files, Yukon Expedition, NGS Archives, Washington, D.C.

176. In 1906, the 141st Meridian was established as the boundary between Alaska and the Yukon. The International Boundary Commission carried out expeditions to survey this region from 1906-1913. The original lines of demarcation between Russian and British possessions in North America was established in 1825; see "Alaskan Boundary," 272-76. Russian survey parties made it a practice to bury plates to confirm their discoveries. For information pertaining to this practice in Alaska, see Pierce and Doll, "Alaskan Treasure," 2-7. See also Hodges, *The Alaska-Canada Boundary Dispute.* For the boundary survey of 1913 see Barnard, *Report of The International Boundary Commission,* 92-101; Green, *The Boundary Hunters,* 168-75.

177. Tarr and Martin, *Alaskan Glacier Studies,* 11.

178. BW to Gilbert Grosvenor, November 6, 1934. Gilbert Grosvenor files, Yukon Expedition.

179. *Ibid.*

180. Gilbert Grosvenor to BW, November 15, 1934. Gilbert Grosvenor files Yukon Expedition.

181. BW to Gilbert Grosvenor, November 21, 1934. Gilbert Grosvenor files Yukon Expedition.

182. BW to Gilbert Grosvenor, January 3, 1935. Gilbert Grosvenor files Yukon Expedition.

183. Gilbert Grosvenor to BW, January 16, 1935. Gilbert Grosvenor files Yukon Expedition.

184. *Ibid.*

185. *Ibid.*
186. Gilbert Grosvenor to L. S. Peck, January 24, 1935, Gilbert Grosvenor files Yukon Expedition.
187. BW, "National Geographic Society Yukon Expedition," n.d., BWC, 7, 11.
188. Tarr and Martin, "Glaciers and Glaciation," 154-55; see also Tarr and Martin, *Alaskan Glacier Studies*, 109.
189. *Ibid.*, 104.
190. Although Washburn's expedition was the first to attempt a crossing of the St. Elias Range, there are reports of significant penetrations into the range before 1935. See Rohn, "Survey and Opening Up of a Military Road," 780-84; Tarr and Martin, *Alaskan Glacier Studies*, 160.
191. BW, "National Geographic Society Yukon Expedition," 8; BW to NGS, March 1, 1935, 1-2, Gilbert Grosvenor files Yukon Expedition. The National Geographic Society," *Geographic News Bulletin,* Gilbert Grosvenor Files Yukon Expedition, March 8, 1935, 1.
192. Field, *Mountain Glaciers*, 225. It has now been established that the Bering Glacier, also located in the St. Elias Range, is the largest and longest glacier in North America; a complex glacier with a piedmont lobe and valley glacier segment. See Molnia and Post, "Holocene History of Bering Glacier," 87.
193. BW to NGS, Gilbert Grosvenor files Yukon Expedition, Gilbert Grosvenor Files Yukon Expedition, March 9, 1935, 1-2.
194. BW, "National Geographic Society Yukon Expedition," 33. King George V expressed "sincere appreciation for the compliment which the National Geographic Society Yukon Expedition" bestowed upon the crown. See John Simon to BW, one page laminated copy of

letter found in 1935 Yukon Expedition Diary, BWC, NGS Yukon Expedition, Box 2, file 1.
195. See Melville Grosvenor to BW, June 25, 1965, Mount Kennedy files 5021.182 F-1.
196. BW, "The Mapping of Mount Hubbard," 249-50.
197. *Ibid.*, 253-59.
198. Gottfried Konecny to BW, June 24, 1966 with attachment entitled *Mount Kennedy-Yukon Mapping Project, 1965/66.* Copy provided to author from BW included within Dr. Washburn's personal files.
199. BW, Kennedy, and Whittaker, "Canada's Mount Kennedy," 5.
200. Newman Bumstead to BW, Mt. Kennedy File 5021.182 F-1, NGS Archives.
201. NGS News Release, March 17, 1965. Mt. Kennedy File 5021.182 F-1, NGS Archives.
202. BW, Kennedy, and Whittaker, "Canada's Mount Kennedy," 5-33.
203. BW, "The Mapping of Mount Hubbard," 252-53.
204. BW, Kennedy, and Whittaker, "Canada's Mount Kennedy," 5-33.
205. *Ibid.*, 28.
206. BW, "The Mapping of Mount Hubbard," 253.
207. BW, Kennedy, and Whittaker, "Canada's Mount Kennedy," 6.
208. *Ibid.*, 9.
209. Melville Grosvenor to BW, June 25, 1965. Burr Franklin Award File 549-147. NGS Archives.
210. BW continued this practice of aerial reconnaissance and photographs in support of ground-based survey and climbing efforts throughout his career. BW, "National Geographic Society Yukon Expedition," 39.
211. BW, "National Geographic Society Yukon Expedition," D,12-13; BW to NGS, March 9, 1935, Gilbert Grosvenor files Yukon Expedition, 1-2.

212. BW, "National Geographic Society Yukon Expedition," 29-40.

213. BW, *Exploring the Unknown,* 65.

214. *Ibid.*

215. *Ibid.,* 68.

216. *Ibid.,* 70.

217. *Ibid.*

218. *Ibid.*

219. *Ibid.,* 73.

220. *Ibid.,* 75.

221. *Ibid.,* 77.

222. *Ibid.*

223. *Ibid.,* 77, 79.

224. *Ibid.,* 79.

225. *Ibid.,* 81.

226. John Simon to BW, BWC, NGS Yukon Expedition, Box 2, file 1.

227. Gilbert Grosvenor to BW, June 6, 1935, Gilbert Grosvenor Files, Yukon Expedition.

228. *National Geographic News Bulletin,* The NGS, June 28, 1935. Gilbert Grosvenor Files, NGS, Yukon Expedition.

229. BW to Gilbert Grosvenor, February 26, 1938, Gilbert Grosvenor files, Yukon Expedition.

230. See, for instance, Molnia and Post, "Holocene History of Bering Glacier," 87-92.

231. *Ibid.,* 98.

232. BW to Thomas Bagley Jr., 12 July, 1995; Thomas Bagley to BW, May 30, 1995, BWPP. BW and Terris Moore also made the first ascents of Mount Agnes, named by Col. James Bagley for his wife. However, as it is prohibited to name any geographic feature after a living person, the name was changed to Mount Marcus Baker.

233. BW to Gilbert Grosvenor, 13 January, 1936, Gilbert Grosvenor files Yukon Expedition.

234. BW, "Exploring Yukon's Glacial Stronghold," 715-748.

235. BW to Gilbert Grosvenor, January 3, 1935. Gilbert Grosvenor files Yukon Expedition.

236. BW to Gilbert Grosvenor, November 20, 1935, Gilbert Grosvenor files Yukon Expedition.

237. *Ibid.*

238. See Thrower, *Maps and Civilization,* 163.

239. On Lowell's views, see Doel, *Solar Systems Astronomy in America,* 6, 26-29.

240. Harvard University, *Harvard University Handbook: An Official Guide,* 82-84.

241. Fairchild Aviation, "A Complete College Course in Aerial Photography," 1-3, Harvard University Archives, HUF 418.400, Harvard University. The creation of the institute angered many Harvard geology faculty who believed Rice, a medical doctor, "bought" his rank of full professor. They also complained that he held such a title in a discipline in which he held no academic credentials. According to BW, contempt for Rice ran so deep that geology faculty refused to allow their students to enroll in geography classes that were supported by the Institute; personal communication, BW to Mike Sfraga, September 12, 1996. See for instance Smith, "Academic War Over the Field of Geography," 160-161. Through the later 1930s, and well into the 1940s, Harvard President James B. Conant disdained the discipline of geography, stating that "geography is not a university subject" (cited in Smith, "Academic War," 159); see also Livingstone, *The Geographical Tradition,* 304-12. Conant, a champion of "pure science," found little verifiable "science" within the social sciences. See Hershberg, *James Conant,* 94. Geography at Harvard was eliminated in 1948 and as a result, Hamilton Rice withdrew all funding for the Institute. See "Dr. Rice Ends Aid to Institute At

Harvard," *Boston Herald*, October 1951, p. 2; William F. Homer, "Harvard 'Unappreciative,' Dr. Rice Cancels Gift," *Boston Herald*, October 1951, p. 1, Harvard University Archives, HUF 418.400, Harvard University.

242. "Geographic News Bulletin," *National Geographic Society*, June 28, 1935.

243. Smith, *John Buchan,* 407.

244. Wood, "The Wood Yukon Expedition of 1935," 228-46.

245. The Department of Technical Training of the American Geographical Society had first introduced this technique in Labrador. See Forbes, "Surveying in Northern Labrador," 30-60; Forbes, "A Flight to Cape Chidley, 1935," 48-58.

246. Miller, *Progress Report of the Juneau Ice Field Research Project.* JIRP is still in operation today, having trained scores of professional glaciologists, the results of which can be seen in a plethora of published research accounts and substantial financial support for graduate student research. Over the years, JIRP has extensively used aerial transport and photography as well as the most advanced scientific equipment.

247. Sharp, *Living Ice,* 151. Washburn's photographs are used throughout this text; See for instance pages 31, 38, 72, 116, 137, 142. Thousands of Washburn's technical photographs have been published over the decades in hundreds of books, journals, and popular accounts. See for instance Shelton, *Geology Illustrated,* 211, 216-218, 223, 226; Dyson, *The World of Ice,* plates V, XIV, XV, XVII, XX; Sharp, *Glaciers,* 12, 64; Wahrhaftig, "The Alaska Range," Plate 1.

248. BW, "A Preliminary Report," 222. Geologist Dr. Troy Pewe believes Washburn's photographs provide an invaluable record of Alaska's glaciers from which their movement may be studied. Pewe, telephone interview with Mike Sfraga, Tucson, Arizona, January 28, 1996.

249. Bruce Molnia, in *Satellite Image Atlas of Glaciers of the World : U.S. Geological Survey Professional Paper 1386-K,* forthcoming. Interview with Mike Sfraga, October 24, 2003.

250. BW, taped interview with Mike Sfraga, June 18, 1992, Cambridge, Massachusetts.

251. Roberts, *Escape from Lucania.*

252. Rock*, Museum of Science, Boston,* 2.

253. *Ibid.*, 215.

254. BW, "How Bradford Washburn Became Director of the New England Museum of Natural History (Now Boston's Museum of Science) December 28, 1939." Memorandum sent to author and housed with BW's private papers.

255. *Ibid.*

256. *Ibid.*

257. In 1949, a new location along Boston's Charles River was purchased for a new museum facility. The New England Museum of Natural History was relocated to "Science Park" and its name changed to Boston's Museum of Science. See Rock, *Museum of Science, Boston,* 55.

258. *Ibid,* 23. BW retained his position of Instructor of Geography at Harvard until the outbreak of World War II.

259. BW, "How Bradford Washburn Became Director of the New England Museum of Natural History." See also Barbara Washburn and Lew Freedman, *The Accidental Adventurer.*

260. "The First Woman to Climb Difficult Mt. Bertha, Alaska," *The Illustrated London News*, August 16, 1941, 217-218. In 1912, Dora Keen had scaled Mt. Blackburn (16,286

feet), the highest point in the Wrangell Mountains. For an abbreviated discussion and reflection of this climb, see editors' note, "Mountain Climbing in Alaska: The First Expedition to Mt. Blackburn," *Appalachia*, June 15, 1995, 87-89.

261. BW, "The First Ascent of Mount Hayes," 3-7. In 1947 Barbara Washburn joined her husband on an expedition to Mount McKinley, on which she became the first woman to scale the peak.

Chapter 3

1. For a discussion of the military's efforts to train and equip U.S. servicemen in harsh environments during World War II, see Baxter, *Scientists Against Time.*

2. For a much broader discussion of the role of environment on human mortality, see McNeill, *Plagues and People.*

3. Ariev, "Fundamental Outlines.". See also Grattan, "Trench Foot," 169-77. It is reported that approximately 10,000 Greek soldiers suffered "mass freezing" in the mountains of Armenia while retreating from Babylon to the Black Sea.

4. Thatcher, *Military Journal of the American Revolution,* 127, 188.

5. Larrey, *Mémoires,* 1-2.

6. *Medical and Surgical History,* vol. 2; MacPherson, "The Russo-Japanese War," 242; Page, "Gangrene in War," 386-88.

7. Whayne and DeBakey, *Cold Injury, Ground Type,* 43.

8. *Ibid.,* 47. American Expeditionary Forces served also in Siberia, with clothing in use at the time at a number of Alaskan military garrisons. Other U.S. forces in Russia relied on equipment supplied by the British.

9. See also Chew, *The White Death*; Aleksander Moiseevich, *22 June, 1941*; Tanner, *The Winter War.*

10. Engle and Paananen, *The Winter War,* 9, 8.

11. *Ibid.,* 4.

12. Gregory, *Mountain and Arctic Warfare,* 102. The Finns employed tactics devised to attack specific targets by means of swift movement. *Sissi* combat relied on surprise attack in a limited area with hit and run tactics. *Motti* tactics relied on small teams of troopers surrounding the enemy in a ring of gunfire. In both cases, Finnish troops relied on their ability to move about in small numbers and to use the environment as an ally. See Center for Military History, *Effects of Climate on Combat,* 65.

13. Engle and Paananen, *The Winter War,* 43.

14. Gregory, *Mountain and Arctic Warfare,* 102.

15. Nikita Khruschev, quoted in Engle and Pannnanen, *The Winter War,* 122.

16. Robert Bates, taped interview with Mike Sfraga, Exeter, New Hampshire, July 15,1992.

17. Public Information Officer Headquarters, *The Army's Role,* 26-40.

18. Nielson, *An Interpretive Survey,* 6, 90. The acronym WAMCATS was used for the Washington-Alaska Military Communications and Telegraph System.

19. *Ibid.,* 84-85.

20. Pitkin, *Quartermaster Equipment,* 1.

21. War Department Quartermaster Corps, *Specifications No. 1171,* 3-11.

22. Pitkin, *Quartermaster Equipment,* 1.

23. *Ibid.,* 9.

24. War Department, *Basic Field Manual,* 4-10. The manual does, however, provide a detailed discussion by Dr. Vilhjalmur Stefansson on the construction of domed snow houses and Nordic ski techniques.

25. House, "Mountain Equipment," 225.

26. Historical sources on Roosevelt and the United States' entry into World War II are vast; for an introduction to the literature see Dallek, *Franklin D. Roosevelt and American Foreign Policy;* Leuchtenburn, *Franklin D. Roosevelt and the New Deal.*

27. Moore, taped interview with Mike Sfraga, Cambridge, Massachusetts, January 15, 1993. For additional information on Henry Stimson, see Morison, *Turmoil and Tradition.*

28. The Quartermaster Corps will hereafter be referred to as QMC. These efforts were among dozens of research programs launched by the government at this time. See Owens, "The Counterproductive Management of Science," 515-76. There is a general void yet to be filled in the literature pertaining to the importance and role of the OSRD. Owens points out that "OSRD has not attracted the attention it deserves despite a growing volume of studies of wartime and Cold War Science." *Ibid.*, 516-17.

29. House, "Mountain Equipment," 226. Robert Bates was a member of numerous expeditions to Alaska under the direction of BW, including Mount Crillon in 1933, the 1935 National Geographic Society's Yukon Expedition, and the first ascent of Mount Lucania in 1937.

30. Bates, taped nterview with Mike Sfraga, Exeter, New Hampshire, July 15, 1992.

31. Pitkin, *Quartermaster Equipment*, 3.

32. Bates, taped interview with Mike Sfraga, Exeter, New Hampshire, July 15, 1992.

33. Langer and Gleason, *The Undeclared War,* 31. The 1940 Tripartite Agreement signed by Japan, Germany, and Italy mandated the declaration of war against the U.S. by the latter two nations.

34. Center for Military History, *Effects of Climate*, 18.

35. Carter, "Mountain Intelligence," 245.

36. Moore, taped interview with Mike Sfraga, Cambridge, Massachusetts, January 15, 1993. As author Ben Read suggests, Terris Moore had "forgotten more about Alaska's mountains than most of us will ever be privileged to learn." See Read, "An Interview," 16.

37. Montgomery, *In Search of L. L. Bean,* 24-25.

38. For a discussion of problems with limited materials for adequate military clothing, see Risch, *U.S. Army in World War II,* 58-74.

39. House, "Mountain Equipment ," 225.

40. Stefansson details his theories in *The Friendly Arctic.*

41. BW, taped interview with Mike Sfraga, Boston, Massachusetts, June 18, 1992.

42. Bates, taped interview with Mike Sfraga, Exeter, New Hampshire, July 15, 1992.

43. Pitkin, *Quartermaster Equipment,* 5.

44. *Ibid.*, 227.

45. BW, "Personal Equipment," 235. For the unique clothing requirements of the AAF, see also BW, quoted in Purtee, *Development of Army Air Force Clothing* (Air Technical Service Command), 4. (Hereafter cited as ATSC.)

46. BW, "Personal Equipment," 227.

47. *Ibid.*

48. Simon Buckner to Commanding General, Ninth Corps Area, quoted in Pitkin, *Quartermaster Equipment,* 11.

49. Sweeting, *Combat Flying Clothing,* 2.

50. BW, "A Report and Recommendations on the Emergency Equipment of the Army

Air Corps," March 1942, in Pitkin, *Quartermaster Equipment,* 136.

51. BW, interview with Mike Sfraga, Denver, December 5, 1993. See also Pitkin, *Quartermaster Equipment,* 136.

52. *Ibid.*, 137.

53. Major General W. G. Kilner to Brigadier General H.C. Pratt, March 19, 1932; Brigadier General H. C. Pratt to Major General W. G. Kilner, April 7, 1932, in Purtee, *ATSC,* 1.

54. *Report of the U.S. Army Alaskan Test Expedition, 1942,* vol. 2, plates 38, 151, 152, 77, 109, 100.

55. *Report of the U.S. Army Alaskan Test Expedition*, Vol. 1, ii. The Fourth Armored Division conducted Field exercises in the early winter of 1942 at Pine Camp, New York. However, the equipment tested was developed primarily for armored divisions and did not include mountain or Arctic gear. Still, these maneuvers marked the first wartime, large-scale field testing of winter equipment by the QMC. Equipment developed specifically for ground troops engaged in mountain and Arctic terrain was tested in the late spring of that same year on Mt. Rainier in Washington State. Robert Bates, taped interview with Mike Sfraga, Exeter, New Hampshire, July 15, 1992; Albert Jackman, taped interview with Mike Sfraga, Denver, December 6, 1993.

56. BW, interview with Mike Sfraga, Denver, Colorado, December 5, 1993. See also BW, *Association with the Material Center.* See also Pitkin, *Quartermaster Equipment,* 137.

57. Bates, "Mt. McKinley, 1942," 2.

58. Moore, *Mt. McKinley: The Pioneer Climbs,* 161.

59. Albert Jackman, interview with Mike Sfraga, Denver, December 6, 1993. Jackman was a member of the 1942 Mount Rainier Expedition as

well as the 1942 U.S. Army Alaskan Test Expedition.

60. *Report of the U.S. Army Alaskan Test Expedition*, vol. 1, iii.

61. *Ibid.*, 2; BW, taped interview with Mike Sfraga, Boston, June 18, 1992; BW, *United States Army Air Forces.*

62. *Report of the U.S. Army Alaskan Test Expedition*, vol. 1, 11. See also War Department to Lieutenant Colonel Frank G. Marchman, May 22, 1942, Albert Jackman Papers, 10th Mountain Division Collection, Western History Department, Denver Public Library.

63. Walter Wood used the airplane in support of previous scientific expeditions along the Canadian side of the Wrangell-St. Elias Range in the Yukon Territory. See Wood, "The Wood Yukon Expedition of 1935;" Wood, "Parachuting of Expedition Supplies," 36-55; Wood, "Report of the Wood Yukon Expedition," Section II, TDS, 5-10, 12,15, 37-43, Albert Jackman File, 10th Mountain Division Collection.

64. BW, "Over the Roof of the Continent," 78-98.

65. BW, *Mount McKinley Alaska: 1942,* D, 1942, 6, Box 2. BWC.

66. *Ibid.*, 9. On June 3, 1942 the Japanese Imperial Air Force bombed the small Alaskan community of Dutch Harbor. See *The New York Times*, "Japanese Bomb Dutch Harbor, Alaska, Twice," June 4, 1942, 1. For thorough review of the Aleutian campaign, see Garfield, *The Thousand Mile War.*

67. Frank Been, "Superintendent's Narrative: Supplemental Monthly Report, January 1941-1943," June 10, 1942, Superintendent Records, Denali National Park and Preserve Archives, Denali, Alaska.

68. Bates, "Mount McKinley, 1942," 5.

69. BW, "Mount McKinley Alaska: 1942," 55.

70. For a thorough analysis of use of parachutes in troop deployment and supply during both world wars, see Sweeting, *Combat Flying Equipment,* 73-119. For a discussion of the problems associated with aerial supply during this expedition, see BW, "Mount McKinley Alaska: 1942," 6.

71. Read, "An Interview," 16.

72. Bates, "Mount McKinley, 1942," 10.

73. Moore, *Mount McKinley: The Pioneer Climbs,* 168.

74. BW, "Mount McKinley Alaska: 1942," 78. BW's climbing account has been documented by himself, Robert Bates, Terris Moore and others. Citations describing this climb can be found in this chapter's footnotes as well as the bibliography. It is worth noting that since Washburn's mountaineering accomplishments have been discussed in numerous publications through his career, they are not discussed in great detail here.

75. Bates, "Mount McKinley, 1942," 11.

76. *Ibid.,* 13.

77. *Report of the U.S. Army Alaskan Test Expedition, 1942,* vol. 4, 107, 118, plate 161.

78. BW, "Mount McKinley Alaska: 1942," 93.

79. *Ibid.,* 95, 107.

80. BW, *Alaska: August 25, 1942 - March 14,1943,* D, 11, Box 2, BWC, Elmer E. Rasmusen Library, University of Alaska Fairbanks.

81. *Ibid.,* 13.

82. *Ibid.,* 14.

83. BW, interview with Mike Sfraga, December 6, 1993. See also Purtee, *ATSC,* 5; Pitkin, *Quartermaster Equipment,* 142.

84. BW, *Alaska: August 25, 1942-March 14, 1943,* 15.

85. *Ibid.,* 20.

86. *Ibid.,* 26.

87. *Ibid.,* 30.

88. *Ibid.,* 32.

89. *Ibid.*

90. *Ibid.,* 33.

91. BW, phone conversation with Mike Sfraga, January 10, 1997. Because of the sensitivity of the situation, BW did not document this event. This information was shared with the author.

92. BW, *Alaska: August 25, 1942 - March 14, 1943,* 39. BW was appointed Special Liaison between the Quartermaster General and the Commanding General of the Alaska Defense Command, Simon Buckner. Later meetings were convened at Wright Field to discuss the use of several types of clothing and materials. As Pitkin points out, military officials who stated that such items were "not entirely adequate over a wide range of environmental conditions" supported Washburn's assertion that significant problems existed with AAF cold-weather clothing. Pitkin, *Quartermaster Equipment,* 143. BW believed that a separate research and development program, staffed by qualified experts with direct input from the combat troops, would be the only practical solution to the AAF's clothing and equipment problems. BW, interview with Mike Sfraga, December 6, 1993, Denver.

93. Loyal Davis to Brigadier General Paul Hawley, Chief Surgeon, E.T.O.U.S.A., February 18, 1943, Loyal Davis personal papers, hereafter cited as LDPP. Dr. Davis placed a great deal of personal correspondence regarding this issue with Bradford BW, who graciously allowed me access to these personal files. Davis was the first to identify high altitude frostbite, see Davis et al., "High Altitude Frostbite," 561-75. Davis was also interested in the identification of pathological

processes of frostbite and the development of successful treatments. Although frostbite was well documented at the time, the exact physiology was still to be identified.

94. *Ibid.* The Aero Medical Laboratory (AML) at Wright Field studied the effects and causes of cold on the human body. For a review of the AML's history and mission, see Sweeting, *Combat Flying Equipment*, 3-20. In June of 1942, the NRC began a review of research programs pertaining to human physiology and the development of effective military clothing for various theaters of war. A subcommittee, composed of members of the Harvard Fatigue Laboratory, the Medical Research Laboratory at Fort Knox, Office of the Air Surgeon, the Surgeon General of the Army, and others studied these issues. See for instance Newburgh, *Physiology of Heat Regulation*.

95. Lt. Col. Loyal Davis to Chief Surgeon, Brigadier General Paul Hawley, ETO, August 31, 1943, LDPP.

96. Davis, *From One Surgeon's Notebook* (C.C. Thomas, 1967), 121-22, LDPP.

97. Whayne and DeBakey, *Cold Injury, Ground Type,* 130-32.

98. *Ibid.,* 132.

99. *Ibid.,* 143.

100. BW, interview with Mike Sfraga, December 6, 1993, Denver; BW, *Alaska: March 15, 1943-November 14,* 1945, D, 39, Box 2, BWC.

101. [Anonymously] BW and Henry Field, "Report on A.A.F. Material Center, Wright Field," August 30, 1943, Army Air Force File OF 25-U, Franklin D. Roosevelt Collection, Franklin D. Roosevelt Library, Hyde Park, New York. Neither BW nor Field retained a copy of the

memorandum, to preserve their anonymity, but the author was able to find the original document in the Franklin D. Roosevelt Collection. I would like to thank Mr. Raymond Teichman, Supervisory Archivist for his assistance. BW makes cursory reference to the memorandum in his wartime diary, only after the document had been delivered to the president, and even then such a reference is cryptic. See Henry Field to BW, April 20, 1981. This and subsequent correspondence between BW, Field, and Davis has been given to Mike Sfraga by BW for use in this study. Hereafter, such correspondence will be cited as BWPP. See also BW, *Alaska March 15-November 14, 1943.*

102. Dr. Loyal Davis to BW, April 28, 1981, LDPP.

103. BW to Loyal Davis, March 31, 1981, BWPP; BW, *Alaska: March 15, 1943 - November 14, 1945,* 96.

104. *Ibid.,* 100-101.

105. *Ibid.,* 103.

106. *Ibid.,* 105.

107. *Ibid.*; BW to Loyal Davis, March 31,1981. Washburn's interest in the subject of cold injury and frostbite continued well after the war. See for instance BW, "Frostbite," 974-89.

108. *Ibid.*

109. BW, *Alaska: August 15, 1943-November 14, 1945,* 106.

110. Franklin D. Roosevelt to Henry Hopkins, 28 September 1943. Army Air Force File OF 25-U, Franklin D. Roosevelt Collection.

111. Robert Lovett to Henry Hopkins, October 1, 1943. Army Air Force File OF 25-U, Franklin D. Roosevelt Collection.

112. *Ibid.*

113. Sweeting, *Combat Flying Equipment,* 10.

114. *Ibid.* General Arnold witnessed firsthand the degree to which

American flyers were suffering from frostbite during his visit to England. As a result, he placed all AAF clothing research and development under the personal supervision of Major General Charles Branshaw, Commanding General, Material Command. Branshaw then selected Gagge to direct the new AAF Clothing Section.

115. BW, *Alaska: March 15, 1943 - November 14, 1945*, 121.
116. *Ibid.*, 136.
117. *Ibid.*, 125.
118. Purtee, *ATSC*, 7, 9.
119. Whayne and DeBakey, *Cold Injury, Ground Type*, 132.
120. Purtee, *ATSC*, 15.
121. Purtee, *ATSC*, 16.
122. *Ibid.*
123. BW, *Alaska: March 15, 1943-November 14, 1945*, 120.
124. BW, interview with Mike Sfraga, January 10, 1997.
125. *Ibid.*
126. BW, interview with Mike Sfraga, December 6, 1993, Denver.
127. BW to Henry Field, April 17, 1981, BWPP.
128. BW, interview with Purtee, in *ATSC*, 17.
129. *Ibid.*, 34.
130. Chief, Experimental Engineering Section to Continental Mills, Inc., June 24, 1940, in, Purtee, *ATSC*, 35.
131. Memorandum EXP-M-54-653-18, July 24, 1940 in *Ibid.*, 36.
132. *Ibid.*
133. *Ibid.*, 37-38.
134. Frank L. Walton, Deputy Chief, Textile, Clothing and Leather Branch, War Production Board to Colonel W. F. Volandt, AAF, November 2, 1942, in Purtee, *ATSC*, 39.
135. Field tests of shearling and other AAF clothing were carried out in Alaska, Ladd Field, under the command of Colonel Gaffney during the winter of 1942-43. Gaffney found that although shearling provided adequate protection in extreme winter conditions, it should be replaced for AAF personnel with a less bulky garment. See *Report of Cold Weather Test Detachment*, 111-13. The reports recommended strongly the use of alpaca with wind-proof overgarments for wind protection, added warmth, and flexibility, 114-15.

136. Purtee, *ATSC*, 41.
137. Major General W. H. Frank to Commanding General, AAF, August 4, 1943, in *Ibid.*, 42.
138. BW, interview with Purtee, February 17, 1945, in *Ibid.*, 54.
139. Lt. Stewart Seass, interview with Purtee, February 19, 1945, in *Ibid.*, 55.
140. Purtee, *ATSC*, 60, 59; *Report of Cold Weather Test Detachment*, 114-15.
141. Whayne and DeBakey, *Cold Injury, Ground Type*, 132.
142. Gray, *Science at War*, 224-26, 239-43.
143. BW to Loyal Davis, March 31, 1981, BWPP.
144. BW, "Alaskan Field Test—U.S. Air Force Emergency Equipment and Food: October 17-December 9, 1944," D, i, BWC.
145. T.W Cummins, "Preliminary Narrative Report – Accident 5738,"2, September 28, 1944. Memorandum to D.J. King, BWPP.
146. *Ibid.*, 1.
147. *Ibid.*, 2.
148. *Ibid.*
149. *Ibid.*
150. *Anchorage Daily Times*, September 20, 1944.
151. BW, "The First Ascent of Mount Deception," 94.
152. Cummins, 1.
153. *Ibid.*, 4.

154. The nineteen missing passengers were listed as follows: Roy Proebstle, Pilot, Peter Blivens, Co-Pilot, Private James George, Flight Clerk, Major Rudolph Bostelman, First Lieutenant Orlando Buck, Private Anthony Kasper, Technical Four Grade Maurice Gibbs, Sergeant William Backus, Technical Fifth Grade Edward Stoering, Corporal Charles Dykema, Private First Class Clifford Phillips, Private Howard Pevey, Private Charles Ellis, Chief Warrant Officer Floyd Appleman, Private First Class Alfred Madison, Lieutenant Athel Gill, Seaman First Class Bernard Ortego, and Mr. Carl Harris. War Department, Bureau of Public Relations, Press Branch. 19 "Reported Missing Aboard ATC Plane in Alaska." October 4, 1944, BWPP.

155. Cummins, 4.

156. *Ibid.*, 3.

157. Cummins, 4.

158. *Ibid.*

159. Letter to Mrs. Peter Blevins from Harry Gray, via Congressman Buck, October 21, 1944, BWPP.

160. Grant Pearson, Mount Deception Diary, 1, BWPP.

161. Cummins, 5.

162. *Ibid.*

163. War Department memo to Congressmen Buck, September 28, 1944. Memorandum sent to author by BW.

164. Pearson, 1.

165. Lindley "Mt. McKinley," 33-44.

166. Pearson, 1.

167. *Ibid.*

168. BW, Diary: "June 4, 1944—March 10, 1945." BWPP.

169. BW, "Alaskan Field Test Diary, October 17-December 9, 1944," 1.

170. *Ibid.*, 1.

171. Bates, "Mt. McKinley, 1942."

172. Pearson, 1.

173. "Report of U.S.A.A.F. Expedition to the Scene of the C-47 Crash." December 7, 1944, 10. BWPP. A copy of the report was given to the author by BW.

174. BW Diary, "June 4, 1944 - March 10, 1945,"58-59.

175. USAAF, 31.

176. BW Diary, "June 4 1944 - March 10 1945," 60.

177. *Ibid.*

178. *Ibid.*, 63.

179. BW, "First Ascent of Mount Deception," 96.

180. *Ibid.*

181. *Ibid.*, 95-96.

182. Congressman Buck to Mount Deception families. December 1, 1944. Walker private papers and included in BWPP.

183. Interview with Nancy Buck Ransom, daughter of Congressmen Buck. Anchorage, Alaska, December 19, 1994.

184. *Ibid.*

185. BW Diary, "June 4 1944 - March 10 1945," 65.

186. C-47 Accident Final Report, United States Army Air Force, 1945, 17, BWPP.

187. BW, interview with Mike Sfraga, September, 19, 1994.

188. C-47 Accident Final Report, United States Army Air Force, 1945, 17, BWPP.

189. BW, "First Ascent of Mount Deception," 97.

190. *Ibid.*, 96.

191. BW, "Alaskan Field Test Diary, October 17-December 9, 1944," 16-17.

192. *Ibid.*

193. *Ibid.*

194. *Ibid.*

195. BW, "First Ascent of Mount Deception," 100.

196. BW, "Alaskan Field Test Diary, October 17-December 9, 1944," 23.

197. *Ibid.*

198. BW to Mike Sfraga, personal correspondence, July 15, 2003.
199. *Ibid.*
200. *Ibid.*
201. C-47 Accident Final Report, 20.
202. Interview with BW, September 18, 1994.
203. Pearson, 5.
204. *Ibid.*
205. *Ibid.*, 6.
206. *Ibid.*
207. BW, "First Ascent of Mount Deception," 104.
208. A subsequent survey by BW placed the height of the mountain at 11,826 feet.
209. BW, "First Ascent of Mount Deception," 105.
210. *Ibid.*, 105.
211. BW, "Alaskan Field Test Diary, October 17-December 9, 1944," 54.
212. BW Diary, "June 4 1944 - March 10 1945," 77.
213. Interview with BW, September 18, 1994.
214. Lowrey. "Tragedy of the C-47," 10.
215. Pearson, 7.
216. Congressman Buck to Mount Deception families, January 8, 1945. BWPP.
217. *Alaskan Field Test of AAF Emergency and Survival Equipment: March to May 1945* (Dayton: Air Technical Service Command, 1945), 21-138, BWPP.
218. BW, "Personal Equipment," 243.
219. BW to Mr. and Mrs. Henry B. Washburn, September 1, 1945, BWPP. Great strides had been made by 1945 in equipment for AAF flyers, and for ground troops as well. Although research continued after the war on such issues, with the outbreak of the Korean War the United States once again faced cold-weather clothing problems. During the winter of 1950, over four thousand soldiers experienced significant cold injury and were transported to a special Cold Injury Section at Osaka Hospital. See Orr and Fainer, *Cold Injuries in Korea,* 2.
220. BW, "A New Map of Mount McKinley, Alaska," 160.
221. *Ibid.*
222. *Ibid.*, 161. See Military Engineer, "Elevation of Mt. McKinley," 384.

Chapter 4

1. Rock, *Museum of Science,* 26.
2. *Ibid.*, 31.
3. *Ibid.*
4. *Ibid.*, 31-32.
5. *Ibid.*, 27-28.
6. *Ibid.*, 32-33.
7. BW has published a wide range of popular and scholarly articles. His work has appeared in such popular publications as the *National Geographic Magazine, Life* and the *American Alpine Journal.* More scholarly work on the subject of morainic banding has appeared in the *Bulletin of the American Geological Society of America* (co-authored with Richard Goldthwait), *The Royal Geographical Journal,* and the *Dennison University Bulletin* (an article on surveying co-authored with Harvard geologist Kirtley Mather). BW has also worked with a number of the world's most celebrated scientists and cartographers, including Harvard astrophysicist Harlow Shapley, University of Chicago physicist Marcel Schein, and renowned cartographer Erwin Raisz.
8. BW, *On High.*
9. Leslie, *The Cold War and American Science,* 1.
10. Sapolsky, "Academic Science and the Military," 379.
11. See Moore, *Mount McKinley, The Pioneer Climbs*; and Brown, *A History of the Denali-Mount McKinley Region,* especially 1-58.

12. The significance of William Field's glacial research in Southeast Alaska in the early twentieth century and his influence on BW was discussed in chapter two.

13. In 1866 Boston scientist'and naturalist William Dall explored the interior of Alaska, then Russian-America. With English artist Frederick Wymper, Dall noted vast mountain range in the territory's interior. He named this extensive chain of glaciated peaks the "Alaskan Range," now referred to as the Alaska Range. See Dall, *Alaska and Its Resources,* 286.

14. Wahrhaftig, "The Alaska Range," 48. See also Field, *Mountain Glaciers,* 574; Thomas Griffiths, "Glacial Geomorphology," 331-36.

15. Elias, *The Ice-Age History,* 61-62. For a review of early glacial observations along the Alaska Range, see Brooks, "A Reconnaissance in the Tanana and White River Basins," 425-94; Brooks, "Mountain Exploration," 1-22; Brooks, "The Mount McKinley Region," 125-29.

16. Elias, *The Ice-Age History*, 64-70.

17. In sharp contrast, Native Alaskans had long traveled ancestral trails throughout the Alaska Range. See Kari, "The Tenada-Denali-Mount McKinley Controversy," 349.

18. For a discussion of Native typonomy related to the McKinley region, as well as the long-standing controversy regarding such issues, see Kari, *ibid.* 347-51. The most popular and perhaps most accepted indigenous name for the peak is Denali. See also Wickersham, "The Creation of Denali," 1-10.

19. George Vancouver, *Voyages of Discovery,* 210-11.

20. See for instance Farquhar, "The Exploration and First Ascents of Mount McKinley," 95; Moore, *Mount McKinley, The Pioneer Climbs*, 1.

21. Wrangell, *Statistische und Ethnographische Nachrichten.* For a description of Glazunov's reference to Mount McKinley and ensuing expedition, see 137-60. Wrangell's map, which identifies for the first time the location of Mount McKinley, Mount Foraker, and the Alaska Range, is on 322. I thank Dr. Terris Moore for assistance in the translation of this document and for detailed discussions related to this topic. Among other explorations in the McKinley region, C. Grewingk included the Alaska Range, referred to then as the Tehigmit Mountains, on a map published in the 1850s. See Grewingk, "Beitrage," 24.

22. Brooks, *The Mount McKinley Region,* 24. Among the early explorers of this region were a small group of men including Alfred Mayo and Arthur Harper. The latter was the father of the first man to reach the top of Mount McKinley as a member of Hudson Stuck's 1913 expedition. See Stuck, *The Ascent of Denali.*

23. Moore, *Mount McKinley, The Pioneer Climbs,* 8.

24. Allen, *Report of an Expedition,* 69.

25. Spurr, "A Reconnaissance in Southeastern Alaska," 95; Brooks, *The Mount McKinley Region*, 25.

26. William Dickey, "Discoveries in Alaska," *New York Sun,* Sunday, January 24,1897, reprinted version in *American Alpine Journal* (1951-1953). For a specific reference to the height of the mountain, see 131. Dickey's map indicating the location and height of McKinley is reprinted in Moore, *Mount McKinley: The Pioneer Climbs,* 16.

27. *Ibid.* As previously noted, a controversy continues to rage over the appropriate name for Mount McKinley. As linguist James Kari points out, Alaska Native peoples have long referred to the mountain by several traditional names. In

addition to Mount McKinley, the peak possesses another "official" name, bestowed upon it in 1965. With the death of British statesman Sir Winston Churchill, President Lyndon Johnson honored the former Prime Minister of England by naming the twin summits of the mountain "Churchill Peaks." This little-known fact can be seen in current USGS maps of the mountain, which place "Churchill Peaks" between the two summits of the massif; Korsmo and Sfraga, "Churchill Peaks," 131-38. See Office of the White House Press Secretary, press release, October 23, 1965, Lyndon Baines Johnson Collection, file PA2/Winston Churchill, Lyndon Baines Johnson Library, Austin.

28. Sherwood, *Exploration of Alaska,* 171-72; Rabbitt, *Minerals, Lands and Geology,* 280-83.

29. *Ibid.*; Brooks, *The Mount McKinley Region,* 27.

30. Eldridge, "A Reconnaissance on the Sushitna Basin," 8. Muldrow's diary refers to Mount McKinley by its Russian name, Mt. Bulshia (also known on several Russian maps as Bulshia Gora, meaning either "big mountain" or "great mountain"). His personal notes indicate the following initial computation of the mountain's height: "Located Mt. Bulshia. Ela. over 19,000 feet. Ela." See Henry Lowndes Muldrow, *U.S. Geological Survey Expedition to Alaska 1898.* The diary was given to BW by the Muldrow family and is included in the BWPP. In the same year, a USGS party led by Josiah Spurr made the first crossing of the Alaska Range, on which Spurr noted: "marvelous-appearing mountains . . . I would not be surprised if they were among the highest in the world." Many years later Spurr recalled the

exciting fact that his expedition had "seen the highest mountain in North America (McKinley), the position and altitude of which were determined during the same summer by the Eldridge-Muldrow party." See Spurr and Spurr, *The Log of the Kuskokwim,* 23.

31. The War Department dispatched Lieutenant F. W. Glenn and USGS field geologist William Mendenhall to Alaska, where they carried out numerous surveys along the Alaska Range. See Mendenhall, "A Reconnaissance," 265-340. Lieutenant J. Castner was also under orders to explore various areas near McKinley; see Castner, "A Story of Hardship," 686-709. In 1899, Lieutenant Joseph Herron, in search of an all-American route to the Klondike, explored the unknown region between the areas traversed by Spurr (along the Kuskokwim) and by Allen (along the Tanana) and produced a map detailing the area he covered. See Herron, *Explorations.* On this expedition, Herron named Mount Foraker, the tall peak adjacent to Mount McKinley. See Farquhar, "Naming Alaska's Mountains," 211-12.

32. Brooks, "An Exploration to Mount McKinley," 407-25. Brooks' reference to first setting foot on the mountain is noted on 420-21: "My objective was a shoulder of the mountain about 10,000 feet high." However, he soon was convinced that it would be "foolhardy, alone as I was, to attempt to reach the shoulder for which I was headed, at 7,500 feet I turned and cautiously retraced my steps, finding the descent to bare ground more perilous than the ascent." At his highest point, Brooks left a record of the ascent: "On a prominent cliff near the base of the glacier on which

I had turned back I built a cairn, in which I buried a cartridge shell from my pistol, containing a brief account of the journey, together with a roster of the party." This note was found nearly five decades later by John Reed. See Reed, "Record of the First Approach to Mt. McKinley," 78-83. Brooks prepared a detailed sketch map of the Alaska Range and the expedition's route, and it soon became an invaluable resource for subsequent USGS parties and several groups of adventurous mountaineers. Brooks's map is in "An Exploration to Mount McKinley," 410.

33. Brooks, "The Mount McKinley Region, Alaska," 29; Brooks and Raeburn, "Plan for Climbing Mt. McKinley," 30-35.

34. Eleven expeditions attempted McKinley during the decade following Brooks' article. None of the parties attempting the mountain from the south succeeded, while three of the four that came from the north established a route that led to the first ascent in 1913.

35. Wickersham, *Old Yukon: Tales, Trails and Trials,* 203-320. The north wall, on which Wickersham climbed, has long been known to mountaineers as the "Wickersham Wall."

36. For an account of Cook's 1903 expedition, see Cook, "America's Unconquered Mountain," parts I and II. The 1903 expedition is also described in Cook, *To the Top of the Continent,* 1-91. See also the articles in *Outing Magazine* by Dunn, "Across the Forbidden Tundra," "Into the Mists of Mt. McKinley," "Storm-Wrapped on Mt. McKinley," "Highest on Mt. McKinley," and "Home by Ice and by Swimming from Mt. McKinley." His highly critical account of Dr. Cook's leadership and climbing skills is

documented in Dunn, *Shameless Diary of an Explorer.*

37. In addition to citations in previous chapters, including recent discussions about Dr. Cook's claim to both the North Pole and the summit of Mount McKinley, see his *To the Top of the Continent,* "The Conquest of Mt. McKinley," and *My Attainment of the Pole* See also Browne, *The Conquest of Mount McKinley,* especially 68-72; BW, Carter, and Carter, "Dr. Cook and Mount McKinley," 1-30. Bryce, *Cook & Peary.* Also the BBC documentary *Mountain Men: The Mystery of Mount McKinley* (London: British Broadcasting Corporation, 2001) for which Dr. Michael Sfraga served as on-screen historian.

38. Expeditions around this time brought back rich information about Mt. McKinley and its environment. The Sourdough Expedition of 1910 scaled McKinley's shorter north peak (*New York Sun*, "Four Climb Mt. McKinley," April 13, 1910, p. 1-2). The expedition's success was questioned due to the rather exaggerated claims of the team's organizer Thomas Lloyd, who himself did not reach the north peak; see Rusk, "On the Trail of Dr. Cook," 62. See also Cole, *The Sourdough Expedition.* In 1910, an expedition led by the Oregon Mountaineering Club, the Mazamas, attempted to retrace Dr. Cook's 1906 expedition to p[rove the truth of Cook's claim. The team dismissed his ascent as impossible. See Rusk, "On the Trail of Dr. Cook." Also in 1910, Belmore Browne and Herchel Parker, both members of Dr. Cook's 1906 expedition, returned to the mountain and photographed a small peak nearly twenty miles distant from the true summit of McKinley, matching this to the one that Dr.

Cook offered as "the summit." This photo is reproduced in Browne, *The Conquest,* 122a. Two expeditions attempted the mountain in 1912, neither attaining the summit; see Browne, *The Conquest.* The *Fairbanks Daily Times Expedition,* led by Ralph Cairns, also failed to reach the summit. See *Fairbanks Daily Times,* "Time's Expedition Enroute M'Kinley," p. 1; Cairns "Hazards." The first ascent of McKinley is documented in Stuck, *The Ascent of Denali.*

39. Allen Carpè to Francis Farquhar, January 10, 1932, quoted in Moore, *Mount McKinley, The Pioneer Climbs,* 122.

40. Rossi, *Cosmic Rays,* 2. In 1912, Hess ascended to 16,000 feet in a hot air balloon and recorded, with electroscopes, data indicating "radiation of very great penetrating power enters our atmosphere from above." Quoted in *ibid.* The literature on cosmic rays is quite extensive. See Sekido and Elliot, *Early History of Cosmic Rays* and Laprince-Ringuet, *Cosmic Rays.*

41. Rossi, *Cosmic Rays,* 8-9. Unlike Hess, Millikan employed unmanned sounding balloons equipped with electroscopes that recorded the radiation bombardment in Earth's upper atmosphere. It should be noted that Millikan's techniques were later refined and employed by German physicist Erich Regener, which allowed for more accurate readings. For a historical overview see also DeVorkin, *Science With a Vengeance,* 15.

42. See *New York Times,* "Lindley Expedition Scales Mt. M'Kinley; Descending, Finds Carpè and Koven Dead; Young Scientists Fell Into a Crevasse," May 17, 1932, p. 1; *New York Times,* "Carpe, Koven Died In a Feat of Daring," May 18, 1932, p.1, 12. Beckwith, "The Mt. McKinley

Cosmic Ray Expedition, 1932," 45-68; "'Cosmic Ray' Party Comes to Grief," *Park Service Bulletin* 2, no. 4, June, 1932.

43. Compton, "A Geographic Study," 387. In addition to Carpe's Mount McKinley Expedition in Alaska, other high altitude networks were set up around the world, such as Colorado, Switzerland, Peru, Mexico, Hawaii, South Africa, Panama, and New Zealand. *Ibid.,* 388. For additional discussion of the Latitude Effect, see Compton, "Cosmic Rays as Electrical Particles," 1119-20, and Rossi, *Cosmic Rays,* 73-75. According to A. M. Hillas, 1932 was "selected as an international magnetic year. See Hillas, *Cosmic Rays,* 14.

44. Compton, "A Geographic Study," 387-403; Kevles, *The Physicists,* 240-41.

45. DeVorkin, *Science With a Vengeance,* 15, 247.

46. Jay Bonafield to Paul Hollister, January 29, 1947. BWC, Operation White Tower, box 3, file 1 (hereafter referred to as OWTF).

47. Paul Hollister to BW, October 7, 1946, *Ibid.*

48. BW, *Operation White Tower,* undated post expedition report, OWTF, file 6, 1.

49. Paul Hollister to Roy Larsen, October 1, 1946, OWTF. Ullman, *The White Tower.*

50. BW, *Operation White Tower,* 1.

51. Editor's note, Ullman, *The White Tower.*

52. *Ibid.*

53. Paul Hollister to BW, October 7, 1946, OWTF.

54. *Ibid.*

55. BW to Paul Hollister, October 14, 1946, OWTF.

56. *Ibid.*

57. Dorrit Hoffleit, "Two Days and Thirteen Hours," December 22, 1946, 1-2, Dorrit Hoffleit private

papers, quoted in David DeVorkin, *Science With a Vengeance,* 249.

58. Dupree, *Science and the Federal Government,* 374. ONR support was secured through Navy contract N6ori, Task Order XVIII. See Carr, Schein and Barbour, "Cosmic-Ray Investigation on Mt. McKinley,"1419.

59. BW to Mike Sfraga, telephone conversation, December 5, 1996; BW, "Mapping Mt. McKinley," unpublished keynote address presented at the Alaska Surveyors Conference, Anchorage, Alaska, March 11, 1991, 10. BWPP. Sapolsky, "Academic Science and the Military," 386. The Office of Naval Research was the conduit through which a considerable amount of scientific research was funded during the years immediately following World War II. For example, Sapolsky points out that even the "Atomic Energy Commission then used ONR as its preferred mechanism for the support of university-based research" (*Ibid.*). Moreover, ONR played a key role throughout the post-war years in establishing models for collaborative scientific research programs between universities and the U.S. government (*Ibid.*), 380. For a concise and informative history of ONR, see Sapolsky, *Science and the Navy.* The way in which science was organized and funded went through a significant transformation just prior to World War II. By 1940, new and dynamic research partnerships were formed between scientific communities, universities and government. Historian A. Hunter Dupree has called the creation of such partnerships and their subsequent arrangements for scientific investigations, the "Great Instauration of 1940." Dupree, "The

Great Instauration of 1940," 443-465. For additional discussion of the history of ONR, see for instance Sapolsky, *Ibid.*, 378-400. For a discussion as to ONR's research interests in and funding of cosmic ray research, as well as vehicles on which such experiments could be conducted, see, for instance, Kevles, *The Physicists,* 353-56, 363-64, 420-21; DeVorkin, *Science With a Vengeance,* 256-67; Leslie, *The Cold War and American Science,* 144-48.

60. "The Military Aspects of the Geophysics Branch Program," undated report, SIO Subject Files, Records, 1903-1981, box 26, 81-16, F.36. "U.S. Navy. Office of Naval Research, February 1947-1948," Scripps Institution of Oceanography Archives, University of San Diego.

61. BW to Paul Hollister, October 16, 1946, OWTF.

62. In 1936, BW had carried out the first systematic aerial photographic survey of Mount McKinley. The photographic work he suggested to Hollister would complement and update his work of a decade earlier. See BW, "Over the Roof of the Continent," 78-98. A detailed map of the mountain did not exist at this time. The U.S. Army's 1942 McKinley Expedition, on which BW participated (see chapter 3), used both aerial photographs and a map prepared by Alfred H. Brooks during his 1902 McKinley Geological Survey expedition.

63. BW to Paul Hollister, October 16, 1946, OWTF. Although Washburn's proposed observatory was the highest established in North America, the highest in the world was located on the 19,200-foot summit of El Misti, a dormant South American volcano. Scientists of the Harvard College Observatory for astronomical work and Scott

Forbush of the Department of Terrestrial Magnetism carried out cosmic ray studies on the summit in the 1930s. See Forbush, "Some Recollections of Experiences," 174.

64. *Ibid.* BW projected that the expedition could be accomplished for the sum of $15,000.

65. On January 20, 1947, a written contract between RKO Pictures and BW established the New England Museum Alaskan Expedition 1947, Inc., OWTF, file 6.

66. Donald Menzel replaced Shapley as Director of the Harvard College Observatory in the early 1950s. In 1939, Menzel founded the High Altitude Observatory in Climax, Colorado. See Doel, "Redefining a Mission," 139-152.

67. Harlow Shapley to Paul Hollister, October 31, 1946, OWTF, file 1.

68. Marcel Schein to Harlow Shapley, December 3, 1946, OWTF, file 3.

69. Schein, Jesse and Wollen, "Intensity and Rate of Production of Mesotrons," 847-854.; Schein, Jesse, and Wollan, "The Nature of the Primary Cosmic Radiation," 615.

70. DeVorkin, *Science With a Vengeance,* 248. The use of aircraft in cosmic ray research, in particular the high-flying B-29, had begun immediately following the war. See *Ibid.*, 255, 270-71. Such programs were carried out by Bruno Rossi, who employed B-29s at altitudes to thirty-five thousand feet. See Rossi, Sand, and Sard, "Measurement of the Slow Mesotron Intensity," 122. It stands to reason that Schein's concern for a pristine and controlled environment attracted him to the cosmic ray research possibilities on McKinley's upper regions. The use of balloons in high-altitude research, including celestial radiation is well documented. In addition to the McKinley expedition, Schein was involved in a number of high-altitude balloon programs related to upper-atmosphere radiation, including Project Skyhook in the fall of 1947. The project was an ONR funded program utilizing high-altitude balloons that subsequently reached altitudes in excess of 31,000 feet; David DeVorkin, *Race to the Stratosphere,* 296.

71. Marcel Schein to BW, January 12, 1947, OWTF; Schein to BW, January 24, 1947. *Ibid.* As an indicator of the importance of Air Force participation, a nine-by-nine-by-six foot cosmic ray hut was built in Anchorage, Alaska and air dropped to an altitude of eighteen thousand feet. BW to Schein, March 18, 1947, *ibid.*; BW, *Operation White Tower,* 2. The expedition was also to use and test new Army Air Force cold weather clothing, a subject BW knew intimately (see chapter 3). He submitted a report outlining the effectiveness of such clothing at the close of the expedition. See BW to Commanding General, Army Air Forces, August 22, 1947, OWTF, file 6.

72. "Army Ground Forces Representative Joins Mt. McKinley Expedition," press release, War Department, Public Relations Division, March 19, 1947, BWPP; BW, *Operation White Tower,* 2.

73. Paul Hollister to Ernest Gruening, November 23, 1946, OWTF, file 1. Although preliminary plans had called for the inclusion of an actress on the expedition, it was decided that Mrs. Washburn, who had previous Alaskan mountaineering experience, would be included. For Barbara Washburn's account of her pioneering ascent as the first woman to reach the summit of Mount McKinley, see BW, *The Accidental Adventurer.*

74. Paul Hollister to Ernest Gruening, November 27, 1946.

75. Ernest Gruening to BW, February 28, 1947.

76. BW, OWT, 1.

77. *Ibid.*, 3.

78. BW, "Mount McKinley January 19-July 10, 1947 ('Operation White Tower')" BWC, 14, Box 2, file 1 (hereafter referred to as OWT). Croil Hunter, president of Northwest Airlines, supplied free transport for expedition members and nearly four thousand pounds of equipment from Minneapolis to Anchorage. *Ibid.*, 2.

79. Air logistical support was carried out by the Alaska Air Command stationed at Fort Richardson, Anchorage. BW, OWT, 17.

80. BW, *Operation White Tower*, 4. ·

81. *Ibid.* Browne Tower is 16,600 feet above sea level.

82. *Ibid.*, 5.

83. *Ibid.*, 6.

84. *Ibid.*

85. *Ibid.*, 5

86. *Ibid.*, 8.

87. *Ibid.*

88. BW, OWT, 57.

89. *Ibid.*, 9.

90. "Good Camping Trip, Courtesy of the Army," *Anchorage Hi-Life*, April 16, 1947, 1-2.

91. "McKinley Climb Filmed By Rugged Movie Cameraman," *Fairbanks Daily News-Miner*, June 4, 1948, 1.

92. BW, OWT, 60.

93. *Ibid.*, 61.

94. BW, *Operation White Tower*, 9.

95. BW, OWT, 62.

96. *Ibid.*, 74.

97. *Ibid.*

98. BW, *Operation White Tower*, 10.

99. BW, "Mapping Mount McKinley," 10.

100. *Ibid.*

101. Barbara Washburn, *The Accidental Adventurer*, 111.

102. BW, OWT, 75.

103. *Ibid.*, 76

104. BW, *Operation White Tower*, 11.

105. BW, OWT, 76

106. Barbara Washburn, *The Accidental Adventurer*, 114.

107. BW, OWT, 76-77.

108. BW, *Operation White Tower*, 13.

109. *Ibid.*

110. BW, OWT, 78-83; BW, *Operation White Tower*, 14.

111. *Ibid.*, 14.

112. BW, *Operation White Tower*, 14. The USGS was preparing a map of the region, albeit far less detailed than Washburn's effort.

113. Carr, Schein, and Barbour, "Cosmic-Ray Investigation," 1419, 1423.

114. BW, "National Geographic-Mt. McKinley Flights: 1936," D, BWPP, 12. Linc Washburn was a member of BW's Mount Crillon Expeditions.

115. BW, "Over the Top of the Continent," 97.

116. *Ibid.* For a discussion regarding the existence of Mount Hunter, see Farquhar, "Naming Alaska's Mountains," 222-24.

117. BW to Gilbert Grosvenor, Gilbert Grosvenor file 11-15.759—Washburn, Bradford, 1937 McKinley, July 13, 1936. BW, "Aerial Photography," 20. For a brief but informative history of the Fairchild Camera Company, see Brandt, "Sherman Fairchild Looks at the World," 96-99. Stevens had used the camera on a number of high altitude aerial explorations. See his "Exploring the Valley of the Amazon," 401, and "Flying the Hump of the Andes," 595-636. See also Clark, *Photography by Infra Red*, 269. In 1933, Stevens took the farthest photograph of earth thus far attained. He was one of the first to pioneer the use of infra red photography, a technique BW used to photograph McKinley in 1936.

See BW, "National Geographic Flights—Mt. McKinley Flights: 1936," 13.

118. BW, "A New Map of Mount McKinley," 160.

119. BW to Gilbert Grosvenor, Gilbert Grosvenor file 11-15.759-Washburn, Bradford, 1937 McKinley, 1 October 1937.

120. BW, "A New Map of Mount McKinley," 160.

121. "Mount McKinley National Park," 1:250,000 (Washington, D.C.: Government Printing Office, 1952); BW, "A New Map of Mount McKinley," 164.

122. For a description of BW's use of helicopters on Mount McKinley, in particular the Sikorsky H5G, see Gahagan, "The Mountain Tamer," 18-20.

123. BW, "A New Map of Mount McKinley," 164-79.

124. Miltary Engineer, "Elevation of Mt. McKinley," 384; BW, "Mapping Mount McKinley," 12; BW, "Reconnaissance of Mt. McKinley: July 26-August 30," D, BWC, 92-147, box 3; BW, "Alaska Field Observation-1952," *Ibid.*; BW, "Mt. McKinley Field Observation: 1953," *Ibid.;* BW, "Field Observations: 1959," *Ibid.*

125. BW, "Mount McKinley from the North and West," 283-93. BW had discovered this route, accessible along the Kahiltna Glacier, during his numerous reconnaissance flights and by having twice scaled the peak from the north.

126. The samples have long-since been lost. Independent attempts to locate the collection by BW and the author have failed.

127. BW, "Mount McKinley: The West Buttress, 1951," 214-15; William Hackett, "Report on 1951 Mount McKinley Expedition: sponsored by Boston Museum of Science, University of Denver, University of

Alaska," 2, October 31, 1951, BWPP. BW to Mike Sfraga, telephone conversation, December 5, 1996. The implementation of improved vehicles such as high altitude-aircraft, balloons and rockets made the project less attractive. See DeVorkin, *Science With A Vengeance,* 265. For a discussion of accelerators, see Kevles, *The Physicists,* 270-71.

128. Adolph Murie to Otto Geist, October 28, 1949. Geist Collection, box 15, Alaska and Polar Regions Archives, Rasmuson Library, University of Alaska Fairbanks. My thanks to Tim Rawson for identifying this source.

129. BW, *Exploring the Unknown,* 90-91.

130. *Ibid.,* 91.

131. *Ibid.,* 92.

132. *Ibid.*

133. *Ibid.,* 94. BW, "Mount McKinley: The West Buttress: 1951," 215.

134. *Ibid.*

135. *Ibid.,* 96.

136. *Ibid.,* 100.

137. *Ibid.,* 103.

138. *Ibid.,* 104.

139. *Ibid.*

140. *Ibid.,* 108.

141. *Ibid.*

142. *Ibid.,* 111.

143. *Ibid.,* 112.

144. *Ibid.,* 116-22.

145. *Ibid.,* 126.

146. *Ibid.*

147. BW, Kasper, and Huber, *Mount McKinley,* 5. See also BW, "A New Map of Mount McKinley," 159-86.

148. *Ibid.,* 3-6.

149. BW, *A Map of Mount McKinley, Alaska.*

150. Ambroziak and Ambroziak, *Infinite Perspectives.* Washburn's McKinley map and the author's quote appear on p. 75.

151. Military Engineer, "Elevation of Mt. McKinley," 384. In 1977 BW, with the assistance of two climbing parties

from the National Outdoor Leadership School (NOLS) made the first laser measurements of McKinley. See BW, "The First Laser Measurements," 381-86.

152. BW, "Mapping Mount McKinley," 12. A role of nine-and-one-half-inch U-2 negatives was given to the author and deposited in the BWC at the University of Alaska Fairbanks, 91-024, box 3, file 6. For an insightful discussion and analysis into the development and employment of Cold War reconnaissance satellites and aircraft, see Gaddis, *The Long Peace,* 195-214.

153. BW, "Mount McKinley (Alaska): History and Evaluation," 80-81.

154. Cassin, "The South Face of Mount McKinley," 27-37. For further insight into one of the world's celebrated mountaineers, see his *Fifty Years of Alpinism.*

155. Roberts, "The Legacy of Washburn," 134.

156. BW to Mike Sfraga, telephone interview, July 20, 1992.

Chapter 5

1. BW, "The Heart of the Grand Canyon." The map was co-produced by the NGS and Boston's Museum of Science. For a summary of Washburn's mapping program, see page 37. See also Garrett, "Grand Canyon: Are We Loving it to Death?," *ibid.,* 16-51.

2. BW, "The First Laser Measurements," 382; BW, "Alaska 1977 Laser Angles," D, BWC, 90-146, box 1, envelope 4.

3. See BW to Editor, *Earth Magazine,* March 29, 1994. BWPP.

4. Rock, *Museum of Science, Boston,* 1.

5. *Ibid,* 2.

6. *Ibid.,* 216.

7. *Ibid.,* 65, 69.

8. *Ibid.,* 73, 77, 79.

9. *Ibid.,* 88, 110.

10. *Ibid.,* 151, 177, 180.

11. Graham and Mead, *Manual of Aerial Photography,* 298.

12. BW, "Mapping Mount Everest," speech presented at the University of Alaska Fairbanks, May 1990, Fairbanks, Alaska, 2-33. BWPP. BW, "Mount Everest: Surveying the Third Pole," 653-659. For an artistic representation of the role of the space shuttle *Columbia,* see page 655.

13. BW, "The Altitude and Position of Mount Everest," unpublished report, 1-12. BWPP. BW, "Mount Everest's Surveying History," Trimble Navigator's User Conference, Sunnyvale, California, October 15, 1998. Copy of speech sent to author by BW.

14. BW to David Rawle, January 31, 1996. BWPP.

15. For a lively yet scholarly investigation of the Lewis and Clark expedition and the role of Thomas Jefferson in its development, see Ambrose, *Undaunted Courage.*

16. For a discussion of scientific patronage in the mid twentieth century, see Sapolsky, "Academic Science and the Military." Although BW used military funding in the post-war era, he retained strong ties with personal networks that he had developed prior to the war. These private and corporate patrons were an important component of his funding formula. He continues to use this style today, providing a means through which funding can be obtained for such geographic research as Mount Everest. "Washburn Photographs Illuminate Geologic Features," *GSA Today* 5, no. 10 (October 15, 1995): 200-201.

17. NRC, *Rediscovering Geography,* 30.

18. BW, "Geography—Dynamic Catalyst for Science," printed address at the annual dinner of the

American Geographical Society, New York, NY, December 3, 1964, 6. BWPP.

19. Bryce, "The Relationship of History and Geography," 426.

20. BW, "Geography—Dynamic Catalyst for Science," 6.

21. *Ibid.,* 7. See also Livingstone, *The Geographical Tradition,* 191-92.

22. Mackinder, "On the Scope and Methods of Geography," quoted in Livingstone, *The Geographical Tradition,* 190. Livingstone's quote is found on the same page.

23. Smith, "Academic War Over the Field of Geography," 155-72; Putnam, "Geography is a Practical Subject," 395.

24. Historians and scholars have only recently begun to address the development of interdisciplinary fields; for an introduction, see Bowler, *The Norton History of Environmental Sciences;* Doel, "The Earth Sciences and Geophysics," and Toulmin, *Cosmopolis.*

25. BW, interview with Tom Stepp, Holderness, New Hampshire, July 1, 1993. Transcribed tape recording, 1-2. BWPP.

26. BW, taped interview with Mike Sfraga, Boston, July 18, 1992.

27. Schulten, *The Geographical Imagination,* 158.

28. *Ibid.,* 171.

29. Waddington, "Wave Ogives." For a personal and professional tribute to the scientific and aesthetic value of Washburn's photographs, see Post, "Annual Aerial Photography of Glaciers," 17.

30. Kuklick and Kohler, "Science in the Field, Introduction," 1.

31. BW to Gilbert Grosvenor, November 20, 1935, Gilbert Grosvenor files: Yukon Expedition.

32. BW and Decaneas. *Bradford Washburn: Mountain Photography,* 15.

Literature Cited

Abbreviations

AAJ American Alpine Journal
BGSA Bulletin of the Geological Society of America
GJ Geographical Journal
GR Geographical Review
HMM Harper's Monthly Magazine
JG Journal of Glaciology
NGM National Geographic Magazine

NGSRR National Geographic Society Research Reports
OM Outing Magazine
PG Physical Geography
PR Physical Review
USGSB United States Geological Survey Bulletin
USGSPP U.S. Geological Survey Professional Paper

Abramson, Howard. *National Geographic: Behind America's Lens on the World.* New York: Crown Publishers, 1987.

Ahlmann, Hans Wilson. "Forward." *Journal of Glaciology* 1 (1947).

"Alaskan Boundary." *Bulletin of the American Geographical Society* 857 (June 1889).

Allen, Henry. *Report of an Expedition to the Copper, Tanana and Koyukuk Rivers, in the Territory of Alaska.* Washington, D.C.: Government Printing Office, 1887.

"Alpine Special." *High Mountain Sports* (February 1995).

Ambrose, Stephen. *Undaunted Courage: Meriwether Lewis, Thomas Jefferson and the Opening of the American West.* New York: Simon and Schuster, 1996.

Ambroziak, Brian, and Jeffrey R. Ambroziak, *Infinite Perspectives: Two Thousand Years of Three-Dimensional Mapmaking.* New York: Princeton Architectural Press, 1999.

Amundsen, Roald. My Life as an Explorer. New York: Doubleday, Page, 1927.

———. *The North West Passage: Being the Record of a Voyage of Exploration of the Ship Gjo 1903-1907.* London: Constable, 1908.

———. *The South Pole.* Trans. A. G. Chater. London: John Murray, 1925.

———. "To the North Magnetic Pole and Through the Northwest Passage." *Geographical Journal* 29.

Ariev, T. V. "Fundamental Outlines of Present Day Knowledge of Frostbite." Trans. and ed., Earl Hope. *Frostbite.* Ottawa: Earl R. Hope, 1950.

Bagley, James W. "The Use of the Panoramic Camera in Topographic Surveying." *USGSB* 657. Washington, D.C.: 1917.

Barnard, E. C. *Report of The International Boundary Commission* (1918). Washington, D.C.: Government Printing Office, 1921.

Bartlett, Richard A. *Great Surveys of the American West.* Norman: University of Oklahoma Press, 1962.

Bates, Robert. "Mt. McKinley, 1942," *American Alpine Journal* (1943).

Baxter, James Phinney. *Scientists Against Time.* Cambridge, MA: The M.I.T. Press, 1952.

Beckwith, Edward. "The Mt. McKinley Cosmic Ray Expedition." *AAJ* (May 1932).

Berton, Pierre. *The Arctic Grail: The Quest for the North West Passage and the North Pole.* New York: Penguin Group, 1988.

Blake, William P. "The Glaciers of Alaska, Russian American." *American Journal of Science* 2nd series 44 (1867).

Boddington, Jennie. *Antarctic Photographs: Herbert Ponting and Frank Hurley.* New York: St. Martin's Press, 1979.

Bolles, Edmund Blair. *The Ice Finders: How a Poet, a Professor, and a Politician discovered the Ice Age.* Washington, D.C.: Counterpoint, 1999.

Bork, Kennard Baker. *Cracking Rocks and Defending Democracy: Kirtley Fletcher Mather, Scientist, Preacher, Social Activist. 1888-1978.* San Francisco: AAS, 1994.

Botsford, A. "Catching Up With Bradford Washburn." *Appalachia* (January/February 1986).

Bowler, Peter. *The Norton History of The Environmental Sciences.* New York: W.W. Norton & Company, 1993.

Brandt, Anthony. "Sherman Fairchild Looks at the World: How a Millionaire Inventor Got the Bugs Out of Shutters and Made Accurate Aerial Photography Possible." *Air & Space* (October/November 1990).

Breashears, David, and Audrey Saulkeld. *Last Climb: The Legendary Everest Expeditions of George Mallory.* Washington, D.C.: National Geographic Society: 1999.

Brockamp, B., and Hans Mothes. "Seismische Untersuchungen auf dem Pasterzengletscher 1, *Zeitschrift furGeophysik* 6 (1930).

Brooks, Alfred H. *An Exploration to Mount McKinley, America's Highest Mountain.* Smithsonian Institution Annual Report, 1903. Washington, D.C.: Government Printing Office, 1904.

———. *The Mount McKinley Region, Alaska.* USGSPP 70. Washington, D.C.: Government Printing Office, 1911.

———. "Mountain Exploration in Alaska." *Alpina Americana* 3. [*Alpina Americana* was the journal of the American Alpine Club. It has since been renamed *American Alpine Journal.*]

———. *Preliminary Report on the Ketchikan Mining District, Alaska, with Introductory Sketch of the Geology of Southeastern Alaska.* Washington, D.C.: Government Printing Office, 1902.

———. *A Reconnaissance in the Tanana and White River Basins, Alaska, in 1898.* USGS, 20th Annual Report, VIII: *Explorations in Alaska in 1898.* Washington, D.C.: Government Printing Office, 1900.

———, and D. L. Raeburn. "Plan for Climbing Mount McKinley." *NGM* (January 1903).

Brown, William. *A History of the Denali-Mount McKinley Region, Alaska.* Santa Fe: National Park Service, 1991.

Browne, Belmore. *The Conquest of Mount McKinley.* Boston: Houghton Mifflin Company, 1956.

Bryan, C. D. B. *The National Geographic Society: 100 years of Adventure and Discovery.* New York: Harry N. Abrams, 1987.

Bryce, James. "The Relationship of History and Geography." *Contemporary Review* 49 (1886).

Bryce, Robert M. *Cook and Peary: The Polar Controversy Resolved.* Mechanicsburg, PA: Stackpole Books, 1997.

Buwalda, John P., in John Muir, *Studies in the Sierra.* Intro. by William Colby, foreword by John P. Buwalda. San Francisco: Sierra Club, 1950.

Byrd, Richard Evelyn. "The Conquest of Antarctica by Air." *NGM* (August 1930).

———. *Little America: Aerial Exploration in the Antarctic.* New York: G.P. Putnam's Sons, 1930.

Cairns, Ralph. "Hazards of Climbing Mount McKinley." *Overland Monthly* (February 1913).

Carr, Thomas, Marcel Schein, and Ian Barbour. "Cosmic-Ray Investigations on Mt. McKinley." *PR* 73: 12 (15 June 1948).

Carter, Adams H. "Mountain Intelligence." *AAJ* (1946).

Cassin, Ricardo. *Fifty Years of Alpinism.* Seattle: The Mountaineers, 1982.

———. "The South Face of Mount McKinley," *American Alpine Journal* (1962): 27-37.

Castner, J. C. "A Story of Hardship and Suffering in Alaska." in U. S. Congress, Committee on Military Affairs, *Compilation of Narratives of Exploration in Alaska.* Washington, D.C.: Government Printing Office, 1900.

Center for Military History. *Effects of Climate on Combat in European Russia.* Washington, D.C.: Government Printing Office, 1952.

Chamberland, R. T. "Instrumentation Work on the Nature of Glacier Motion." *GJ* 36 (1928).

Chew, Allen F. *The White Death: The Epic of the Soviet-Finnish Winter War.* East Lansing: Michigan State University Press, 1971.

Clark, Ronald William. *The Alps.* New York: Alfred Knopf, Inc., 1973.

———. *The Splendid Hills: The Life and Photographs of Vittorio Sella.* London: Phoenix House Limited, 1948.

Clark, Walter. *Photography by Infra Red.* New York: John Wiley Co., 1939.

Cole, Terrence. *The Sourdough Expedition.* Anchorage: Alaska Journal, 1985.

Collins, Henry B. *Science in Alaska.* Washington, D.C.: The Arctic Institute of North America, 1952.

Compilation of Narratives of Explorations in Alaska. U. S. Congress, Committee on Military Affairs, Washington, D.C.: Government Printing Office, 1900.

Compton, Arthur. "A Geographic Study of Cosmic Rays." *PR* 42, no. 6 (15 March 1933).

———. "Cosmic Rays as Electrical Particles." *PR* 50 (December 15, 1936).

Cook, Frederick. "America's Unconquered Mountain." *HMM* (January and February 1904).

———. "The Conquest of Mount McKinley." *HMM* (May 1907).

———. *My Attainment of the Pole.* New York: The Polar Publishing Co., 1911.

———. *Return from the Pole.* Ed. Frederick J. Pohl. New York: Pelligrini & Cudahy, 1951.

———. *To the Top of the Continent.* London: Hodder & Stoughton, 1909.

Crone, D. R. "Mapping from the Air." *GJ* 84 (July 1934).

Cronin, Thomas, Thomas Gaisser, and Simon Swordy. "Cosmic Rays at the Energy Frontier." *Scientific American* (January 1997).

Cronon, William, George Miles, and Jay Gitlin. "Becoming West: Toward a New Meaning for Western History," in Cronon, Miles, and Gitlin, eds., *Under an Open Sky: Rethinking America's Western Past.* New York: W.W. Norton, 1992.

Dall, William. *Alaska and Its Resources.* Boston: Lee and Shepard, 1870.

———. *Coast Pilot, Alaska,* Pt. 1 Washington, D.C.: Government Printing Office, 1883.

———. *Report on Mount Saint Elias, Mount Fairweather, and Some of the Adjacent Mountains.* USCS Annual Report 1875 (Washington, D.C.: Government Printing Office, 1875.

Dallek, Robert. *Franklin D. Roosevelt and American Foreign Policy, 1932-1945.* New York: Oxford University Press, 1981.

Davis, Loyal. *From One Surgeon's Notebook.* Springfield, IL: C.C. Thomas, 1967.

———, et al. "High Altitude Frostbite: Preliminary Report." *Surgery, Gynecology and Obstetrics* 77 (December 1943).

De Filippi, Filippo. *The Ascent of Mount St. Elias.* Westminster: Archibald Constable, 1900 and New York: Frederick A. Stokes, 1900.

DeVorkin, David. *Race to the Stratosphere: Manned Scientific Ballooning in America*. New York: Springer-Verlag, 1989.

———. *Science With a Vengeance: How the Military Created the US Space Sciences After World War II*. New York: Springer-Verlag, 1992.

Dickey, William. "Discoveries in Alaska (1896)." *AAJ* (1951-1953).

Doel, Ronald. "Defining Cooperative Research: The Harvard Experimental Geophysics Committee, 1931-1940, as Basis for Interdisciplinary Work," paper presented at the History of Science Society, October 16, 1994.

———. "The Earth Sciences and Geophysics." In John Krige and Dominque Pestre, eds., *Science in the Twentieth Century*. London: Hartwood Academic Press, 1997. Reprinted in Stephen E. Toulmin, *Cosmopolis: The Hidden Agenda of Modernity*, New York: Free Press, 1990.

———. "Expedition and the CIW: Comments and Contentions." In Gregory Good, ed., *The Earth, the Heavens and the Carnegie Institution of Washington*. Washington, D.C.: American Geophysical Union, 1994.

———. "Redefining a Mission: The Smithsonian Astrophysical Observatory on the Move." *Journal for the History of Astronomy* 21 (1990).

———. *Solar Systems Astronomy in America: Communities, Patronage, and Interdisciplinary Science, 1920-1960*. New York: Cambridge University Press, 1996.

Dolnick, Edward. *Down the Great Unknown: John Wesley Powell's 1869 Journey of Discovery and Tragedy Through the Grand Canyon*. New York: HarperCollins, 2001.

Dunn, Robert. "Across the Forbidden Tundra." *OM* (January 1904).

———. "Highest on Mt. McKinley," *OM* (April 1904).

———. "Home by Ice and by Swimming from Mt. McKinley." *OM* (May 1904).

———. "Into the Mists of Mt. McKinley." *OM* (February 1904).

———. *Shameless Diary of an Explorer*. New York: The Outing Publishing Co., 1907.

———. "Storm-Wrapped on Mt. McKinley." *OM* (March 1904).

Dupree, A. Hunter. "The Great Instauration of 1940." In Gerald Holton, ed., *Twentieth Century Sciences: Studies in the Biography of Ideas*. New York: Norton, 1972.

———. *Science and the Federal Government: A History of Politics and Activities*. Baltimore: The Johns Hopkins University Press, 1986.

Dyson, James. *The World of Ice*. New York: Alfred Knopf, Inc., 1962.

Eames, Hugh. *Winner Lose All: Dr. Cook & the Theft of the North Pole*. Boston: Little, Brown and Company, 1973.

Editor. "Washburn Photographs Illuminate Geologic Features." *GSA Today* 5, no. 10 (15 October 1995).

Eldridge, George. "A Reconnaissance on the Sushitna Basin and Adjacent Territory, Alaska, in 1898." *Twentieth Annual Report of the United States Geological Survey 7*. Washington, D.C.: Government Printing Office, 1898-1899.

"Edward J. Hall: Vice-president of the American Telephone and Telegraph Co., Died at Watkins, N.Y. September 17, 1914." *The Telegraph Review* (October 1914).

"Elevation of Mt. McKinley." *Military Engineer* 48 (1956).

Elias, Scott. *The Ice-Age History of Alaskan National Parks*. Washington, D.C.: Smithsonian Institution Press, 1995.

Engle, Eloise, and Lauri Paananen. *The Winter War: The Soviet Attack of Finland 1939-1940*. Harrisburg, PA: Stackpole Books, 1992.

Fagen, George V. "Philip Washburn: 'A Thorough Colorado Man.'" The Colorado Magazine (Fall 1972).

Fairchild Aviation. "A Complete College Course in Aerial Photography: Institute for Geographical Exploration of Harvard University Gives Students Practical Training with Modern Fairchild Equipment." *Fairchild Aviation News* (February 1937).

Farquhar, Francis. "The Exploration and First Ascents of Mount McKinley." *Sierra Club Bulletin* (June 1949).

———. "Naming Alaska's Mountains," *American Alpine Journal.*

"Father Hubbard's Alaskan Explorations." *NGM* (May 1934).

Field, William. "The Fairweather Range: Mountaineering and Glacier Studies." *Appalachia* (December 1926).

———. *Geographic Study of Mountain Glaciation in the Northern Hemisphere: Alaska and Adjoining Parts of Canada,* Part 2a. New York: American Geographical Society, 1958.

———. "Glaciological Research in Alaska." In Henry B. Collins, *Science in Alaska.* Washington: The Arctic Institute of North America, 1952.

———. *Mountain Glaciers of the Northern Hemisphere.* Hanover: Cold Regions Research and Engineering Laboratory. 1927.

———. *Some Aspects of Glaciers and Glaciology.* Washington, D.C.: Naval Operations for Polar Projects, 1956.

———, and C. Suzanne Brown, *With a Camera in My Hands: William Field as told to Suzanne Brown.* Fairbanks: University of Alaska Press, 2003.

Fisher, J. E. "Forbes and Alaskan 'Dirt' Bands on Glaciers and Their Origins." *American Journal of Science* 245 (1947).

———. "The Formation of Forbes Bands." *JG* 1 (1958).

Flemer, J. A. *Photographic Methods and Instruments.* United States Coast and Geodetic Survey Report for 1897. Washington, D.C.: Government Printing Office, 1898).

Fleming, James. *Meteorology in America: 1800-1896.* Baltimore: The Johns Hopkins University Press, 1990.

Forbes, Alexander. "A Flight to Cape Chidley, 1935." *GR* 29 (1936).

———. "Surveying in Northern Labrador." *GR* 22 (1932).

Forbes, John D. *Travels Through the Alps of Savoy.* Edinburgh: Simpkin, 1843.

———. *The Theory of Glaciers.* Edinburgh: Simpkin, 1859.

Forbush, Scott. "Some Recollections of Experience Associated with Cosmic-Ray Investigation." In Yataro Sekido and Harry Elliot, eds., *Early History of Cosmic Ray Studies: Personal Reminiscences With Old Photographs.* Dordrecht and Boston: D. Reidel, 1985.

Fox, Stephen R. *John Muir and His Legacy: the American Conservation Movement.* Boston: Little, Brown 1981. Repr Madison: University of Wisconsin Press, 1985.

Freeman, Andrew. *The Case for Dr. Cook.* New York: Coward-McCann, Inc., 1961.

Gaddis, Lewis. *The Long Peace: Inquiries Into the History of the Cold War.* New York: Oxford University Press, 1987.

Gahagan, Neil. "The Mountain Tamer." *Bee-Hive* (January 1950).

Garfield, Brian. *The Thousand Mile War: World War II in Alaska and the Aleutians.* New York: Bantam, 1982.

Garrett, W. E. "Grand Canyon: Are We Loving it to Death?" *NGM* (July 1978).

Gilbert, Grove Karl. *Glaciers and Glaciation.* Washington, D.C.: Smithsonian Institution, 1910.

———. *Harriman Alaska Expedition,* vol. 3. New York: Doubleday, Page & Co., 1903.

Goddard, George. "The Unexplored Philippines from the Air." *NGM* (September 1930).

Goetzmann, William. *Exploration and Empire: The Explorer and the Scientist in the Winning of the American West.* New York: Norton, 1978.

———. *New Lands, New Men: America and the Second Great Age of Exploration.* New York: Viking Penguin Inc., 1987.

———. "Paradigm Lost." In Nathan Reingold *The Sciences in the American Context: New Perspectives.* Washington D.C.: Smithsonian Institution Press, 1979.

———, and Kay Sloan, *Looking Far North: The Harriman Expedition to Alaska, 1899.* Princeton: Princeton University Press, 1982.

Goldthwait, Richard. "Dating the Little Ice Age in Glacier Bay, Alaska. Report on the International Geological Congress 21st Session." *Norden* (1963).

———. "Seismic Sounding on South Crillon and Klooch Glaciers." *GJ* 87 (June 1936).

———, Ian McKeller, and Casper Cronk. "The fluctuations of Crillon Glacier System, Southeast Alaska." *Bulletin of the International Association of Sci. Hydrology* 8 (1963).

Graham, Ronald, and Roger Mead. *Manual of Aerial Photography.* London: Focal Press, 1986.

Grattan, H. W. "Trench Foot." In *History of the Great War Based on Official Documents.* London: His Majesty's Stationery Office, 1922.

Gray, George. *Science at War.* Freeport: Books for Libraries Press, 1972.

Green, Lewis. *The Boundary Hunters.* Vancouver: University of British Columbia, 1982.

Gregory, Barry. *Mountain and Arctic Warfare: From Alexander to Afghanistan.* Wellingborough: The Bath Press, 1988.

Grewingk, C. "Beitrage zur Kenntniss der orographischen und geognostischen Beschafenheit der Nordwest Kuste Amerikas," in Alfred H. Brooks, *The Mount McKinley Region, Alaska* (Washington, D.C.: Government Printing Office, 1911).

Griffiths, Thomas. "Glacial Geomorphology on the Mt. McKinley Massif, Alaska." *Proceedings of the VIIIth General Assembly-XVIIth Congress, International Geographical Union* (1952).

Grosvenor, Gilbert. *The National Geographic Society and Its Magazine.* Washington, D.C.: National Geographic Society, 1957.

Hambrey, Michael, and Jurg Alean. *Glaciers.* Cambridge, England: Cambridge University Press, 1992.

Hamilton, Thomas, Katherine Reed, and Robert Thorson, eds. Glaciation in Alaska: The Geologic Record. Anchorage: Alaska Geographic Society, 1986.

Harvard University Handbook: An Official Guide. Cambridge: Harvard University Press, 1936.

Henson, Matthew. *A Negro Explorer at the North Pole.* New York: Stokes, 1912.

Herbert, Wally. *The Noose of Laurels: Robert Peary and the Race to the North Pole.* New York: Atheneum, 1989.

Herron, Joseph. *Explorations in Alaska, 1899.* Washington, D.C.: War Department, 1899.

Hershberg, James. *James Conant: Harvard to Hiroshima and the Making of the Nuclear Age.* New York: Alfred Knopf, Inc., 1993.

Hevly, Bruce. "The Heroic Age of Glacier Motion." *Osiris* 11 (1996).

Hillas, A. M. *Cosmic Rays.* Oxford: Pergamon Press, 1972.

Hodges, Thomas. *The Alaska-Canada Boundary Dispute.* Toronto: William Tyrell and Co., 1903.

Holzel, Tom, and Audrey Saulkeld. *First on Everest: The Mystery of Mallory and Irvine.* New York: Paragon House Publishers, 1988.

House, William. "Mountain Equipment for the U.S. Army." *AAJ* (1946).

Hunt, William. *Mountain Wilderness.* Washington, D.C.: Government Printing Office, 1991.

———. *To Stand at the Pole.* New York: Stein and Day, 1981.

Huntford, Roland. *The Last Place on Earth.* New York: Atheneum, 1986.

Kamb, Barclay, et al. "Glacier Surge Mechanism: 1982-1983 Surge of Variegated Glacier, Alaska." *Science* 227: 4686 (February 1985).

Kari, James. "The Tenada-Denali-Mount McKinley Controversy." *Names* 34: 3 (September 1986).

Kerr, Mark Brickell. *Mount St. Elias and Its Glaciers.* New York, 1987.

Kevles, Daniel. *The Physicists: The History of a Scientific Community in Modern America.* Cambridge: Harvard University Press, 1995.

King, C., and W. Lewis. "A Tentative Theory of Ogive Formation." *JG* 3 (1961).

Kirwin, L. P. *A History of Polar Exploration.* New York: Norton, 1960.

Klotz, O. J. "Notes on the Glaciers of Southeastern Alaska and Adjoining Territory." *GJ* 14 (1899).

Kohler, Robert. *Partners in Science: Foundations and Natural Scientists, 1900-1945.* Chicago: University of Chicago Press, 1991.

———. "Place and Practice in Field Biology," *History of Science* xl, (2002).

Korsmo, Fae, and Mike Sfraga, "Churchill Peaks and the Politics of Naming" *Polar Record* 36 (197).

Krashieninnikov, Stephan P. *Explorations of Kamchatka: 1735-41.* Portland: Oregon Historical Society, 1972.

Kuklick, Henrika, and Robert Kohler, eds. "Science in the Field." *Osiris* 11 (1996).

Langer, William Leonard, and S. Everett Gleason. *The Undeclared War.* New York: Harper and Brothers Publishing, 1953.

La Perouse, Jean Francis Galaupe, Comte de. *A Voyage Around the World,* Vol. 1. London: Joseph Bumstead, 1799.

Laprince-Ringuet, Louis, Trans., Fay Ajzenberg. *Cosmic Rays.* New York: Prentice Hall, 1950.

Larrey, Dominique Jean, baron. "Mémoires d'un Chirurgien Militaire, et de Campagnes (1812-1817)." In Hans Killiam, *Cold Injuries With Special Reference to German Experience During World War II.* Washington, D.C: United States Navy, 1952.

Leslie, Stuart. *The Cold War and American Science: The Military-Industrial-Academic Complex at MIT and Stanford.* New York: Columbia University Press, 1993.

Leuchtenburn, William E. *Franklin D. Roosevelt and the New Deal: 1932-1940.* New York: Harper & Row, 1963.

Lever, Trevor, H. "Vilhjamur Stefansson, the Continental Shelf, and a New Arctic Continent," *British Journal for the History of Science* 21 (1988).

Lindley, A. D. "Mt. McKinley, South and North Peaks, 1932," *American Alpine Journal* (1933).

Livingstone, David. *The Geographical Tradition: Episodes in the History of a Contested Enterprise.* Oxford, England and Cambridge, MA: Blackwell, 1993.

Lowrey, Paul B. "Tragedy of the C-47." *Alaska Life* (April 1945).

Lucier, Paul. "Commercial Interests and Scientific Disinterestedness: Consulting Geologists in Antebellum America." *Isis* 86: 2 (June 1995).

Lunn, Sir Arnold. *A Century of Mountaineering: 1857-1957.* London: George Allen & Unwin Ltd., 1957.

Lutz, Catherine, and Jane Collins. *Reading National Geographic.* Chicago: The University of Chicago Press, 1993.

Mackinder, Sir Halford John. "On the Scope and Methods of Geography." *Proceedings of the Royal Geographical Society* 9 (1887).

MacPherson, W. H. "The Russo-Japanese War." In *Medical and Sanitary Reports from Officers Attached to the Japanese*

Forces in the Field. London: His Majesty's Stationery Office, 1908.

Mather, Keith, and Bradford Washburn. "The Telescopic Alidade and Plane Table, as used in Topographic and Geologic Survey," *Dennison University Bulletin* (April 1938).

Mathis, F. E. "Glaciers." *Hydrology, Physics, of the Earth* IX. New York: Dover, 1942.

McKinley, Ashley C. *Applied Aerial Photography.* New York: John Wiley & Sons, Inc., 1929.

McNeill, William. *Plagues and People.* Garden City: Anchor Press, 1976.

Medical and Surgical History of the British Army During War Against Russia in Years 1854-56. London: His Majesty's Stationery Office, 1858.

Mendenhall, William. "A Reconnaissance From Resurrection Bay to Tanana River, Alaska." *Twentieth Annual Report of the United States Geological Survey 7.* Washington, D.C.: Government Printing Office, 1900.

Merriam, Clinton Hart, ed. *Harriman Alaska Expedition.* 13 vols. Washington, D.C.: Smithsonian, 1910 - 1914.

Mertie, J. B. "Geography and Geology of Lituya Bay." In Phillip Smith, *Mineral Resources of Alaska.* Washington, D.C.: Government Printing Office, 1930.

Miller, Maynard. "Observations on the Regimen of Glaciers of Icy Bay and Yakutat Bay, Alaska, 1946-47." Master's Thesis. New York: Columbia University, 1948.

———. *Observations on the Regimen of the Glaciers of Icy Bay and Yakutat Bay, Alaska: 1946-1947.* Special Report: Foundation for Glacial Research. Seattle: Foundation for Glacial Research, 1955.

———. *Progress Report of the Juneau Ice Field Research Project.* New York: American Geographical Society, 1949.

———. "The Role of Diastrophism in the Regimen of Glaciers in the St. Elias District, Alaska." *JG* 3 (1958).

Moiseevich, Aleksander. *June 22, 1941: Soviet Historians and the German Invasion.* Trans. and ed. Vladamir Petrov. Columbia: University of South Carolina Press, 1968.

Molnia, Bruce. *Alaska's Glaciers.* Anchorage: Alaska Geographical Society, 1982.

———, and Austin Post. "Holocene History of Bering Glacier, Alaska: A Prelude to the 1993-94 Surge." *PG* 16 (March-April 1995).

Montgomery, M. R. *In Search of L.L. Bean.* Boston: Little, Brown & Company, 1984.

Moore, Katrina. *Borestone to Bering Strait* (Boston: Katrina H. Moore and Katrina M. Smathers private printing, 1999).

Moore, Terris. *Mount McKinley, The Pioneer Climbs.* Fairbanks: University of Alaska Press, 1967.

Morison, Elting Elmore. *Turmoil and Tradition: A Study of the Life and Times of Henry L. Stimson.* Boston: Houghton Mifflin, 1960.

Mothes, Hans. "Dickenmessungen von Gletschereis mit Seismischen Methoden." *Zeitschrift furGeophysik* 3 (1927).

Mount Everest. Washington: D.C.: *NGM*, 1988.

"Mount McKinley National Park," 1:250,000 map (Washington, D.C.: Government Printing Office, 1952.).

"Mountain Climbing in Alaska: The First Expedition to Mt. Blackburn," *Appalachia* (June 15, 1995).

Mountain Men: The Mystery of Mount McKinley. London: British Broadcasting Corporation, 2001, documentary.

Muir, John. *John Muir: Travels in Alaska.* Boston: Houghton Mifflin Company, 1979.

Munro, John. *Geophysics at Harvard.* Cambridge: Harvard University Press, 1940.

Nash, Gerald D. *Creating the West: Historical Interpretations, 1890-1900.*

Albuquerque: University of New Mexico Press, 1991.

National Research Council, *Rediscovering Geography: New Relevance for Science and Society* (National Academy Press: Washington, D.C., 1997),

Needell, Allan. *Cold War and the American State: Lloyd V. Berkner and the Balance of Professional Ideals.* Amsterdam: Harwood Academic Press, 2000.

———. "Lloyd Berkner and Science-Statesmanship." In Peter Galison and Bruce Hevly, eds., *Big Science: The Growth of Large-Scale Research.* Palo Alto: Stanford University Press, 1992).

Newburgh, Louis. *Physiology of Heat Regulation and the Science of Clothing.* Philadelphia: W.B. Saubders, 1949.

Nielson, Jonathan. *An Interpretive Survey of Alaska's Military Heritage: 1867-1980.* Anchorage: Alaska Historical Commission, 1980.

"Note on Mount Logan." *American Geologist* 13 (1894).

Oleson, Alexander, and John Voss, eds. *The Organization of Knowledge in Modern America, 1860-1920.* Baltimore: The Johns Hopkins University Press, 1979.

Orr, K. D., and D. C. Fainer. *Cold Injuries in Korea During Winter 1950-51.* Fort Knox: Army Medical Research Laboratory, 1951.

Owens, Larry. "The Counterproductive Management of Science in the Second World War: Vannevar Bush and the Office of Scientific Research and Development." *Business History Review* 68, no. 4 (Winter 1994).

Page, C. M. "Gangrene in War." *British Medical Journal* 2 (August 1914).

Pauly, Philip. "The World and All That's in It: The National Geographic Society, 1888-1918." *American Quarterly* 31: 4 (1979)

Peary, Josephine. *The Snow Baby.* Cambridge: The University Press, 1901.

Peary, Robert E. *The North Pole.* New York: Stokes, 1910.

Pierce, Richard, and Alexander Doll. "Alaskan Treasure: Our Search for the Russian Plates." *Alaskan Journal* 1: 1 (1971).

Pitkin, Thomas. *Quartermaster Equipment for Special Forces.* Washington, D.C.: Quartermaster Corps Historical Studies, 1944.

Post, Austin. "Annual Aerial Photography of Glaciers in Northwest North America: How it All Began and Its Golden Age." *Physical Geography* 16: 1 (January-February 1995).

———. *Effects of the March 1964 Alaskan Earthquake on Glaciers.* USGSPP 544-D (1967).

Powell, John Wesley. *The Exploration of the Colorado River and Its Canyons.* New York: Penguin Books, 1987.

Public Information Officer Headquarters. *The Army's Role in the Building of Alaska.* Seattle: Headquarters United States Army, Alaska, 1969.

Purtee, Edward. *Development of Army Air Force Clothing and Other Personal Equipment Peculiar to Air Operation.* Dayton, Ohio, Wright Field: Air Technical Service Command (ATSC), 1945.

Putnam, D. P. "Geography Is a Practical Subject." In Griffith Taylor, ed., *Geography in the Twentieth Century: A Study of Growth, Fields, Techniques, Aims and Trends.* New York: Philosophical Library, 1951.

Pyne, Stephen. "From the Grand Canyon to the Marianas Trench: The Earth Sciences After Darwin." In Reingold, Nathan. *The Sciences in the American Context: New Perspectives.* Washington, D.C.: Smithsonian Institution Press, 1979.

———. "A Third Great Age of Discovery." In Martin Collins and Sylvia Kraemer, eds. *Space: Discovery and Exploration.* Hong Kong: Hugh Lauter Levin Associates, 1993.

Rabbit, Mary. *Minerals, Lands, and Geology for the Common Defence and General Welfare.* 3 vols. Washington D.C.: Government Printing Office, 1979.

Rawlins, Dennis. *Peary at the Pole: Fact or Fiction?* New York: Robert B. Luce, Inc., 1973.

Read, Ben. "An Interview with Bradford Washburn and Terris Moore." *Climbing* (April 1993).

Read, Harry Fielding. "Studies of Muir Glacier, Alaska." *NGM* 4 (21 March 1892).

Reed, John C. "Record of the First Approach to Mt. McKinley." *AAJ* (1955).

Reingold, Nathan. *The Sciences in the American Context: New Perspectives.* Washington, D.C.: Smithsonian Institution Press, 1979.

Report of Cold Weather Test Detachment: Winter of 1942-1943, Laboratory Reports. Vol. 2 (Dayton and Fairbanks: United States Army Air Corps, n.d.)

Report of the U.S. Army Alaskan Test Expedition, 1942. Washington, D.C.: Office of the Quartermaster Corps, 1942.

Riffenburgh, Beau. *The Myth of the Explorer: The Press, Sensationalism, and Geographic Discovery.* London: Bellhaven Press, 1993.

Risch, Erna. *U.S. Army in World War II, The Quartermaster Corps: Organization, Supply and Services.* Vol. 1. Washington, D.C.: Government Printing Office, 1953.

Roberts, David. "Bradford Washburn," *American Photographer* (April 1983).

———. *Escape from Lucania: An Epic Story of Survival.* New York: Simon & Schuster, 2002.

———. *Great Exploration Hoaxes.* San Francisco: Sierra Club Books, 1982.

———. "The Legacy of Washburn." In Bradford Washburn and David Roberts, *Mount McKinley: The Conquest of Denali.* New York: Harry N. Abrams, 1991.

Robinson, Arthur H. "Geographic Cartography." In Preston James and Claren F. Jones, eds., *American Geography: Inventory and Prospect.* Syracuse: Syracuse University Press, 1954.

Rock, Mary Desmond. *Museum of Science, Boston: The Founding and Formative Years, The Washburn Era 1939-1980.* Boston: Museum of Science, 1989.

Rohn, Oscar. "Survey and Opening Up a Military Road from Valdez to Copper Center, 1899." *Compilation of Narratives of Explorations in Alaska.* Washington, D.C.: Government Printing Office, 1900.

Ross, Dorothy. *The Origins of American Social Sciences.* New York: Cambridge University Press, 1991.

Rossi, Bruno, Mathew Sand, and Robert Sard. *Cosmic Rays.* New York: McGraw-Hill Book Company, 1964.

———. "Measurement of the Slow Mesotron Intensity at Several Altitudes." *PR* 72 (15 July 1947).

Rusk, Claud. "On the Trail of Dr. Cook." *Pacific Monthly* (January 1911).

Russell, Israel. "An Expedition to Mount St. Elias, Alaska." *NGM* 29 (May 1891).

———. *Glaciers of North America.* Boston: Ginn & Company, 1897.

Salt, J. S. "Photographs From the Mount Everest Flight." *GJ* 82 (July 1933).

Sapolsky, Harvey. "Academic Science and the Military: The Years Since the Second World War." In Reingold, Nathan. *The Sciences in the American Context: New Perspectives.* Washington, D.C.: Smithsonian Institution Press, 1979.

———. *Science and the Navy: The History of the Office of Naval Research* (Princeton: Princeton University Press, 1990).

Sargent, R. H., and F. H. Moffit. "Aerial Photographic Surveys in Southeastern Alaska." *USGSB* 797-E. Washington,

D.C.: Government Printing Office, 1929.

Saulkeld, Audrey. "Skinning One Skunk at a Time." *Mountain* 126 (March/ April 1989).

Schein, Marcel, William Jesse, and E. D. Wollen. "Intensity and Rate of Production of Mesotrons in the Stratosphere." *PR* 57 (1940).

———. "The Nature of the Primary Cosmic Radiation and the Origin of the Mesotron." *PR* 69 (1941).

Schulten, Susan. *The Geographical Imagination in America, 1880 -1950.* Chicago: The University of Chicago Press, 2001.

Schweber, S. S. "Writing the Biography of a Living Scientist: The Challenges and the Reward," paper presented at the "Interviews in Writing Recent Science," conference, Stanford University, 28-30 April, 1994.

Scott, Robert F., and Leonard Huxley, eds. *Scott's Last Expedition: Being the Journals of Captain R.F. Scott, R.N., C.V.O.* London: Smith, Elder & Co., 1913.

———. *Scott's Last Expedition: The Journals.* London: Murray, 1987.

Sekido, Yataro, and Harry Elliot, eds. *Early History of Cosmic Rays: Personal Reminiscences with Old Photographs.* Dordrecht and Boston: D. Reidel Publishing Company, 1985.

Seligman, Gerald. "Research on Glacier Flow." *Geografiska Annaler* 1-2 (1949).

Sella, Vittoria et al. *Summit: Vittorio Sella: Mountaineer and Photographer: The Years 1879-1909.* Aperture: New York, 1999.

Sharp, Robert. *Glaciers.* Eugene: University of Oregon, 1990.

———. *Living Ice.* Cambridge, England: Cambridge University Press, 1988).

———. *Living Ice: Understanding Glaciers and Glaciation.* New York: Cambridge University Press, 1992.

Shelton, John. *Geology Illustrated.* San Francisco: W.H. Freeman and Company, 1966.

Sherwood, Morgan. *Exploration of Alaska: 1865-1900.* Fairbanks: University of Alaska Press, 1993.

Simpitch, Frederick. "Skypaths Through Latin America." *NGM* (January 1931).

Smith, Janet Adam. *John Buchan.* London: Rupert Hart-Davis, 1965.

Smith, Neil. "Academic War Over the Field of Geography: The Elimination of Geography at Harvard, 1947-1951." *Annals of the Association of American Geographers* 77: 2 (June 1987).

Soderquist, Thomas. "After the 200th Hour: The A/Effects of Long-Term Interviewing for Science Biography," paper presented at the "Interviews in Writing Recent Science" conference, 28-30 April, 1994.

Solomon, Susan. *The Coldest March: Scott's Fatal Antarctic Expedition.* New Haven: Yale University Press, 2001.

Sorrenson, Richard. "The Ship as Scientific Instrument in the Eighteenth Century." *Osiris* 11 (1996).

Spurr, Josiah. "A Reconnaissance in Southeastern Alaska in 1898." *Twentieth Annual Report of the United States Geological Survey 7.* Washington, D.C.: Government Printing Office, 1900.

———, and Stephen Spurr. *The Log of the Kuskokwim: An Exploration in Alaska.* Petersham: Spurr, 1950.

Stefannson, Vilhjalmur. *The Friendly Arctic.* New York: The Macmillan Company, 1943.

Steller, George Wilhelm. *Journal of a Voyage with Bering 1741-1742.* Palo Alto: Stanford University Press, 1988.

Stevens, Albert. "Exploring the Valley of the Amazon in a Hydroplane." *NGM* (April 1926).

———. "Flying the Hump of the Andes." *NGM* (May 1931).

———. "Photographing the Eclipse of 1932 From the Air: Five Miles Above the Earth Surface . . . ." *NGM* (November 1932).

Stuck, Hudson. *The Ascent of Denali: A Narrative of the First Complete Ascent of the Highest Peak in North America.* Lincoln: University of Nebraska Press, 1914.

———. *The Ascent of Denali.* Lincoln: University of Nebraska Press, 1989.

Sweeting, C. G. *Combat Flying Clothing.* Washington, D.C.: Smithsonian Institution Press, 1984.

———. *Combat Flying Equipment: U.S. Army Aviators' Personal Equipment, 1917-1945.* Washington, D.C.: Smithsonian Institution, 1989.

Tanner, Väinö Alfred. *The Winter War: Finland Against Russia, 1939-1940* (Palo Alto: Stanford University Press, 1957).

Tarr, Ralph Stockman. "Recent Advances of Glaciers in the Yakutat Bay Region." *BGSA* 18 (1907).

———. "The Yakutat Bay Region, Alaska: Part 1, Physiography and Glacial Geology." *United States Geological Survey Professional Paper 64.* Washington, D.C.: Government Printing Office, 1912.

———, and Lawrence Martin. *Alaskan Glacier Studies.* Washington, D.C.: National Geographic Society, 1914.

———. "Glaciers and Glaciation of Yakutat Bay, Alaska." *American Geographical Society* 38 (1906).

Taylor, Griffith, ed., *Geography in the Twentieth Century: A Study of Growth, Fields, Techniques, Aims and Trends.* New York: Philosophical Library, 1951.

Tevor, Lever H. "Vilhjamur Stefansson, the Continental Shelf, and a New Arctic Continent." *British Journal for the History of Science* 21 (1988).

Thatcher, James. *Military Journal of the American Revolution.* Hartford: Hurlbert William and Co., 1862.

Thrower, Norman, J. W. *Maps and Civilization: Cartography in Culture and Society.* Chicago: The University of Chicago Press, 1996.

Tissot, Roger. *Mont Blanc.* London: The Medici Society Limited, 1924.

Toulmin, Stephen E. *Cosmopolis: The Hidden Agenda of Modernity.* New York: Free Press, 1990.

Turner, Frederick Jackson. *The Frontier in American History.* New York: Henry Holt and Company, 1921.

Ullman, James Ramsey. *The White Tower.* Philadelphia: J.B. Lippincott Company, 1945.

Vancouver, George. *A Voyage of Discovery to the North Pacific Ocean.* London: Hakluyt Society, 1801.

Waddington, E. D. "Wave Ogives." *JG* 32 (1982).

Wahrhaftig, Clyde. "The Alaska Range." In Howel Williams, ed., *Landscapes of Alaska: Their Geological Evolution.* Berkeley: University of California Press, 1958.

War Department. *Basic Field Manual: Operations in Snow and Extreme Cold.* Washington, D.C.: Government Printing Office, 1941.

War Department Quartermaster Corps. *Specifications No. 1171 for Alaskan Clothing.* Washington, D.C.: Government Printing Office, 1914.

Washburn, Albert Lincoln. "Memorial to Richard Parker Goldthwait: 1911-1992," *The Geological Society of America* 23 (1993).

Washburn, Barbara. *The Accidental Adventurer.* Kenmore: Epicenter Press, 2001.

Washburn, Bradford. "Aerial Photography: Alaska and the Alps. In Malcolm Barnes, ed., *The Mountain World.* Chicago: Rand McNally & Company, 1961.

———. *Among the Alps with Bradford.* New York: G.P. Putnam's Sons, 1927.

———. *Association with the Material Center, Wright Field, Dayton, Ohio, from January 1942 Until March 1943.* Dayton: United States Army Air Corps, 1943.

———. "Back-Packing to Fairweather." *The Sportsman* (April 1931).

———. "A Boy on the Matterhorn." *The Youth's Companion* (17 March 1927).

———. *Bradford on Mt. Fairweather.* New York: G.P. Putnam's Sons, 1931.

———. *Bradford on Mt. Washington.* New York: G.P. Putnam's Sons, 1928.

———. "The Conquest of Mount Crillon." *NGM* (March 1935).

———. *Exploring the Unknown* (Kenmore, WA: Epicenter Press, 2001).

———. "Exploring Yukon's Glacial Stronghold." *NGM* (June 1936).

———. "The First Ascent." *The Sportsman* (March 1930).

———. "First Ascent of Mount Deception." *Sierra Club Bulletin* 36: 5 (1951).

———. "The First Ascent of Mount Hayes," *The Backlog* 18: 4 (December 1941).

———. "First Laser Measurements to the Summit of Mount McKinley." *AAJ* (1978).

———. "Fishing: What a Boy Thinks." *The Churchman* (31 May 1919).

———. "Frostbite: What It Is—How to Prevent It—Emergency Treatment." *New England Journal of Medicine* 266 (10 May 1962).

———. "The Harvard-Dartmouth Alaskan Expeditions," *GJ* 87 (June 1936).

———. "The Heart of the Grand Canyon." *NGM* (July 1978).

———. "I Climb Mont Blanc." *The Youth's Companion* (30 June 1927).

———. *A Map of Mount McKinley, Alaska.* Wabern: Swiss Federal Institute of Topography, 1960.

———. "The Mapping of Mount Hubbard and Mount Kennedy, 1965." *NGSRR 1965 Projects.* Washington, D.C.: National Geographic Society, 1971.

———. "Morainic Banding of Malaspina Glacier and Other Alaskan Glaciers." *BGSA* 46 (1935).

———. "Mount Everest: Surveying the Third Pole." *NGM* (November 1988).

———. "Mount McKinley (Alaska): History and Evaluation." In Malcolm Barnes, ed., *The Mountain World.* New York: Harper & Brothers, 1957.

———. "Mount McKinley from the North and West." *AAJ* (1947).

———. "Mount McKinley: The West Buttress, 1951." *AAJ* (1952).

———. "A New Map of Mount McKinley, Alaska: The Story of a Cartographic Project." *GR* 51 (April 1961).

———. "Oblique Aerial Photography of the Mount Hubbard-Mount Kennedy Area on the Alaska-Yukon Border." *NGSRR 1966 Projects.* Washington, D.C.: National Geographic Society, 1971.

———. *On High.* Washington, D.C.: National Geographic Society, 2002.

———. "Over the Roof of the Continent." *NGM* (July 1938).

———. "Personal Equipment." *AAJ* (1946).

———. "A Preliminary Report on the Studies of the Mountains and Glaciers of Alaska." *GJ* 98 (1941).

———. *The Trails and Peaks of the Presidential Range of the White Mountains.* Worcester: The Davis Press, 1926.

———. *United States Army Air Forces: Report on Results of Field Tests and Conferences on Equipment, Alaska, June-July-August, 1942.* Dayton: United States Army Air Forces, 1942.

———, Adams Carter, and Ann Carter. "Dr. Cook and Mount McKinley." *AAJ* (1958).

———, and Peter Cherici. *The Dishonorable Dr. Cook: Debunking the Notorious Mount McKinley Hoax.* Seattle: The Mountaineers Books, 2001.

———, and Anthony Decaneas. *Bradford Washburn: Mountain Photography.* Seattle: The Mountaineers Books, 1999.

————, and Richard Goldthwait. "Lituya Bay and Mount Crillon District." *GJ* 87, supplement (June 1936).

————, and ————. "Movement of South Crillon Glacier, Crillon Lake, Alaska." *BGSA* 48 (1 November 1937).

————, Hugo Kasper, and Ernst Huber. *Mount McKinley, Alaska: A Reconnaissance Topographic Map by Bradford Washburn*. Waben: Neue Zurcher Zeitung, 1960.

————, Robert Kennedy, and James Whittaker. "Canada's Mount Kennedy." *NGM* (July 1965).

————, and David Roberts. *Mount McKinley: The Conquest of Denali*. New York: Harry N. Abrams, 1991.

Waxell, Sven Larsson. *The American Expedition*. Tr. M. A. Michael. London: William Hodge and Company, 1952.

Whayne, Tom, and Michael DeBakey. *Cold Injury, Ground Type*. Washington, D.C.: Government Printing Office, 1958.

Wickersham, James. "The Creation of Denali (Mount McKinley), By Yako, the Athabascan Adam: A Legend of the Yukon Tena Indians." *Alaska Magazine* 1: 1 (January 1927).

————. *Old Yukon: Tales, Trails and Trials*. Washington, D.C.: Washington Law Book Co., 1938.

Wilson, J. T. "Glacial Geology of Part of Northwestern Quebec." *Transactions of The Royal Society of Canada* 32: 4 (May 1938).

————. "Structural Features in the Northwest Territories." *American Journal of Science* 239 (1941).

Wood, Walter A. "Parachuting of Expedition Supplies: An Experiment by the Wood Yukon Expedition of 1942." *GR* 32 (January 1942).

————. "The Wood Yukon Expedition of 1935: An Experiment in Photographic Mapping." *GR* 26 (1936).

Worster, Donald. *A River Running West: The Life of John Wesley Powell*. New York: Oxford University Press, 2001.

Wrangell, Ferdinand P. von. *Statistische und Ethnographische Nachrichten uber die Russischen Bestzungen an der Nordewestkuste von Amerika*. St. Petersburg: Imperial Academy of Science, 1839.

Wright, Frederick G. "The Muir Glacier." *American Journal of Science,* series 3:33 (1887).

Wright, John K. "The Field of the Geographical Society." In Griffith Taylor, ed., *Geography in the Twentieth Century: A Study of Growth, Fields, Techniques, Aims and Trends*. New York: Philosophical Library, 1951.

Zaslow, Morris. *Reading the Rocks: The Story of the Geological Survey of Canada 1842-1972*. Toronto: The Macmillan Company of Canada Limited, 1975.

Newspapers Cited

Anchorage Daily News
Anchorage Hi-Life
Boston Herald
Champaign-Urbana News
Fairbanks Daily News-Miner
Fairbanks Daily Times
New York Sun
New York Times
The Illustrated London News
Third Form Weekly